CREATING A CAMPUS-WIDE CULTURE OF STUDENT SUCCESS

Offering a new approach to institutional practices, this book describes evidence-based strategies to create a campus culture conducive to truly supporting *all* students. We are at a critical crossroads in higher education, where large numbers of low-income, racially minoritized, and first-generation college students – referred to in this book as "at-promise students" – are attending college in greater numbers than ever, yet access has not translated to significantly improved retention and graduation rates. This book, therefore, proposes a realignment of existing initiatives to create campus-wide support through a new model of coordination.

The ideas presented in this book are the culmination of one of the largest studies of comprehensive college support programs for at-promise students. Chapters include illustrations of the key concepts and promising practices of the Promoting At-promise Student Success (PASS) Project, as well as guiding questions that can be used to facilitate conversations on campus. In this helpful resource, the authors address *how* student supports are delivered in validating ways, rather than focusing solely on *what* supports are offered, as has typically been the way institutions address the issues that at-promise students face.

This book is intended to provide guidance and support to educators who want to be a part of changing how higher education supports at-promise students toward increased equity.

Ronald E. Hallett is a lead research associate at the Pullias Center for Higher Education in the Rossier School of Education at the University of Southern California and a Professor of Education in the LaFetra College of Education at the University of La Verne, USA.

Adrianna Kezar is Dean's Professor of Leadership, Wilbur-Kieffer Professor of Higher Education, at the University of Southern California, USA, and Director of the Pullias Center for Higher Education within the Rossier School of Education.

Joseph A. Kitchen is an Associate Research Professor in the Pullias Center for Higher Education at the University of Southern California, USA.

Rosemary J. Perez is an Associate Professor in the Center for the Study of Higher and Postsecondary Education at the University of Michigan, USA.

Campus-wide Culture of Student Success offers higher education a much-needed new way of thinking by introducing a culture of ecological validation and outlining the necessary shifts in institutional practice that move from fragmented support to comprehensive approaches, build collaborative and trusting relationships, and engage educators in professional development."

Jillian Kinzie, *Associate Director, National Survey of Student Engagement, Indiana University Center for Postsecondary Research*

"Grounded in rigorous mixed methods and longitudinal research, this book offers an array of actionable strategies to broaden opportunity structures for communities that typically have not been well served in higher education. It is highly recommended reading for higher education leaders and practitioners who want to transcend individualistic approaches and implement collaborations to enact collective responsibility for student success."

Anne-Marie Núñez, *Executive Director, Diana Natalicio Institute for Hispanic Student Success; Distinguished Centennial Professor, Educational Leadership and Foundations, The University of Texas at El Paso*

CREATING A CAMPUS-WIDE CULTURE OF STUDENT SUCCESS

An Evidence-Based Approach to Supporting Low-Income, Racially Minoritized, and First-Generation College Students

Ronald E. Hallett, Adrianna Kezar, Joseph A. Kitchen, and Rosemary J. Perez

Routledge
Taylor & Francis Group

NEW YORK AND LONDON

Designed cover image: © Getty Images

First published 2024
by Routledge
605 Third Avenue, New York, NY 10158

and by Routledge
4 Park Square, Milton Park, Abingdon, Oxon, OX14 4RN

Routledge is an imprint of the Taylor & Francis Group, an informa business

© 2024 Taylor & Francis

The right of Ronald E. Hallett, Adrianna Kezar, Joseph A. Kitchen, and Rosemary J. Perez to be identified as authors of this work has been asserted in accordance with sections 77 and 78 of the Copyright, Designs and Patents Act 1988.

ISBN: 978-1-032-58128-6 (hbk)
ISBN: 978-1-032-58151-4 (pbk)
ISBN: 978-1-003-44371-1 (ebk)

DOI: 10.4324/9781003443711

Typeset in Galliard
by MPS Limited, Dehradun

CONTENTS

FOREWORD

The current student stressors, including the worsening global political and social divides, violence in our communities, widening financial inequality, access to health care, and mental health, as well as the social media, news cycles, and of course, the COVID pandemic, have been unkind, very unkind to higher education, but particularly so to our students. These and other stressors have had a major impact across many sectors of our society that will endure for the foreseeable future. There is also little question that it has been particularly unkind to students pursuing an undergraduate degree, particularly those referred to here as at-promise students, or better known as low-income, racially minoritized, and first-generation college students. This cohort of students, although demographically increasing in undergraduate programs, has struggled mightily for decades with myriad factors superimposed upon the recent changes caused by the COVID pandemic of 2019.

In many ways, this period of time brought out challenges and, at the same time, opportunities to intervene, to creatively support this cohort of students upon whom we will rely increasingly as our nation and world strive to meet workforce and societal needs. There have been many strategies, programs, policies, and anecdotal experiences to address barriers for at-promise students. Many have related to financial support, some have approached individual cultural and supportive related opportunities, but few, if any, have brought together a comprehensive, wraparound experience not only supporting the very fragile financial needs of at-promise students, but also demonstrating meaningful and sustainable interactions with educators who provide a host of services to enhance their journey through higher education and into all that follows.

The authors of this manuscript have reported on a unique and exciting series of interventions and outcomes to support at-promise students in postsecondary institutions. This microcosm of the state of Nebraska has demonstrated that when highly coordinated, organized approaches are implemented, and ongoing support services are widely available and proactive, one can ensure that at-promise students not only have a stronger sense of belonging and self-efficacy, but also outperform their peers in academic achievement, promotion, and indeed, degree completion.

These authors demonstrate clearly that in addition to the full financial support that is frequently necessary, a host of wraparound services to create a strong sense of belonging and to identify the environmental hurdles that these students will face is equally important to their success. The Promoting At-promise Student Success (PASS) Project reports on six years of intense efforts including data collection, analysis of the students at promise, as well as a peer matched group looking for similarities and differences in academic outcomes plus in a host of psychosocial outcomes, which include the all-important belonging, self-efficacy, and so many other factors that determine the success of pathways through postsecondary education.

As the authors conclude, "a culture of ecological validation is a strengths-oriented, proactive, identity-conscious, and developmental approach that holistically creates validating experience for at-promise students across the campus context." This culture of ecological validation has formed the foundation of this six-year study, and it appears to be foundational as well to the necessary programs supporting a broad cohort of at-promise students. Indeed, this ecological validation framework appears to be as important and, in many instances, more important, than the pure financial support these students frequently need.

As the Provost and Executive Vice President of the University of Nebraska System, it has been an incredible pleasure and true honor to work with The Susan Thompson Buffett Foundation, which supported this unique project and to work with the authors on this aspect of the research and many others. Although the long-term research-practice partnership among the NU campuses, our system office, the foundation, and of course, the research team is relatively unique, it is broadly applicable as an exemplar for our campuses and those outside of our system. As such, this work actively continues on all of our undergraduate campuses, not as a special program, but as a set of programs that are increasingly weaving best practices for academic and student success into our campus culture.

This manuscript and the extensive reference base that has been created provide an open and transparent look into an attempt to deal with one of our society's greatest challenges and, at the same time, greatest opportunities.

Yes, there is no question that the pandemic has been unkind, particularly for these at-promise students. However, there is also a clear pathway forward for these students, with higher earnings capability, greater job satisfaction, and a wide spectrum of long-term benefits for both individuals and society.

Jeffrey P. Gold, M.D.
Provost and Executive Vice President
University of Nebraska System

ACKNOWLEDGMENTS

A project of this size would not have been possible without the many people who offered their guidance, support, and time. We have been fortunate to be part of a team of talented researchers who are dedicated to improving opportunities and success for at-promise college students. The PASS Project had several scholars who provided leadership throughout the project in addition to the coauthors of this book, including Nick Bowman, Darnell Cole, Zoë Corwin, Tatiana Melguizo, and Robert Reason. We also appreciate the thought partnership of the many researchers who have been a part of the PASS Project since it began in 2015, including Arely Acuña Avilez, Genie Bettencourt, Edward Chi, KC Culver, Tom DePaola, Araceli Espinoza-Wade, Raúl Gamez, Liane Hypolite, Lauren Irwin, Shinji Katsumoto, Angie Kim, Hope McCoy, Mariama Nagbe, Elizabeth Park, Gwendelyn Rivera, Elise Swanson, Ralitsa Todorova, Kristan Venegas, Marissiko Wheaton, and Amber Williams. The PASS Project also had several research consultants who assisted with the study design and analysis, including Paco Martorell, Mark Masterton, Cameron McPhee, Samantha Neiman, Christopher Newman, Evan Nielsen, and Matt Soldner. We also would be remiss if we did not thank Monica Raad and Diane Flores, who work for the Pullias Center for Higher Education and offer many different forms of support that make our research possible. In addition, Zoë Corwin and Christine Rocha assisted with refining the figures that illustrate key concepts throughout the book and coordinated the materials that appear on the PASS website that complement and support ideas presented in this book.

We are grateful to The Susan Thompson Buffett Foundation for providing the funding that made the PASS Project possible. Their support and commitment to supporting at-promise student success through evidence-based practices paved the way for us to identify promising strategies and approaches that promote college success. In particular, Kellie Pickett and Leslie Hawley were important thought partners and collaborators throughout the research project.

The PASS Project had an advisory board that provided guidance on the study design, research publications, and recommendations for informing practice. We appreciate their dedication to the project as well as the many contributions to higher education that they have made. Our advisory board members included Sonja Ardoin, Manuel González Canché, Amalia Daché, Jennifer Keup, Jillian Kinzie, Emily Lardner, becky martinez, Darris Means, Sam Museus, Anne-Marie Nunez, Cecilia Orphan, Leticia Osuguera, Daphna Oyserman, Julie Park, Amalia Parnell, Robert Reason, Kris Renn, and Vincent Tinto.

We want to thank Sam Museus and Susan Elrod, who read a full draft of this book and provided detailed advice about how to strengthen the ideas. In addition, John von Knorring reviewed the manuscript, offered useful insights, and extended the initial book contract.

The PASS Project is an action-oriented project that involves close partnership with the campuses, educators, and students who are highlighted in this book. The University of Nebraska system leadership offered multiple forms of support and thought partnership throughout the design, data collection, and dissemination stages of the project, including David Jackson and Susan Fritz. The leadership on the three campuses enabled us to conduct our research and provided guidance in developing relationships with campus stakeholders as well as feedback throughout the study. In particular, Amy Goodburn, Sarah Edwards, and Mark Ellis served as our points of contact for the research project. The TSLC program staff, peer mentors, office staff, and faculty coordinators gave us a significant amount of their time and many of the resources that enabled us to gain a deep understanding of the programs and how they support students. In particular, the program directors – Dusten Crichton, Kelli King, Jen Harvey, and Lesley Esters – met with us regularly and provided multiple forms of support throughout the project. We are also grateful to the support provided by the faculty coordinators: Julie Campbell, Jerry Cederblom, June Griffen, Courtney Hillebrecht, Rob Luscher, and Gina Matkin. In addition, we deeply appreciate the leadership, staff, faculty, mentors, directors, and staff who trusted us with their stories, perspectives, and experiences.

We had the opportunity to learn from over 80 TSLC students who participated in over 900 interviews and submitted over 900 videos that enabled us to understand their experiences in college, their stories, successes and challenges, and the factors that supported them as they embarked on their college journey. Following their journeys and hearing their honest reflections on their college experience enabled us to develop the frameworks that are presented in this book. We appreciate the time and energy that each of the students devoted to the project.

We also want to thank our colleagues, students, families, partners, and friends who enabled us to dedicate so much of our time and energy to this important work, which included a lot of travel. Their support of our work is often invisible, but essential.

ABOUT THE AUTHORS

Ronald Hallett is a lead research associate at the Pullias Center for Higher Education in the Rossier School of Education at the University of Southern California and a Professor of Education in the LaFetra College of Education at the University of La Verne. Dr. Hallett's research focuses on increasing educational access and success for at-promise students. He has authored several books, monographs, chapters, and research articles that explore the experiences of students and how educational institutions can support their success.

Adrianna Kezar is Dean's Professor of Leadership, Wilbur-Kieffer Professor of Higher Education, at the University of Southern California and Director of the Pullias Center for Higher Education within the Rossier School of Education. Dr. Kezar is a national expert of student success, equity, and diversity, the changing faculty, change, governance, and leadership in higher education. Kezar is well published with 25 books/monographs, over 100 journal articles, and over 100 book chapters and reports. Recent books include: *Shared Leadership in Higher Education* (2021) (Stylus), *The Gig Academy* (2019) (Johns Hopkins Press), *Administration for Social Justice and Equity* (2019) (Routledge Press), and *How Colleges Change (2018) (2nd edition)* (Routledge Press).

Joseph A. Kitchen is an Associate Research Professor in the Pullias Center for Higher Education at the University of Southern California. Dr. Kitchen conducts quantitative, qualitative, and mixed-methods research, and his research agenda spans several areas, with a central focus on the role of college transition, outreach, and support programs and interventions in promoting equitable outcomes and college success among first-generation, low-income, and racially minoritized students. He is committed to translating his research to inform policies and practices that promote social justice and equity in education.

Rosemary J. Perez is an Associate Professor in the Center for the Study of Higher and Postsecondary Education at the University of Michigan. Dr. Perez's scholarship leverages the strengths of student development and organizational theories to explore individual and organizational learning and development, and often uses longitudinal qualitative methods. Dr. Perez's work is informed by her experiences as a student affairs educator and reflects her commitment to engaging in praxis to create a more human, equitable, and just world.

1

INTRODUCTION

We are at a critical crossroads in higher education. Larger numbers of low-income, racially minoritized, and first-generation college students – herein referred to as at-promise students – attend postsecondary institutions in the United States today than at any other time in history (Renn & Reason, 2021; Seidman, 2005). Improved college-going rates demonstrate the importance of high school college preparation programs, improved financial aid policies, shifts in admission processes, and many other efforts championed by practitioners, policymakers, advocates, and researchers. However, equity gaps persist. Increased access has not translated to significantly improved retention and graduation rates (Shapiro et al., 2019). In addition, at-promise students have lower levels of belonging, mattering, self-efficacy, and other outcomes than their peers, which has implications for their transition and success in college.

As increased numbers of at-promise students enter postsecondary institutions, campus leadership, and educators have a responsibility to create systems that encourage the academic success of all students. Educators within these institutions serve the public good by educating citizens, developing community leaders, and preparing future professionals. In addition, postsecondary institutions can be an important vehicle for achieving equity. Earning a postsecondary credential or degree is associated with higher earnings, greater job satisfaction, and many benefits for both individuals and society (Mayhew et al., 2016).

Several strategies, programs, and policies have been implemented to address barriers to at-promise student success. Most attempts involve adding supplemental programming without fundamentally changing the institutional structures, approaches, and culture. These boutique programs

DOI: 10.4324/9781003443711-1

typically support a relatively small group of students by providing them information about how to succeed in the current institutional context and creating a separate space within the broader institution where students can receive additional support. Administrators, instructors, professional staff, and other educators working within these supplemental programs are dedicated to improving the postsecondary experiences and outcomes for at-promise students. These efforts often make a difference for the students served. One challenge is that only the students selected into these programs benefit, and a large number of other at-promise students are left to fend for themselves. In addition, these programs focus on acclimating students to institutions rather than shifting how institutions operate in order to leverage the assets and experiences students bring with them to college (McNair et al., 2016). Instead of creating supplemental programs to change at-promise students, the time has come to rethink our institutional approaches and practices in order to create a campus culture conducive to truly supporting *all* students. Institutional environments need to be recalibrated to meet the needs of the at-promise students they serve.

The current economic realities also mean that postsecondary institutions need to consider effective approaches to supporting at-promise students without additional resources. Federal and state governments have reduced the amount of financial support directed to public colleges and universities. Students – especially those from lower- and middle-income backgrounds – cannot continue to bear the burden of increased tuition. As a result, we need innovative approaches that can be enacted by using the current resources (or, in some cases, with reduced revenue).

The ideas presented in this book are the culmination of one of the largest studies of comprehensive college support programs for at-promise students. The Promoting At-promise Student Success (PASS) Project involved six years of mixed-methods data collection and analysis. As we describe in later chapters, the PASS Project focused on understanding if, how, and why the large comprehensive college transition programs supported the academic and psychosocial outcomes of low-income, racially minoritized, and first-generation college students. We explored nine psychosocial outcomes associated with persistence and graduation in comparison to a control group, including belonging, mattering, and career/major self-efficacy. We found that students in these programs had higher levels of psychosocial and academic outcomes (see Chapter 4).

Based upon our analysis of why the programs were effective, we argue that a culture of ecological validation explains how the programs successfully supported at-promise student success. A culture of ecological validation is a strengths-oriented, proactive, identity-conscious, and developmental approach that holistically creates validating experiences for at-promise students across the campus contexts. A culture of ecological validation has the potential to inform the work of at-promise student support programs, how departments or colleges are structured, and the culture of entire institutions. In addition, ecological validation is an approach that focuses on how educators do their work and does not necessarily require additional revenue or resources. In the next section, we introduce the culture of ecological validation as a new way to think about at-promise student support.

Introducing a Culture of Ecological Validation

A culture of ecological validation is a systemic approach to providing holistic, strengths-oriented, proactive, identity-conscious, and developmental support for at-promise students (see Diagram 1.1). In order to create a culture of ecological validation, educators engage in reflective practices and take a collaborative approach that includes cross-functional work with colleagues across the institution. Drawing from previous research related to ecological and validating approaches to student support, a culture of ecological validation involves educators across campus contexts developing coordinated and aligned approaches to validating students' assets, strengths, and innate capabilities for success (Kezar et al., 2022b; Kitchen et al., 2021e). While the

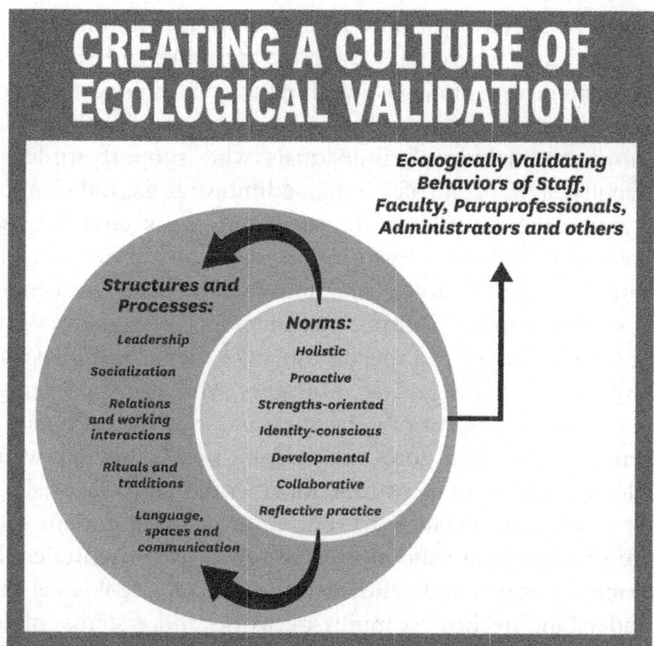

DIAGRAM 1.1   Creating a Culture of Ecological Validation.

norms of ecological validation are not necessarily new to higher education, our approach argues for intentionally enacting each norm and the importance of incorporating all the norms at the same time. Often, scholars and practitioners focus on one of these norms without explicitly exploring how to create an approach that prioritizes the multiple aspects of the student experiences that are influenced by the seven norms we put at the center with ecological validation.

Instead of primarily focusing on *what* supports are offered to students (e.g., advising, peer mentoring, or first-year seminar), a culture of ecological validation focuses on *how* student supports are enacted. Our research confirms that how institutions provide support is more important than the specific program elements available – especially if the support programs are offered within siloed institutional structures that result in fragmented and disconnected supports for at-promise students. We argue that a web of coordinated and connected support contexts sets the stage for validating processes to occur and be reinforced as educators across campus affirm students' assets, strengths, and capabilities for success. In Chapter 6, we provide a more detailed explanation and illustration of a culture of ecological validation. While we focus on at-promise students in this book, we believe that all students would likely benefit if an institution creates a culture of ecological validation. The ideas and strategies presented throughout this book provide a research-based perspective on how to create an institutional culture that is student-centered and where students have affirming and validating experiences in each interaction they have with educators across campus.

Educators are essential to a culture of ecological validation. We use the term *educators* to include all individuals who support student success, including faculty, staff, paraprofessionals, administrators, and campus leaders. Educators across the institution are needed to work cross-functionally to achieve ecological validation. Even individuals who do not directly engage with students (e.g., institutional data and facilities) play important roles in supporting student success. Shifting staff members' perspective of their work from being solely focused on a specific aspect of the institutional functioning toward thinking of themselves as educators who are supporting student success is an important aspect of getting everyone at the university to center the experiences, needs, and goals of students. In Chapter 10, we provide a more detailed discussion of cross-functional work that is essential to creating a culture of ecological validation to support at-promise student success.

A culture of ecological validation draws from two theoretical bodies of work: ecological systems and validation theories. An ecological perspective involves understanding how complex networks and systems influence students' experiences and outcomes. Bronfenbrenner's (1994) Ecological Systems Theory (EST) has been utilized by higher education researchers and practitioners to understand how interactions between students and individuals within their environments shape their educational experiences and development (Renn, 2003). The individual's characteristics and identities (e.g., age, race, gender, personality) influence their ecologies and how they engage with their network of support. Validation is the process of affirming students' backgrounds and identities as assets and recognizing students' innate capabilities for success (Rendón, 1994). However, these two concepts (ecological support systems and validation) have typically been considered separately by researchers and practitioners.

The overarching goal of this book is to draw from research and theory to explain the importance of shifting postsecondary institutional cultures from silos of support that benefit White middle-class students to a more validating ecological approach that supports all students. We recognize that postsecondary institutions may approach the process of shifting culture in different ways. For some institutions, creating a large, comprehensive college transition program that supports a diverse group of at-promise students may be the first step in the process. In particular, Section 2 of this book provides a detailed discussion of the programs we studied. In addition, some academic departments or colleges may be looking for ways to support all the students they serve, and they could draw from the concepts throughout the book to create new cultures within these spaces. And some postsecondary institutions may be ready to shift the entire institutional culture in ways that break down silos in order to create a culture of ecological validation that supports all students. For these institutions in particular, we explore how to scale the findings from our study to an institutional level. As will be discussed in the final section of the book, postsecondary institutions can move toward a culture of ecological validation without necessarily needing to secure additional revenue or resources. A culture of ecological validation involves seven norms that frame the institutional structures and processes and result in ecologically validating educator behaviors, which can positively influence at-promise student experiences and outcomes. We argue that it is not enough to ask faculty and staff to act differently: structures and processes must be created that sustain a new culture.

A culture of ecological validation provides insight into the norms, practices, beliefs, and traditions that influence student success and describes how educators can create change by implementing a culture of ecological validation. Scaling ecological validation at the institutional level ensures that at-promise students have validating experiences during each interaction they have with all educators they engage with throughout their college experiences. Unlike previous discussions of validation as an individual interaction between one educator and one student, ecological validation demonstrates the importance of all postsecondary educators intentionally creating validating experiences for students. The multiple forms of validation that occur over the entirety of the college experience have exponentially more positive influences on student engagement and academic outcomes than a single validating experience.

Audience

We specifically designed this book for postsecondary educators, leaders, and advocates who have been working toward equity but are frustrated that the multiple disconnected programs on their campus have not significantly improved overall at-promise student success. Our audience is educators who believe in the promise of higher education but are disappointed that many of our colleges and universities are not yet reaching their full potential as a path to a better life and more equitable society for all the students they serve. This book is intended to provide guidance and support to educators who want to be a part of changing how higher education supports at-promise students toward increased equity. The chapters include illustrations of the key concepts as well as guiding questions that can be used to facilitate conversations on your campus about ecological validation and lessons learned that could transform how you support at-promise students' success. We have additional resources related to the key concepts on our website (https://pass.pullias. usc.edu/). While the primary audience will likely be current or future educators and educational leaders, we also present new theoretical concepts that may be of interest to researchers in higher education.

Key Assumptions

We review a few key assumptions, such as our use of *at-promise* as a strengths-based alternative to other terms used to identify students who have historically been marginalized in higher education. We discuss the importance of expansive notions of student success that include both academic and psychosocial outcomes. We then explain the importance of institutions shifting perspectives from recruiting students to fit within their structures to being ready as an institution to support all at-promise students. Building upon these ideas, we then argue for postsecondary institutions creating cultures that holistically consider the strengths and challenges of at-promise students instead of creating supplemental programs.

Considering Your Students as At-promise

The term *at-risk* has been used by scholars, policymakers, and practitioners for decades with the intent of identifying students who are "at risk" of failing or dropping out and may need additional resources and support.

Individuals employing this term want to assist students who have historically been marginalized in order to create pathways to improving outcomes. We affirm the desire to work toward unhinging the inequities that exist; however, we acknowledge the underlying deficit assumptions associated with defining students as at-risk. Terms like *at-risk* assume the problem exists within students rather than in structural inequities, which perpetuates deficit-oriented perspectives and solutions. Identifying students as possessing risk as a defining characteristic can create a self-fulfilling prophecy among students, which may limit their ability to achieve their full potential by contributing to their feelings of inadequacy and marginalization (Mireles-Rios et al., 2020).

We join a growing group of scholars and practitioners who use the term *at-promise* to highlight students who have traditionally been, and often remain, underserved (Cheese & Vines, 2017). Our work with at-promise students focuses on low-income students, many of whom are racially minoritized and/or first-generation college students; however, the term also includes other marginalized identities (e.g., gender, sexuality, immigration status, English language learners, and students with disabilities). Shifting to an at-promise view of students involves more than just semantics. Using the term requires a shift in how educators perceive students as well as the institution's role in supporting students (Bettencourt et al., 2023). Educators see the promise or potential in students – and the educators and educational systems promise or commit to providing support for students. The term implies a strengths-based and validating approach that centers on students' potential for success instead of focusing on their risk for failure. In addition, the term assumes institutional responsibility to identify and address structural inequities that result in opportunity gaps (Pendakur, 2016). Using the term *at-promise* changes the narrative to considering students as possessing the ability to succeed, but they may benefit from support designed to help them reach their academic potential (Rios & Mireles-Rios, 2019).

We believe a shift in language can meaningfully influence how instructors, staff, administrators, and policymakers think about students. Instead of focusing on what is wrong with the students, the focus shifts to what is wrong with the systems they are embedded within. The term *at-promise* also aligns with how we use validation theory. In Chapter 5, we discuss how validation is a strengths-based approach that focuses on institutional agents using language that affirms the potential of students.

Expansive Notions of Student Success

We take a broad view of student success, which includes both academic and psychosocial outcomes. Retaining students until degree completion is important since access to college does not have a significant impact on equity if students do not complete their degrees (Tinto, 2012). Developing student-retention efforts often begins by exploring grades and retention data to identify patterns. A student's grade point average and continued enrollment are important outcomes. Running reports to identify patterns among different subgroups of students can highlight inequitable outcomes and may point to key transition points that require attention. For example, data may reveal that students who are the first in their families to attend college are less likely to return after the first semester or African American students are more likely than their White peers to drop a STEM major during their second year. These data can also be leveraged to motivate educators to explore solutions.

Grades and retention patterns do not necessarily explain why students may be struggling or how to resolve the underlying issues. Researchers and practitioners have come to realize that positive mental states (e.g., sense of belonging, mattering, self-efficacy) directly and indirectly influence student success. For example, a gay student may have above-average grades but decide not to return to campus because they do not feel a sense of belonging with a peer group. Or a student from a low-income background working two jobs to pay for tuition and assist her family may disengage from coursework because she does not feel her struggle matters to her instructors or the financial aid office. Indeed, evidence from our study of at-promise student success suggests the link between students' psychosocial outcomes and their academic success (Swanson et al., 2021). As we discuss in Chapter 5, validation is a key lever used to develop a sense of belonging, mattering, and major/career self-efficacy. At-promise students who experience validation during interactions with professional staff, instructors, and other educators are more likely to feel connected to and supported by the postsecondary institution. However, many campuses struggle with developing these psychosocial aspects of student support that researchers have identified as important. We discuss how educators can use both academic and psychosocial outcomes in order to more holistically understand at-promise students' experiences. Focusing just on grades may lead to structural changes that do not actually address the issues that lead at-promise students to depart college or not reach their full potential in college.

In addition to considering the academic and psychosocial outcomes, postsecondary institutions should explore how at-promise students may have goals that differ from White middle-class notions of success. For example, a student may have priorities related to family, community, and other issues that they want (or need) to direct their time to instead of extracurricular activities, graduating in four years, or earning a 4.0 GPA. Goals of the student may not always align with the goals of the institution.

An expansive and inclusive definition of success includes academic outcomes, psychosocial outcomes, and an understanding of at-promise students' goals. A singular focus on grades or graduation rates may inhibit an institution's ability to create equitable structures, policies, and practices that support at-promise students. As the next section explains, institutions need to shift from trying to force at-promise students to fit within current systems and move toward creating new approaches that center the student and their goals for college.

Institutions Becoming Student Ready

For several decades, practitioners and policymakers have focused on how to improve the college readiness of at-promise students. The underlying assumption suggests that the reason that at-promise students have not been retained and graduated is that they were not given the tools they needed in high school. Some of these efforts have led to important changes in the K-12 system, such as ensuring students in low-income communities have access to advanced placement courses, college advising, and waivers of college application fees. These structural changes matter. Continued efforts are needed to address opportunity gaps and structural barriers that create inequitable access to higher education.

While improved connections between high school and postsecondary education are important, the focus on college readiness often involves deficit thinking about both at-promise students and the high school educators who worked with them instead of focusing on structural and societal issues. As a result, many postsecondary institutions have focused on finding at-promise high school students who demonstrate the ability to succeed in college without significant support instead of exploring how the institutional culture, systems, and practices could be adjusted to support all students who want to pursue higher education. Focusing just on identifying "college ready students" who are perceived as high achieving academically and self-directed reinforces the social stratification that continues marginalizing low-income, first-generation college, and racially minoritized communities. McNair et al. (2016) argue for institutions to change the narrative and focus on becoming *student ready* – meaning that colleges and universities should change their policies, practices, and pedagogy to meet the needs of the students who attend their institutions. The idea of student readiness means that at-promise students are not the problem to be fixed; rather, institutions have the responsibility for creating new cultures, structures, and practices that support all students.

Central Arguments

Having reviewed our underlying assumptions, we now describe our central arguments that support implementing ecological validation: forging trusting relationships, moving from fragmented support to comprehensive approaches, and prioritizing institutional culture change (not siloed programs). We discuss each of these arguments before situating our argument within the conversations about at-promise student success.

Forging Trusting Relationships

We join an emerging body of research that argues for the importance of establishing trusting relationships between students, staff, faculty, administrators, and other stakeholders on campus. While some research focuses on specific relational dynamics (e.g., student-instructor), the current movement focuses on moving toward an institutional culture that focuses on fostering relationships between everyone at the institution (e.g., student-student, student-instructor, instructor-instructor, student affairs-academic affairs) in order to create the context for at-promise student success. As Felton et al. (2016) argue, "Strong institutions value strong relationships, and they do not leave these to chance. Relationships are cultivated and nurtured intentionally at all levels" (p. 6).

Establishing trusting relationships with peers and campus stakeholders early in a student's academic career lays an important foundation upon which students establish academic relationships, engage with academic content, navigate challenges, make decisions about opportunities, and determine majors and career goals throughout their time in college (Chambliss & Takacs, 2014). Trusting relationships enable at-promise students to fully engage in learning and develop a sense of belonging on campus (Felton et al., 2016; Nunn, 2021). Conrad and Lundberg (2022) explore how some minority-serving institutions are redefining post-secondary education as a shared relational endeavor focused on sustaining students and their communities. They explain how the institutions created structures and an institutional culture focused on building trusting relationships between students, faculty, and staff, which positively influenced retention and persistence of all students. Their book – among others – note the importance of creating intentional approaches to building relationships.

Postsecondary institutions have come to recognize the importance of building relationships for students. Often, these efforts focus on creating programming the first semester or year (e.g., peer mentoring, learning communities, involvement fairs, and first-year seminars). However, these efforts rarely shift the overall institutional culture. While individual actions of educators or staff may create meaningful experiences for individual students at a specific point in time, these isolated efforts are not enough to significantly improve academic experiences and outcomes for at-promise students (Felton et al., 2016). Scholars have begun calling for trusting relationships to be a foundation of the postsecondary institutional culture.

Relationships between at-promise students and campus stakeholders rarely happen accidentally and should not be left to chance. Similarly, relationships between stakeholders in different spaces on campus do not organically develop. The lack of connection among educators across campus leads to fragmented and difficult-to-navigate siloed campus environments. Institutional culture and structures need to be designed to facilitate interactions and prioritize the development of trusting relationships between stakeholders who can collaborate on student success. The idea of centering relationships in higher education works against the individualistic foundation of higher education that involves the student and faculty member focusing on their personal pursuits (Conrad & Lundberg, 2022; Guiffrida et al., 2012). Institutions need to create pathways for relationships to be established since current structures inhibit trusting interactions that can positively influence student experiences and then celebrate when relationships are established in ways that influence student outcomes (Felton et al., 2016).

How to create institutional culture and structures that support trusting relationships continues to need additional theorizing and research. We contribute a research-based framework that provides guidance for institutions interested in finding ways to create a culture of trusting relationships that support at-promise student experiences and outcomes. In particular, we discuss how to create a culture with institutional structures that facilitate a web of relationships with all stakeholders on campus, including students, staff, administrators, and faculty.

Moving from Fragmented Support to Comprehensive Approaches

Postsecondary institutions, foundations, and national organizations have developed multiple interventions to support at-promise students, including peer mentoring, culture centers, supplemental instruction, first-year seminars, learning communities, and summer bridge programs (Kezar, 2019). Current institutional efforts tend to focus on supporting small groups of students in fragmented supplemental programs that attend to a single part of a student's identity during a targeted transition point in the early stages of college. Even though these supplemental efforts have existed for decades, postsecondary institutions continue to struggle in improving academic and psychosocial outcomes for at-promise students (Bailey et al., 2015; Mayhew et al., 2016; Seidman, 2005). Although large program efforts, such as TRIO, College Pathways, and Accelerated Study in Associate Program (ASAP), exist to provide comprehensive support for at-promise students, there are still large numbers of students who do not get into these programs.

The problem is that postsecondary education has been focused on creating supplemental programs instead of shifting institutional culture. At-promise students may feel validation, belonging, mattering, and other psychosocial outcomes within the supplemental program, but they do not necessarily feel the same way in the general campus context. Tinkering at the edges of the problem has hindered our collective ability to meaningfully address seemingly intractable disparities in at-promise students' success on a broad scale. The time has come to pull lessons learned from supplemental programs and explore ways to shift institutions in ways to create validating experiences for students throughout their time in college.

Changing institutional structures is challenging. Traditional campuses are organized with each functional area operating in a restricted fashion that focuses on a fixed set of services with little knowledge of other areas. The bureaucratic systems in higher education involve units separated by tasks (e.g., student support services, academic units, and administrative units focused on finance, alumni, and other specializations), which have developed their own subcultures and siloed work structures with little incentive to collaborative across units (Kezar & Lester, 2009; Kuh et al., 2006; Manning et al., 2014). Creating supplemental programming has been seen as easier than changing the structures of higher education. Scholars have called for fundamental shifts to improve the college experiences and outcomes for at-promise students. As mentioned, McNair et al. (2016) call for postsecondary institutions to become "student ready" instead of students becoming "college ready." Our work provides an opportunity to empirically support the work of McNair and colleagues.

Museus (2011) developed the Culturally Engaging Campus Environment (CECE) that discusses how to support racially minoritized students through creating a humanizing postsecondary environment. Similar to the culture of ecological validation, Museus calls for proactive and holistic approaches to become the norm in higher education. In addition, he was hypothesizing what a culture could look like since empirical examples did not exist. Our study adds more nuance by providing research-based support for some of the ideas that Museus argues are needed. We also encourage postsecondary institutions to consider exploring how to incorporate the CECE model into their work as they build a culture of ecological validation.

Some foundations and institutions have heeded the call of scholars who argue for more comprehensive approaches to supporting at-promise students. Comprehensive college transition programs (CCTPs) have emerged as a way for postsecondary institutions to implement holistic, proactive, and identity-conscious approaches to supporting at-promise students (Dawson et al., 2020). CCTPs – including Dell Scholars Program, Accelerated Study in Associate's Program (ASAP), Carolina Covenant, and Stay the Course – coordinate multiple forms of support (e.g., financial, social, academic, major/career support) to holistically consider the multiple needs and success of at-promise students. Our study and other robust quasi-experimental studies of CCTPs suggest that comprehensive, coordinated, and holistic forms of support increase student success (Clotfelter et al., 2017; Page et al., 2019). While CCTPs can be an important first step to providing support for at-promise students and may serve as a hub of innovation, they still do not address issues of institutional culture that impede at-promise students. The ideas we present throughout this book move from conversations about supplemental programs and look at broader institutional shifts that can support all students.

Prioritizing Institutional Culture Change, Not Siloed Programs

Throughout this book, we argue for exploring how to shift institutional culture in ways that support at-promise students instead of designing more supplemental programs. Many postsecondary institutions have a multitude of disconnected programs and efforts designed to address a specific need. Although students are complex individuals with multiple identities, many programs take a fragmented approach to addressing students' needs. In addition, many postsecondary programs serve only a fraction of the number of students on their campus who could benefit from support.

Adding more programs does not address the reality that postsecondary institutions were designed for and by White cisgender men from privileged backgrounds. The policies, structures, and culture of postsecondary institutions often create challenges for at-promise students because they were not designed with these students in mind. Supplemental programs attempt to create supportive spaces on campus and teach students how to decode the system. These supplemental efforts continue to be necessary because educators have not figured out new ways to imagine a higher educational system that supports all students. We present an alternative approach that focuses on shifting institutional culture that draws from a rigorous study of comprehensive college transition programs, engagement with theory, and an exploration of the current research related to at-promise students, institutional culture, and student support programs.

Situating Our Argument

The student success literature has focused predominantly on silver bullet interventions, programs on the side, technology tools and solutions, and predictive analytics. Our research demonstrates that the focus of many current efforts is not going to help at-promise students or institutions in achieving their student success goals. We argue that institutions should focus more on altering campus culture through approaching work differently – collaborating and building trusting relationships – and engaging administrators, staff, and faculty in professional development. There are others that have made similar arguments, such as Freeman Hraboswski at the University of Maryland Baltimore County. We are not arguing that programs, technology, or data are not valuable, but that they are over-relied on and not an approach that will generally create the knowledge, capacity, and scale to support at-promise students. Work on data systems, in particular, has evolved and can be an important tool to help support the type of culture change we are arguing for. But using the data systems alone will not generally create the desired ends. We encourage campuses to expand their approach to focus more on human and cultural solutions than technocratic ones.

Organization of the Book

This book provides a new way of thinking about how postsecondary institutions can provide educational opportunities and support for at-promise students – creating a culture of ecological validation. Underlying our arguments is a belief that higher educational institutions have the onus to shift in order to meet the needs of students, not the other way around. To illustrate the ideas presented throughout the book, we leverage a large mixed-methods study of comprehensive college transition programs as well as our experiences doing research in other contexts.

Our book is divided into three sections. Section 1 – "Understanding the Institutional Challenges to Serving At-promise Students" – contains three chapters that lay the foundation for the rest of the book. Chapter 2 provides an overview of research related to the challenges and inequities that at-promise college students endure. Postsecondary institutions currently admit the most diverse group of students than any time in history; however, academic and psychosocial outcomes of at-promise students are not equitable in comparison to their more privileged peers. Chapter 3 discusses how existing siloed institutional structures undermine at-promise student success by encouraging deficit-oriented, fragmented, reactive, identity-neutral, and nondevelopment practices. Instead of assuming students are the problem that need to be fixed, we focus on aspects of higher education that create challenges for at-promise students. In Chapter 4, we present an overview of the Promoting At-promise Student Success (PASS) Project including a discussion of our study design and research methodology. Given the limited research on comprehensive college transition programs, we provide an overview of the programs we studied and some insights related to program design and implementation. We also highlight the key findings from our longitudinal mixed-methods study that relate to how participation in the CCTP influenced at-promise students' academic and psychosocial outcomes (e.g., belonging, mattering, validation, and academic, career, and major self-efficacy).

Section 2 – "Introducing a Culture of Ecological Validation" – contains five chapters that explain and illustrate how a culture of ecological validation can positively influence at-promise student experiences and outcomes. Chapter 5 summarizes the theoretical foundations of the book, which are rooted in validation, ecological systems, identity-consciousness, and student success cultures. Chapter 6 presents a new approach to supporting at-promise students. A culture of ecological validation supports and develops at-promise students' multiple identities, assets, strengths, and capabilities for success in a coordinated web of student support contexts over time. We discuss how a culture of ecological validation can be created that influences how educators engage with students and other professionals across campus. A culture of ecological validation disrupts the existing dominant White, middle-class, and generationally privileged culture by creating and sustaining an institutional culture that involves seven norms: holistic, proactive, strengths-oriented, identity-conscious, developmental, collaborative, and reflective practice. We also discuss how the culture requires new structures and processes that enable the norms to be sustained and expanded. To further illustrate ecological validation, we provide more detailed examples of educator experiences in Chapter 7 along with promising practices that educators can enact in Chapter 8. We then shift to highlighting the at-promise student experiences with a culture of ecological validation in Chapter 9.

Section 3 – "Expanding a Culture of Ecological Validation Across the Campus" – involves two chapters that explore the process of enacting a culture of ecological validation at the institutional level. Chapter 10 discusses how everyone at an institution plays a role in developing and maintaining a culture of ecological validation, including administrators, professional staff, instructors, peers, and alumni. The goal is to begin a discussion at postsecondary institutions about how people in different roles on campus can shift their perspective toward a culture of ecological validation. Moving from individual approaches to collective action related to a culture of ecological validation, Chapter 11 examines how shared leadership and professional learning communities play an important role in moving an institution toward a culture of ecological validation. We also present professional learning communities as a potential way for post-secondary institutions to engage with our findings and explore how a culture of ecological validation can be created at the institutional level. We also share insights from collaborating with three campuses to develop professional learning communities designed to create a campus-wide culture of ecological validation.

Each of the chapters ends with an opportunity to explore how to connect the ideas to your campus. We avoid providing prescriptive rules since the local context will frame how you apply the ideas and recommendations within this book. As will be discussed later, a collaborative approach is essential in creating and sustaining a culture of ecological validation that supports at-promise student success. We recommend building a team of individuals to explore the ideas within this book. Given that creating a new culture would involve academic affairs, student affairs, faculty, financial aid, and other student services, we encourage you to bring together a diverse group of individuals from across campus. In particular, you may want to begin with those individuals who are already interested in equity issues on your campus.

A few comments about the application of the findings. We studied three very different campuses – a residential research university, an urban commuter campus, and a rural regional campus. All three are public four-year institutions. The findings are likely applicable to private colleges and community colleges. Private liberal arts colleges, Historically Black Colleges and Universities (HBCUs) and Tribal Colleges and Universities (TCUs) often have more attention to relationships and culture. However, the importance of validation is likely applicable to private liberal arts colleges, TCUs, and HBCUs, so we suggest that the student support model offered in our book may also be helpful for these institutions. Community colleges have made significant progress in the last few decades by focusing more on the needs of at-promise students, but their approaches often focus on data and technology. The ideas presented here may help them to balance their efforts with some other approaches. And, while we can make some generalizations by sector/institutional type, there are differences across individual institutions. Therefore, we hope campus leaders will review and consider these arguments with their individual contexts in mind and explore how our ideas can inform the work done to support at-promise student success.

Discussion Questions

- Are there subgroups of students at your campus who continue to have inequitable outcomes even though supplemental programming exists? What data do you have available to understand why these issues persist?
- What assumptions on campus stand in the way of enacting ecological validation?
- How might you consider altering your paradigm of student success and support to be ecological and validating and to be at scale – across the entire campus?

Understanding the Institutional Challenges to Serving At-promise Students

The first section of this book focuses on the challenges and opportunities related to improving at-promise college students' academic and psychosocial outcomes. Chapter 2 provides an overview of the inequities that at-promise college students face. Gaining a deeper understanding of these challenges and inequities enables educators to consider how to transform institutions to better support at-promise students and build upon their strengths toward greater success and a more socially just education system. We also situate our study within current research and practice related to supplemental support programming.

As most educators acknowledge, at-promise students have the potential to be successful in higher education. Educators generally recognize that at-promise students experience challenges navigating higher education and want to assist in improving their academic and psychosocial outcomes. Chapter 3 focuses on the institutional structures and approaches that create challenges for at-promise students. We explore how institutional silos lead to deficit-oriented, fragmented, reactive, identity-neutral, and nondevelopment practices that undermine efforts to improve academic and psychosocial outcomes for at-promise students.

Chapter 4 discusses the research project that serves as the foundation for this book. The Promoting At-promise Student Success (PASS) Project was a six-year mixed methods study of three campus-based comprehensive college transition programs. We describe the program, why it was an ideal site to explore these institutional challenges. The chapter also provides a summary of student outcomes associated with participating in the CCTP as well as some recommendations about program design and implementation.

DOI: 10.4324/9781003443711-2

2

AT-PROMISE STUDENT CHALLENGES AND INEQUITIES

Over the decades, many educators have worked tirelessly to increase at-promise student success, and those efforts have likely made a meaningful difference for students. However, at-promise students continue to face challenges that lead to inequitable retention and completion rates (Engle & Tinto, 2008). Institutions have not fared well in retaining at-promise students and getting them to graduation (Lumina Foundation, 2015). For instance, 6-year completion rates are 67% for White students compared with 46% for Black students and 55% for Latinx students (Shapiro et al., 2019). Only 10% of bachelor's degrees go to students whose families earned under $35,000, and first-generation college students' departure rates are much higher than their continuing generation counterparts (U.S. Department of Education, 2018). These disparities have motivated countless studies that seek to identify, explore, and describe the challenges and inequities faced by at-promise college students.

The inequities and challenges are a result of discriminatory cultures and structures in higher education. U.S. postsecondary education institutions were not designed with the success of at-promise students in mind and instead centered privileged, affluent, White, cisgender, Christian, heterosexual male students and their needs, culture, and values (Espiritu et al., 2019; Hurst, 2012). These postsecondary systems have frequently failed at-promise students. Some have argued that education systems as currently designed simply reproduce social inequities (Espiritu et al., 2019). Understanding at-promise student challenges and inequities in college provides important context to inform institutional solutions and disrupts the reproduction of inequities. While an exhaustive review of at-promise college student

DOI: 10.4324/9781003443711-3

challenges and inequities is beyond the scope of this chapter, we provide an overview of some common challenges and inequities that inhibit at-promise student success to situate the need for institutional action to address these challenges and promote equity. The final section of this chapter discusses how many postsecondary institutions have created supplemental support programs to address the needs of at-promise students. While these efforts often assist the students who get selected to participate, they have not significantly improved the overall outcomes for at-promise students.

College Knowledge and Navigation

At-promise students often do not have the same college preparation as their more privileged counterparts and face challenges such as a lack of a college-educated family or friend network to turn to for guidance navigating college structures that were not designed with at-promise students in mind (Gupton et al., 2008). At-promise students often are challenged to figure out on their own how to access the support they need for issues like financial stress, alienation, and academic barriers (Ardoin & Martinez, 2019; Jury et al., 2017; Soria & Stebleton, 2012). Coming to a college environment alongside students from more privileged backgrounds can lead at-promise students to feel intimidated by college and doubt their capability to succeed (Cushman, 2007). They may be unaware that support exists, and even when they are aware, they may not know where it is or how to access it (Pendakur, 2016). Campuses are typically organized in silos that are difficult to navigate, with little collaboration or communication between silos that makes accessing appropriate support difficult for at-promise students (Kezar & Lester, 2009; Kuh et al., 2006; Manning et al., 2014).

Financial Need

The cost of college has risen much faster than the inflation rate. In the past decade alone, the cost for room, board, fees, and tuition increased by 28% at public colleges and 19% at private nonprofits (National Center for Education Statistics (NCES), 2021). At the same time, there has been an accompanying disinvestment in higher education from many state governments that threatens college access and equity just at a time when higher education is experiencing growth in diversity (Mitchell et al., 2018). A growing number of students are dealing with challenges in college as a result of limited financial resources while also balancing academic, social, and work commitments (Lumina Foundation, 2015; Mitchell et al., 2018). Students from low-income backgrounds commonly experience financial challenges and burdens (Berg, 2010; Carnevale & Smith, 2018). Additional support may be needed navigating complex financial aid policies and aid packages, rules around credit load that bear on financial aid eligibility, or other roadblocks to applying and seeking out financial aid. Many at-promise students also need additional financial support to maintain a reasonable standard of living, to navigate budgets and taxes, cope with food instability and basic needs, pay for auto repairs, pay for healthcare, care for family members, and many other financially related matters that students from wealthier backgrounds need not worry about to the same degree (Hallett et al., 2019a; Lumina Foundation, 2015).

Unmet financial need can contribute an additional layer of college stress and the need to find part-time jobs, ask for financial support from already cash-strapped family members, or request money from private lenders with high interest rates. Financial burdens affect other aspects of at-promise students' college experience like time to study or socialize, limited time and resources for educational enrichment opportunities, or stress created by trying to balance work-life-school commitments. For instance, low-income students are more likely to work during college – more time working for pay is connected to lower grades, retention, and completion (Carnevale & Smith, 2018). Increased financial stress may also influence well-being (Robb, 2017). Comprehensively addressing students' financial needs is a promising way to promote the success of at-promise students; however, most postsecondary institutions lack the resources to do so.

College Engagement

Engagement has been linked to at-promise students' college success (Harper, 2009; Kuh et al., 2007; Quaye et al., 2020). Yet, not all engagement opportunities serve at-promise students well, and not all at-promise students have the same access to college engagement opportunities as their privileged counterparts (Museus et al., 2020; Soria & Stebleton, 2012). For instance, at-promise students may not have the time and energy to engage in co-curricular activities if they must use their time outside of class to meet financial or familial needs. Moreover, engagement opportunities are often one-size-fits-all and not responsive to the needs and identities of at-promise students (Pendakur, 2016).

Curricula that reflect the culture and backgrounds of at-promise students' respective communities promote engagement and success (Kiang, 2009; Museus et al., 2012). Institutions that provide opportunities that speak to the needs, desires, and interests of at-promise students will generally see increased academic engagement (Kitchen & Williams, 2019; Quaye et al., 2020). Educators need to take concerted steps to identify inequities in engagement, address institutional shortcomings, and proactively pursue opportunities to motivate at-promise student involvement by doing things such as bringing engagement opportunities to where many at-promise students already are (e.g., multicultural center, minoritized student organizations or clubs), communicating their commitment to at-promise student engagement, and devising engagement strategies that speak to their unique goals, desires, backgrounds, and interests (Harper, 2009; Kitchen & Williams, 2019).

Furthermore, engagement can be challenging for at-promise students as faculty, staff, and many students on campus have privileged social identities, and at-promise students are unsure whether their lived experiences will be understood by others. In addition, faculty may not incorporate race-conscious and culturally engaging pedagogy that reflects at-promise students' identities and experiences, which may lead to disengagement in the classroom. There are many strategies that promote at-promise student engagement, such as opportunities to give back to cultural communities, culturally oriented organizations, identity-focused peer networks, shifting the time or format of engagement opportunities to accommodate work schedules, and addressing classism, racism, sexism, and other forms of bias in the classroom and co-curriculum (Museus et al., 2020). What is missing is the collective institutional will and consistent follow-through on investing in these kinds of engagement opportunities.

Academic Inequities

At-promise college students, when compared with their privileged counterparts, frequently come to college with lower GPAs, lower standardized test scores, and fewer credits for academically rigorous or advanced coursework (Berg, 2010; Hallett & Venegas, 2011; Reeves & Halikias, 2017). This kind of differential academic preparation is a manifestation of systemic inequalities in schools. For example, at-promise students may come from underresourced school districts, which in turn contributes to a lack of opportunity for nurturing the academic knowledge and skills that would set students up for college success (U.S. Commission on Civil Rights, 2018). Colleges frequently adopt approaches to teaching and learning that perpetuate and exacerbate pre-college academic inequities (Berg, 2010; McNair et al., 2016).

The kinds of knowledge at-promise students bring with them to college often go unacknowledged (Kiyama & Rios-Aguilar, 2017; Yosso, 2005). For example, many at-promise students come to college with hope, determination, and an intense drive to succeed in reaching their goals. Others come to college with a strong desire to promote social justice and equity inspired by what they have learned from their communities or parents. Educators can draw on students' knowledge and capital to help them achieve their goals and contribute to a more student-centered campus culture where all students can succeed (Kuh et al., 2006). For instance, many at-promise students come from cultural backgrounds where community and collaboration are put at a premium in terms of achieving collective goals and success. Such opportunities for collaborative learning could foster at-promise student success (Hurtado et al., 1999; Quaye et al., 2009). However, many colleges and universities celebrate competition and elevate individualistic approaches to learning and achievement. Similarly, higher education privileges certain social class language and ways of communication and stereotypes low-income students' levels of intelligence (Berg, 2010). These institutional norms, values, and approaches to teaching and learning pose challenges for at-promise students who are navigating a system with a conflicting orientation to learning and academic success.

At-promise students also may face a lack of diversity among the educators that serve them. College students are more diverse than the faculty and administrators (Taylor et al., 2020). The lack of faculty or other educators with whom at-promise students can identify may pose barriers to forming trusting relationships that could contribute to students succeeding in college (Guiffrida, 2005). Lack of diversity among faculty, leadership, and staff may result in fewer advocates and individuals on campus who are attentive to institutional policies and practices that may negatively affect at-promise students.

Navigating Major and Career Paths

At-promise students do not have the same exposure to career experiences and preparation in their communities and schools nor as many career role models or mentors with college degrees (Locke & Trolian, 2018; Strayhorn et al., 2013). For instance, some first-generation students who pursue particular career paths (e.g., doctor or engineer) often do not have a family network to turn to for career guidance, lack a professional career network, and do not have access to appropriate college career support (Tate et al., 2015). Racially minoritized students may face challenges finding a same-race peer support network in their major and question whether they can be successful or truly belong in lucrative career paths such as those in STEM where they do not see themselves reflected in the course content or among peers and faculty (Strayhorn et al., 2013). Low-income students who work in college tend to work in the types of jobs (e.g., food services) that will not contribute many of the skills that would benefit them in terms of their future career prospects and preparation (Carnevale & Smith, 2018). At-promise students benefit from opportunities to see the real-world application of course content to future careers that is often not foregrounded in more lecture-oriented teaching (Kitchen et al., 2021c; Strayhorn et al., 2013).

As a result of these challenges, at-promise students may find it difficult to choose a career and major. Without support, students may aimlessly take classes and ultimately graduate from college without a clear career path. While some form of career services exist at most campuses, they are often tucked away, not well advertised or known about, or take one-size-fits-all approaches that do not speak to the unique needs of at-promise students. There is a need for more programming, services, and attention to these issues throughout a student's college career. Moreover, there has long been a strong need for culturally relevant practices to be infused throughout institutional efforts to support the major and career development of at-promise students (Flores & Heppner, 2002).

Psychosocial Development

At-promise students frequently have lower levels of psychosocial outcomes (e.g., belonging, mattering, academic self-efficacy) associated with college success when compared with their more privileged peers (Gopalan & Brady, 2020; Jury et al., 2017; Strayhorn, 2018). Low levels of belonging because of challenging social and cultural experiences in college, for instance, can contribute to negative college outcomes like departure or poor mental health, particularly for racially minoritized and first-generation students (Gopalan & Brady, 2020; Museus & Maramba, 2011; Nunn, 2021; Strayhorn, 2012). Students from at-promise backgrounds may also feel as if their identities and experiences do not matter to institutions, and what they value is rarely represented in the curricula or reflected in the campus milieu.

Negative stereotypes and messages about at-promise students' abilities may put a damper on their academic self-efficacy with implications for academic success and retention (Stewart et al., 2015). At-promise students may have lower confidence in their major and career paths as compared with their more privileged counterparts, with negative implications for college success and degree completion (Gloria & Hird, 1999). All too often, at-promise students' struggle to thrive and cultivate psychosocial outcomes is attributed to individual limitations rather than to the inhospitable institutional environment. Furthermore, institutional efforts to enhance at-promise students' psychosocial development are often siloed in boutique programs rather than integrated into the fabric of the campus environment; this fails to meaningfully address at-promise student psychosocial needs in any broad, appreciable way (Tinto, 2012).

Identity Development

Identity development is an important part of the college experience for all students (Patton et al., 2016). At-promise students, however, are faced with the additional challenge of identity development in collegiate social contexts broadly designed with a different kind of student in mind (primarily White, cisgender men, middle-class or affluent). For instance, many Latinx students need to navigate a bicultural orientation and their Latinx ethnic identity development (Torres, 1999) dealing with cultural forces and expectations within predominantly White college environments in a way that is unique and different from the identity development experiences of their more privileged peers. Students from low-income, first-generation, and working-class backgrounds need to navigate social class identity development in college environments with students from different (and often more privileged) social classes and where the topic of social class is often ignored or actively reproduced to the benefit of those from privileged social classes and the detriment of those from at-promise backgrounds (Bettencourt, 2020). Students from these backgrounds receive messages across environments that their upward mobility and success rests on adopting more privileged middle/upper-class identities, norms, and culture, which may cause anguish and additional identity development challenges uniquely experienced by at-promise students.

As a result of these institutional conditions, at-promise students' healthy identity development benefits from targeted support such as cultural centers, mentors with whom they identify, and identity-based programming. The need for such support may be particularly salient in college contexts with contrasting milieus, such as low-income students at elite institutions or racially minoritized students at predominantly White institutions. Such identity development is a critical aspect of a well-rounded college education (Patton et al., 2016).

Mental Health and Wellness

Mental health challenges and outcomes among college students are a growing concern for higher education. While mental health challenges are not unique to at-promise students, several factors ranging from racism, classism, alienation, challenges navigating campus, being away from family, and financial stress can further exacerbate and compound challenges related to personal wellness for students from low-income, racially minoritized, and first-generation college backgrounds (Becker et al., 2017; Jenkins et al., 2013). For instance, there is evidence that first-generation college students experience more stress and depression symptoms as they navigate college than their continuing generation peers and report less social support from family and friends (Jenkins et al., 2013). Students from minoritized backgrounds must also contend with hostile campus racial climates and feelings of academic stress as a result of assumptions about their identity group, which have been linked to depression and stress (Arbona & Jimenez, 2014; Jochman et al., 2019). Without culturally responsive, identity-conscious mental health support, at-promise students may not be set up for success. Campus environments contribute to at-promise mental health challenges by not explicitly naming the need for being inclusive, not challenging discrimination before it happens, and failing to set up a campus environment where all groups feel safe and a sense of belonging.

Racial, Cultural, and Class Bias and Discrimination

Students from at-promise backgrounds face a variety of challenges related to racial, cultural, and class biases and discrimination (McNair et al., 2016). For instance, scholars have documented that students from lower socio-economic backgrounds who do not adopt traditional middle-class college norms and values may face microaggressions, microinvalidations, and discrimination in college that affect their college experience and success (Berg, 2010; Locke & Trolian, 2018). U.S. society is rife with racial and ethnic discrimination, which extends to college campuses. For instance, research has shown that discrimination on and off campus hinders the academic performance and success of students from racially minoritized backgrounds (Stevens et al., 2018). At-promise students may also face challenges stemming from broader sociopolitical and cultural forces that students from more privileged backgrounds may not contend with to the same degree.

Campus climates that do not elevate, celebrate, and center diversity, equity, and inclusion create conditions ripe for bias, discrimination, and microaggressions that pose barriers to at-promise student success. Furthermore, institutions may enact policies and practices that systematically disadvantage at-promise students. At-promise students who have multiple marginalized identities may face multiple, intersecting forms of oppression that inhibit their success. Students who face racial, cultural, gender, and class-based discrimination may internalize these experiences to their own detriment if institutions do not address the systems that enable this bias and discrimination.

Supplemental Programs Designed to Address Inequities

Advocates, policymakers, administrators, professional staff, and instructors have explored ways to create identity-conscious, holistic, proactive, strengths-oriented and developmental programming for at-promise students in order to improve inequities related to the aforementioned academic and psychosocial outcomes. Institutions of higher education often design supplemental programs (e.g., peer mentoring) intended to support a specific subgroup of at-promise students (e.g., first-generation in college) that targets a specific need identified (e.g., improving sense of belonging) when an inequity emerges while reviewing institutional data (e.g., first-year student surveys). Your institution likely has several of these targeted interventions. Although rare, you may have a comprehensive college transition program at your campus. For the students selected to participate, these supplemental programs may yield positive gains related to the specific need identified.

The programs that exist vary in terms of focus, intensity, timing, and duration (Hallett et al., 2020a). For the most part, these programs are designed to address one or more key transition points. Although not always the case, targeted supplemental programs tend to be shorter in duration and comprehensive programs tend to be longer in duration. In the sections that follow, we discuss the difference between targeted and comprehensive programs.

Targeted Programs

Most efforts to address deficiencies in our higher education system to better support at-promise students have focused on creating small, contained units of supplemental support that are separated from the overall campus environment instead of creating broader systemic change (Ehrmann, 2021; Ting et al., 2000; Toven-Lindsey et al., 2015). Targeted programs include summer bridge programs, peer mentoring, first-year seminars, and first-semester or first-year transition programs. These programs often focus on a specific subgroup of at-promise students (e.g., first-generation college or racially minoritized) with the goal of supporting them through a specific transition. Generally speaking, targeted programs positively influence the small group of students they serve.

One of the issues with targeted programs is that they have not successfully moved the needle in at-promise student success. Challenges exist because most are boutique programs or services that only serve a handful of students, students may not be aware these supports are available to them, and the fragmented approach of targeted programs is not effective in increasing overall at-promise student success in a meaningful way. Creating a laundry list of initiatives and programs often exacerbates the complexity of student support on campus, further confusing students and not addressing the larger problematic campus structures, approaches, and culture that hinder at-promise student success (Bailey et al., 2015; Kuh et al., 2006; Tinto, 2012). Another limitation of standalone initiatives is that they commonly focus on single dimensions of identity and needs. Yet, students have multiple needs and identities, so a singular focus will fall short of holistically addressing student needs. These efforts also commonly – albeit unintentionally – take a deficit approach to at-promise student support, assuming students are lacking something when they come to college, which can prove detrimental to their success (Harper, 2010; McNair et al., 2016; Pendakur, 2016).

Comprehensive Programs

Creating comprehensive college transition and support programs is a relatively new approach that has not been widely adopted. In lieu of introducing a litany of stand-alone supports, scholars have argued for a move toward more interconnected, collaborative, aligned, and comprehensive support systems (Bailey et al., 2015; Tinto, 2012). For instance, one-stop shops and student success centers gained popularity many decades ago (Altieri, 2019). These efforts bring together dispersed student supports, such as advising, financial aid, registration, tutoring, and writing support, to coordinate a system of support in one centralized location, mostly as a matter of convenience to students so they did not need to travel all over campus to access each of these offices. The rationale for these one-stop shops and student success centers is that by co-locating these supports, they could deliver the institution's system of support in a more efficient manner compared with having several siloed supports and functional areas (Buultjens & Robinson, 2011). Despite having been popular, there is limited research on the effectiveness of student success centers; however, students tend to be more satisfied with accessing services in one-stop shops (Altieri, 2019).

Another popular approach to student support is the creation of comprehensive college transition programs (Hallett et al., 2020a). For instance, ASAP, Dell Scholars, CSU STEM collaboratives, and Carolina Covenant are programs that connect many aspects of support to create a comprehensive approach in response to the failure of traditional disconnected siloed campus systems (Angrist et al., 2015; Page et al., 2019; Scrivener & Weiss, 2013). Coordinating comprehensive programmatic support systems is more effective in promoting at-promise students' success. Quasi-experimental studies of Carolina Covenant (UNC-Chapel Hill) have shown that the comprehensive, holistic support that they coordinate for students is linked to higher student GPA and greater likelihood of meeting credit benchmarks to reach graduation (Clotfelter et al., 2017). Evidence from studies of Dell Scholars similarly shows that participation is linked to greater at-promise student success including college persistence and completion (Page et al., 2019). The City University of New York offers the Accelerated Study in Associate Program (ASAP) that coordinates support and promotes student success including increased credit earning and higher graduation rates (Miller et al., 2020; Scrivener & Weiss, 2013; Weiss et al., 2019). There are a number of other such studies of comprehensive college transition programs that suggest this approach to creating student support systems is a promising direction to increase at-promise student success (Dawson et al., 2020). While the emerging influence of comprehensive programs suggests a connection with academic outcomes, the influence on psychosocial outcomes has largely not been explored. Chapter 4 discusses the findings from our study that illustrate the influence of a CCTP on belonging, mattering, validation, and career/major self-efficacy.

Opportunities and Limitations of Supplemental Programs and Centers

Supplemental programs can allow an institution to explore the effectiveness of a specific intervention. Kezar et al. (2022) discuss how college transition programs – particularly comprehensive programs – can be a hub of innovation for postsecondary institutions. Given the finite resources available within higher education, rolling out a costly large-scale effort could be difficult to justify before knowing the potential impact. Piloting targeted interventions within a comprehensive program can be a useful short-term strategy to determine if an intervention works. CCTPs can also allow for unexpected ideas to emerge. The program can be a place to explore and discover new approaches to supporting at-promise students. Instead of mandates only coming from administration, a CCTP can be a place to discover as well as test new approaches that can be scaled to the entire campus. In particular, this can be useful within environments that are resistant to change because an idea can be piloted in order to gather data to make decisions about whether this specific approach works at this specific campus. For critics who may not initially endorse an idea, data from their campus can be persuasive.

One of the most significant critiques of both targeted and comprehensive programs is that these supplemental programs are not designed to change the culture of postsecondary institutions. The underlying structures continue to reflect dominant (e.g., White, middle class, heterosexual, and male) values and experiences. Supplemental programs remain necessary, in this context, to ameliorate the barriers that are embedded within institutional structures. Programs and departments across campus continue to function as silos with particular rules, policies, and expectations. The collection of disconnected programs means that at-promise students rarely get holistic support and guidance. While they may have a validating experience with one instructor or professional staff member, the interaction with the next person may be invalidating. A single invalidating experience in these contexts can create significant barriers for students. Instead of focusing on adding more supplemental programs to try to reduce the impact of invalidating experiences, a culture shift is warranted.

Conclusion

As the U.S. college student population grows increasingly diverse, the success of students, institutions, and U.S. society depends on the will of institutions to fundamentally rethink how they are addressing at-promise student challenges and inequities. This chapter provided an overview of the number of compounding challenges and inequities faced by at-promise students that inform their college experience and shape their college success, including mental health, financial needs and navigation, academic and career preparation, discrimination and bias, college engagement, and psychosocial and identity development. However, the nation's colleges and universities are currently ill equipped to support the increasing numbers of at-promise students matriculating to college. We need transformational change in how educators and institutions support at-promise students. The culture of higher education needs to change, and the way we approach student success needs to be fundamentally reconsidered (Museus, 2014; Pendakur, 2016). As Quaye and Harper (2007) argue, educators must move from negligence toward intentionality in the way they approach supporting at-promise students. Until such time that institutions are set up to serve the increasing proportion of at-promise students who matriculate to college, colleges and universities will never be truly student ready (McNair et al., 2016). The next chapter provides an overview of the limitations of current institutional structures and cultures in higher education that directly influence the challenges described above.

Guiding Questions

- What are some common challenges and inequities that you have encountered in your work with at-promise students?
- What approaches have you adopted to alleviate challenges and inequities faced by at-promise students in your work?
- How has your institution addressed at-promise student challenges and inequities? Where does more work need to be done?

3

SILOED INSTITUTIONAL STRUCTURES THAT LIMIT AT-PROMISE STUDENT SUCCESS

In the last chapter, we discussed the multiple ways that postsecondary institutions continue to struggle in providing support that significantly improves academic and psychosocial outcomes for at-promise students. In this chapter, we discuss the limitations of current structures and cultures in higher education that directly influence the challenges discussed in Chapter 2. In particular, we focus on how the siloed nature of higher education structures undermines efforts to support at-promise students. As a starting point, we share an example from our research of a student navigating siloed educational structures without support.

Ella started college excited and a little nervous. Sitting in Biology 101 on the first day of class marked an important personal and familial milestone – this was the first time anyone in her family had applied, got accepted, and attended college. Hearing each professor give an overview of each class that week, she felt confident about her ability to pass her classes. She also had met a couple of people on her residence hall floor who could potentially become close friends.

As the class progressed, Ella helped tutor one of her friends who lived in her residence hall. The concepts were fascinating. She found herself doing all the optional reading. The only concern that semester was that she earned a B- in her Introduction to Business class. All through high school, she had done well in math and told people she was going to be an accountant. However, the thought of sitting in an office and crunching numbers for a corporation did not seem as fun as she initially thought. A friend of hers had told her that some people who changed majors have to start over with classes and ended up taking another year or two of college. Her university

DOI: 10.4324/9781003443711-4

and Pell grant only covered four years of college, so she decided that changing majors was not an option. She would stick with accounting.

The second semester things changed. In January, her younger brother got into a car accident while driving home from school. He spent a month in the hospital. Their mother let the meat-packing plant know that she would not be able to come back to work until he recovered – she could not bear to have him sitting in the hospital by himself. So, their father tried to pick up some extra shifts. Ella sent some money from the reimbursement check she had received to help cover rent. In February, Ella got a call from her mother who was in tears – she had been fired for not returning to work more quickly. As an undocumented citizen, her mother had no way to fight back. How were her parents and three siblings going to survive? Ella thought about dropping out of college. Her mom convinced her to stay in school. Repeatedly, her mom told Ella that her success was their success.

Ella's roommate mentioned that her friend worked at a hotel and there was a job opening for the overnight shift. Ella figured this was a good way to make money and get business experience. She could work three or four nights a week, which would give her enough to cover her expenses and send money to help her family. She did not anticipate how difficult it would be to engage in classes after working all night. She tried to study at work, but there was always an issue that needed her attention. Normally an upbeat and high-energy person, Ella found herself tired all the time and withdrawing from engaging with friends. Not only was she physically tired, she felt guilty about not going home to help with her brother. In addition, her mid-term exams came back lower than expected: History (C-), Biology 102 (F), English (B-), and Introduction to Accounting (D-). She went into office hours to meet with her biology instructor, who told her to block out more time for studying. Her accounting instructor reminded Ella that she needed a B or higher in order to take the second-year courses. She did not know what to do. She felt guilty that her family sacrificed so much to give her this opportunity and she was wasting it.

By the end of the semester, Ella had stopped going to her biology class and focused all her effort on getting her accounting grade up. She wanted to drop her biology class, but worried that she might not have enough units to be full-time – which might affect her Pell Grant and university scholarship. She finished the semester with a 1.9 GPA, which included an F in biology and a C+ in accounting – just 2% points from a B. Ella was ashamed. A few weeks after moving back home for the summer, she received two letters from the university. One stated that she was on academic probation and the other that she was no longer eligible for the university scholarship because of the requirement of maintaining a 3.0 GPA. She also received an email from her academic advisor that she could not enroll in business classes in the fall because she did not pass accounting. The following week, she got an email from the housing office saying that she needed to submit a deposit or her room would be given to another student.

Every other student seemed to be doing fine. She could not figure out why college was so hard for her. The classes were interesting and she knew how to study, but somehow everything went off the rails. Getting emails and calls from the university made matters worse. While every person was nice, they always focused on what she was doing wrong. Every interaction made her more depressed. At lunch one day, her mom asked if she was getting excited for the fall semester. "Not really," Ella said with a shrug. "Maybe I will take a year off."

While the specifics may differ, you likely work with students with similar stories. Ella's experience represents the complex and overlapping issues we heard at-promise students speak about. Ella had academic challenges as a result of a personal issue that created financial challenges and limited interactions with peers. She came to believe that she was the problem and incapable of completing her goal of a college degree even though she had the academic ability needed to succeed. While supports may have existed on campus, she had a difficult time identifying those resources or figuring out how to access them. Her experience illustrates how siloed structures within higher education can undermine a postsecondary institution's efforts to provide support for students.

In this chapter, we discuss the siloed structures that typically frame how postsecondary institutions operate. Many institutions encourage collaboration between programs, offices, and departments; however, we argue that the ecology of support that emerges from these efforts is still defined by a siloed structure that negatively affects at-promise students. We then shift to highlight five key practices that result from siloed institutional structures: deficit-oriented, fragmented, reactive, identity-neutral, and nondevelopmental approaches to support. Research illustrates how these practices negatively affect the academic and psychosocial outcomes of at-promise students. As Ella's narrative illustrates, at-promise students may have the academic potential to succeed in higher education but have a difficult time navigating all the complex structures that are not designed to encourage their success. We end the chapter with a call for new institutional structures that center at-promise students. Our arguments in this chapter serve as an important foundation for our argument for a new approach to institutional structures – ecological validation – that is presented later in the book.

Siloed Approaches in Higher Education

Throughout this book, we emphasize the value of collaborative and integrated programs that combine several interventions to create a seamless learning environment for supporting students academically, socially, and personally. Scholars have long known that the bureaucratic siloed structures and the resultant institutional culture can undermine student learning and success (Ehrmann, 2021; Felton et al., 2016; Kezar & Lester, 2009; Kuh et al., 2006). Tinto (2012) calls for campuses to halt creating disconnected programs, reevaluate their support programs, and create more connected and aligned student support. Tinto (2012) noted that "too often, institutions invest in a laundry list of actions, one disconnected from another. The result is an uncoordinated patchwork of actions whose impact on student retention is less than it could or should be" (p. 5). In the sections that follow, we discuss two common approaches used to structure postsecondary education: silos of student support and an ecology of student support.

Silos of Student Support

Silos of support exist when each student service, support program, discipline, and academic department functions separately. As Diagram 3.1 illustrates, the professional staff and instructors are at the center of this structure – not the students. Professional staff and faculty members develop a deep level of expertise in their narrow area and rarely work closely with

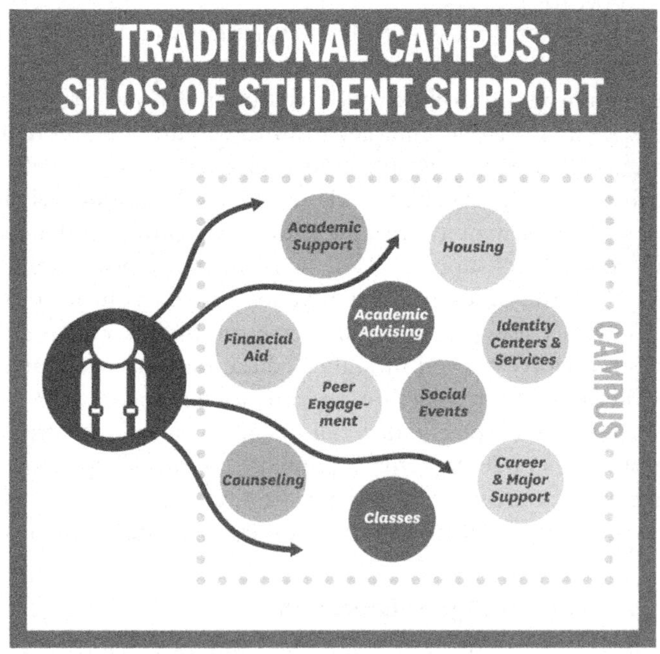

DIAGRAM 3.1 Silos of Student Support.

other areas of campus. Student services provide their specific service, such as financial aid, registrar, student accounts, facilities, and admissions. The professionals in these offices are rewarded for specific tasks without incentive to collaborate across campus to provide holistic student support. For example, the admissions office is expected to bring in a certain number of students with certain qualities; however, the success of students once they arrive on campus is not the concern of the admissions office. The financial aid office focuses on determining students' qualifications and distributing funding; however, the reasons why a student is experiencing financial challenges is not the concern of financial aid. The siloed approach means that professionals focus specifically on their area and avoid engaging students in more holistic, identity-conscious, developmental, or proactive discussions about their experiences, needs, or goals.

Academic departments also exist in silos. Instructors focus on their classes and research without much understanding of the university systems from a student perspective. Instructors may not even know the nuances of the degree requirements for students in their program because this role is delegated to the academic advisors. Advisors often have cross-campus meetings where they learn what resources are available; however, this does not mean that they are collaborating beyond those training sessions. Advisors understand the requirements for their specific content area, but rarely have significant awareness of the other degree programs – especially those outside of their college. Academic advisors are rewarded based upon the number of students in their programs and shortening the length of time to degree. As a result, advisors may be disincentivized from engaging in conversations with students about exploring different majors that may more closely align with the students' strengths and interests. The advisors may have knowledge of the research and internship opportunities offered by faculty in their departments, but they rarely have a close connection with the career and internship office that offers a wide range of opportunities in different fields. In addition, the numbers of students assigned to each advisor means that most are only able to spend 15–30 minutes with individual students during enrollment periods, and in larger departments, they may not see the same students each semester. If the department does not have an academic advising hold on registration, the advisors may not see students after first-semester registration during orientation.

Siloed approaches to student support mean that, at best, professional staff and instructors give students a phone number or email address of another program or department as a referral if an issue emerges that is outside of their expertise. For example, a financial aid staff member may give a student the phone number of counseling if they hear the student discussing feeling anxious about their financial situation. However, the staff member or instructor is not responsible for facilitating a connection for the student to a specific person who can provide support, and they are not required to follow up with the student. The institutional norms encourage educators to focus on their specific area and avoid conversations with students that are outside that area. Clearly, educators should not give advice in areas where they lack knowledge, but that does not mean they cannot holistically engage with students in order to connect them with others on campus. The challenge with silos is that the focus is on discrete tasks, not on building holistic relationships or developmental support as students navigate college. In addition, silos of support are reactive instead of proactive. Many of the interactions with at-promise students result when a student has a problem – such as being on probation or not paying a bill.

As Diagram 3.1 illustrates, silos of student support place the onus on the student to determine that they need support, figure out which office handles that issue, and then find their way to the location. The silos of student support rarely have clear streams of communication between offices, which means that gaps in support often exist. The image demonstrates how students may need support and be unable to figure out where to find assistance on campus. They may go to the wrong department and not be sent to the correct place, or the student may become frustrated trying to find the right place and give up.

Ecology of Student Support

Many postsecondary institutions have seen the limitations of traditional institutional structures that lack communication between different aspects of campus. As Diagram 3.2 illustrates, these institutions create opportunities for professional staff across campus to communicate with each other through an ecology of student support. These ecologies attempt to identify areas where students have unmet needs and areas where policies or practices may be creating challenges for students. For example, the financial aid office may not distribute funding until the second week of the first semester; however, the housing department requires students to pay residence hall fees the first week of classes. Communication between these offices can allow for adjusting policies in ways that benefit students. One-stop shops for student service and student success centers on campus are also examples of this trend. In either of these models of integrated service, campuses organize a variety of service and supports in one area so students do not have to go from office to office seeking out related services. This ensures more communication among these various services as they are more closely linked in location and mission.

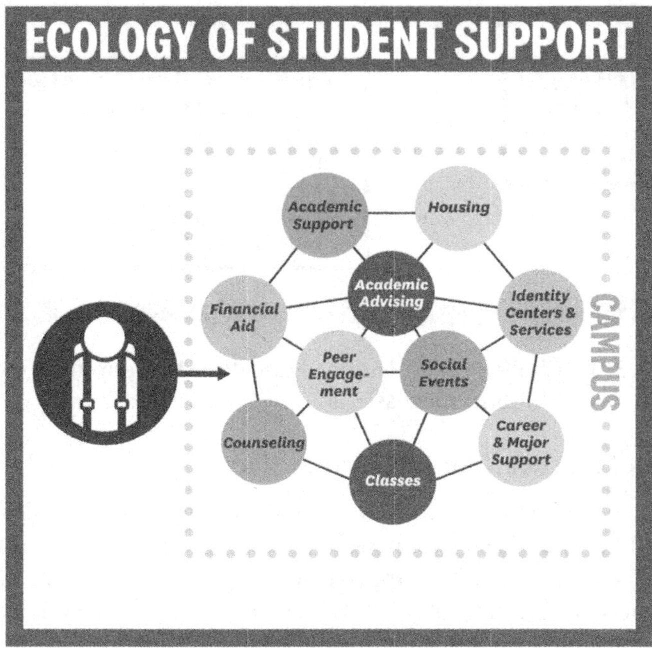

DIAGRAM 3.2 Ecology of Student Support.

While an ecology of student support can improve the bureaucratic structures that negatively affect students, silos still exist. As previously discussed, each program and office has a specific area of expertise. The reward structures and policies within each space on campus are designed with a narrow focus without incentive to significantly shift departmental or institutional culture. Of particular note, an ecology of student support continues to place the onus on the student to initiate support. These campuses do not have educators assigned to each student to provide holistic, developmental, and proactive support. As a result, students may not develop a trusting relationship with a professional staff member whom they can turn to when they experience a challenge or to get guidance on pursuing academic and professional opportunities.

The benefit of an ecology of student support is that more collaboration exists between offices. The problem is that students still do not get centered in this model. The student needs to initiate contact with someone in the ecology in order to get support, resources, and information. For at-promise students in particular, determining if a specific issue could be addressed by someone on campus can be difficult and then figuring out whom to contact can be overwhelming.

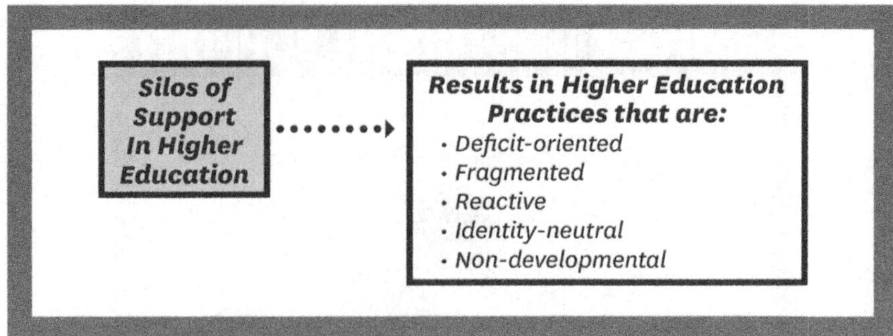

DIAGRAM 3.3 Challenges in Higher Education Undermining At-promise Student Success.

Problems of Practice That Result from Silos

Educators may not be motivated to address the issues of silos without understanding the negative impacts that result from these institutional structures. The silos result in approaches to practice that limit at-promise student success (see Diagram 3.3). Previous research underscores the negative impacts these sorts of practices have on at-promise student experiences and outcomes (Jayakumar & Museus, 2012; Museus, 2014; Tinto, 2012). The culture that emerges from a siloed approach often assumes that students are responsible for figuring out how to navigate college; if a student is unable to figure out the system, they do not deserve a college degree. These assumptions discount the realities we discussed in Chapter 2 – higher education systems were not designed with at-promise students in mind.

The silos that exist in higher education also limit the ability of institutions to create new cultural norms that support at-promise students (i.e., strengths-oriented, holistic, proactive, identity-conscious, and developmental approaches). While individual educators may enact one or more of these approaches within an institution, the overarching siloed structures and institutional norms undermine the ability to create a new culture that supports at-promise student success. In the following sections, we discuss the five approaches that result from silos: deficit-oriented, fragmented, reactive, identity-neutral, and nondevelopmental practices.

Deficit-Oriented Approaches

Many programs and supports created in higher education are deficit-oriented in assuming challenges that exist are a result of students' lack of knowledge, experiences, capability, and motivation – instead of looking at the systemic issues creating those outcomes (Harper, 2010; McNair et al., 2016; Quaye et al., 2020). Researchers also often focus on identifying student deficits with less attention to the institutional deficiencies (Kitchen & Williams, 2019; Museus, 2014). Within siloed systems, the multiple units create their own deficit-oriented subcultures that can negatively influence at-promise students even if one unit adopts a strengths-oriented approach (Kezar & Lester, 2009; Kuh et al., 2006; Manning et al., 2014).

Another approach that educators have identified that is diametrically opposed to a deficit-orientation is a strengths-oriented approach to student support. Strengths-oriented approaches to student support are increasingly popular in higher education and characterized by systematic efforts on the part of educators and practitioners to identify students' innate talents and abilities while engaging students in opportunities to develop those talents and abilities into strengths that empower them to succeed in college (Soria & Stubblefield, 2015). Rather than focus on fixing or mitigating student "problems," a strengths-oriented approach focuses on discovering student characteristics, qualities, and experiences that can be leveraged to achieve success and flourish (Lopez & Louis, 2009). Strengths-oriented approaches to education are guided by the perspective that investing in people's qualities and strengths can empower them to succeed in a way that devoting those same resources to overcoming weaknesses could not (Soria & Stubblefield, 2015).

Some educators and supplemental programs across your campus may already employ a strengths-oriented approach to working with at-promise students. The challenge for postsecondary institutions has been in figuring out ways to move from silos where individual educators or programs use strengths-oriented approaches to creating an institutional norm where every interaction with students focuses on their strengths and unleashing their potential. We argue for creating an institutional culture on campuses where every interaction is strengths-oriented.

Fragmented Approaches

Lack of coordinated and aligned student-support efforts leads to difficult-to-navigate, fragmented, and ultimately ineffective support (Pendakur, 2016; Tinto, 2012). The overall structures work against cross-campus collaboration with faculty organized into programs and departments. Student affairs is generally located in a separate division than academic affairs, and often "the two divisions work in parallel toward the shared goal of student success but without the dialogue necessary to coordinate their efforts" (Weissman et al., 2009, p. 7). Students must seek information and assistance from different parts of campus and often receive conflicting information because of the lack of cross-divisional communication (Bailey et al., 2015).

Fragmented approaches exist when each office, department, and program focuses on a specific aspect of the student experience, learning, identity, or support without attending to other issues, challenges, and opportunities. Educators develop deep levels of expertise in one aspect of higher education, but at-promise students' needs rarely get fully addressed through fragmented interactions with educators. As Ella's story illustrates, the challenges at-promise students experience often involve multiple aspects of their identity and require support from multiple offices on campus. Sending students around to different offices that only attend to a fragmented aspect of an issue without anyone knowing the bigger picture is problematic.

Fragmented approaches and norms lead to fragmented solutions that miss the mark. Sending a student to tutoring may be the correct approach for a student receiving a low grade on a midterm exam – if the reason for the grade is directly connected to a student not understanding the course material. However, a tutor will not be helpful for a student who has the potential to understand the content, but works two jobs to cover personal or family expenses, has a significant personal or family situation that takes much of their mental time or energy, or numerous other situations that your students experience. In our conversations with students, a fragmented solution may lead them to believe that no one on campus understands their situation, and this can discourage them from asking for assistance in the future.

Moving away from fragmented approaches requires taking time to understand why the student is in a specific situation and targeting support to address the underlying issue. Professional staff and instructors avoid assuming that they know the problem before speaking with the student and explore how they arrived at the current situation. A holistic approach works best when students have a trusting relationship with a person on campus. Sharing the details of personal and family issues with every instructor and office on campus can be exhausting and discouraging to students. Most postsecondary institutions do not have systems in place where one person is assigned to build a trusting relationship with each student and gets to know them from a holistic perspective throughout their college experiences.

We want to underscore the importance of taking a holistic approach to both identifying issues and extending opportunities to students. Students experiencing success get to have a conversation with a trusted person on campus about opportunities to build upon their successes. The professional staff or instructor engages with the student about internships, research, job shadowing, student clubs, and other opportunities that specifically connect with the student's interests, abilities, and goals. Holistic approaches are difficult to create within siloed systems that focus on individual processes instead of whole people.

Reactive Approaches

Reactive approaches involve waiting for students to initiate requests for support or reaching out to students after a specific issue has emerged (e.g., failing a class). In order to initiate a request for support, the student must recognize there is an issue, determine if this is an issue that someone on campus may be able to support, figure out whom to contact on campus, find time to share their need, and then explain what their need is. Since at-promise students tend to be unfamiliar with postsecondary education systems, they often do not recognize there is an issue until it has significantly affected their ability to persist in college. Final grades may send a signal that they need assistance; however, that is too late to access support needed to pass the class, and the student may begin to question their ability to be successful.

Educators need to take the responsibility for getting to know and interacting with at-promise students in order to create validating experiences that can positively influence their educational experiences (Rendón, 1994, 2002, 2006; Rendón & Muñoz, 2011). In particular, proactive advising involves the educator reaching out to students early during their time in college and consistently until they complete their degree (Kitchen et al., 2021a, 2021d). Proactive advising includes the traditional support related to selection of courses, choice of major, and academic planning, but also involves discussing career goals, college adjustment, personal issues, time management, strategies for achieving success, and other issues that students may identify as important. This approach to advising often involves educators connecting with students several times a semester in order to track student progress, assess how they are doing at mid-semester, and making connections to appropriate services and opportunities based upon the student's situation and goals (Engle & Tinto, 2008).

The ecology of student support approach has enabled postsecondary institutions to identify gaps in support. Many of the structural solutions have focused on creating responses to student issues as they emerge. For example, many colleges and universities have "red flag" systems where professional staff and instructors can denote in the alert system that an issue exists. Often, the issue is relatively significant by the time a flag gets raised. For example, a student has not attended class for several weeks or a student makes a comment related to suicidal ideation. The online system then sends this information to the department that seems most associated with the issue. A student either gets a standardized email or is contacted by a person whom they have no relationship with who wants to talk about a problem that has been reported. This reactive and impersonal approach can be difficult for students who may receive the message as reinforcing that they are not capable of success and do not belong in higher education.

Postsecondary institutions often use more personalized proactive systems for certain groups of students, such as athletes, Greek systems, honors programs, and students selected for specialized support programs. Drawing from the success of these efforts, you can explore how to extend these proactive opportunities to all at-promise students. For students not in Greek, athletic, honors, or comprehensive college transition programs, the only access to proactive guidance that exists is if a student gets put on academic probation. A student with average grades may be unattended as they navigate college without building a trusting relationship with an educator who could positively influence both academic and career outcomes.

Similar to the holistic approach, a trusting relationship is an important component of being proactive. A professional staff member or instructor who has a trusting relationship with a student is more likely to know when an issue is emerging – before it becomes difficult to resolve. A trusting relationship creates a context where students can feel supported, not tracked. You will not want to create systems that send the message that you assume at-promise students are "at risk" and so you are keeping a close eye on them. As mentioned, proactive systems also allow you to help students identify and prepare opportunities to extend their successes.

Identity-Neutral Approaches

Siloed structures often include identity-neutral approaches to student support. Departments, programs, or centers are responsible for attending to the needs of specific aspects of students' identities. However, the general approach to student support is identity-neutral. Individual interactions with educators across campus do not account for the multiple identities that at-promise students possess. At-promise students bring with them a range of skills, relationships, and identities as they begin college. Beyond having at least one identity that has been historically marginalized by society, they represent the diversity of the United States. In the Diagram 3.4, we provide an illustration of a student wearing a backpack as symbolic of the many different aspects of the student that they bring with them to campus. These skills, relationships, and identities evolve and, at times, shift throughout their time in college. Given the shared experience of marginalization, many of these students find postsecondary institutions difficult to navigate. In this section, we provide a short discussion of many aspects of at-promise students that postsecondary institutions should attend to when developing structures and policies; however, this should not be considered a comprehensive list.

At-promise students' background with higher education vary. Some students have parents, guardians, siblings, or close family members who attended a community college or four-year institution – which may or may

DIAGRAM 3.4   At-promise Student Characteristics and Identities.

not include completion of a degree or certificate. Some students may have connections to individuals in their network who earned a postsecondary degree in another country. Depending upon the high school they attended, at-promise students may have participated in college preparation programs, advanced placement courses, and honors programs. While some at-promise students may have significant college knowledge and may get frustrated by being required to attend seminars with basic information about being successful in college, other students without that experience may benefit from guidance on the basics of college success.

The class background of at-promise students also influences their college experiences. Some at-promise students may be from middle-class family backgrounds while others may qualify for Pell Grants and other forms of need-based support. Their financial background often influences students' perceptions about the costs of education, their decisions about if and how much to work, and their ability to engage in activities with additional costs. The financial guidance and support students need varies. In addition, the comfort or discomfort that students have with the middle-class, or in some cases wealthy, context of the postsecondary institution will likely depend upon their background. For students from lower-income backgrounds, the disconnect between their postsecondary context and home community may create challenges as they navigate these two differently classed spaces.

At-promise students bring racial, ethnic, gender, and sexuality identities with them. Some of these students may find identity and culture centers safe places as they negotiate higher education. For students who are exploring their gender and sexuality, identity centers can provide support – particularly if they come from families and communities that have not been affirming. Other students come from families and communities that have been incredibly supportive and celebrate these students' gender identity and sexuality. Identity and culture centers often serve as important spaces for minoritized college students who benefit from support navigating personal, familial and academic challenges.

At-promise students may also possess other experiences and identities that have been marginalized by society, including immigration or refugee status, homelessness or basic needs insecurity, and parenting or caregiving while a student. The aforementioned aspects of the student's identities and experiences are also fluid. A student may start college with financial stability and then experience a financial crisis. Or they might become more aware of their gender, sexuality, or racial identity as they navigate college. In addition, at-promise students may possess multiple identities and experiences that are marginalized by society. These students often find it difficult to receive intersectional support on campus. For example, a lesbian undocumented Asian student may not find their intersecting identities fully represented in the undocumented student group, LGBTQ+ center, or Asian American club.

Postsecondary institutions often have a difficult time creating a culture that cultivates identity-conscious interactions with students. While individual educators or programs may be identity-conscious, the overarching structures and culture often do not affirm or support at-promise students' multiple identities. Many of the support structures and teaching methods embedded in higher education take a one-size-fits-all approach that ignores or gives only cursory attention to the diversity of students. Support practices and teaching that do not reflect the identities and experiences of at-promise students may create barriers to their learning and success. While many colleges and universities offer identity-based support programming, these efforts often focus on single identities and do not capture intersecting identities.

Research related to student identity argues that new strategies are needed to support the increasingly diverse group of students attending college

(Clotfelter et al., 2017). A typical solution is to create programs or centers that address a specific identity without significantly shifting institutional structures, policies, or culture. Students with privileged identities and backgrounds succeed in a siloed approach because they know how to navigate the system and feel the competitive context reflects their values. As a result, siloed structures reinforce notions of meritocracy and fairness that encourage the success of some students while creating barriers for others. New approaches and institutional norms are needed that push back against classism and racism in order to create identity-conscious cultures in higher education.

Nondevelopmental Approaches

Programming often focuses on a specific point in a student's academic career. Students often get the most support in the transition to college and the first semester. The support provided does not necessarily build over time, nor is there intentional synergy across campus support offices to foster holistic development among students along their college journey. There is not a person who guides students through the process and considers the developmental progression of support. The further students get in college, the less support they may get. Some educators feel that independence is a critical component of a college graduate. However, this discounts that first-generation college students are also the first in their family to pursue a professional career. They benefit from continued support as they move toward the next stage of their education and career.

Whether it be academics, identity, or interpersonal, many scholars have argued that student development unfolds with time (Mayhew et al., 2016; Patton et al., 2016). A developmental approach would harken back to earlier traditions in higher education where a dean was assigned to each incoming college class to work with them over their four years of college to ensure continuity of support. The idea of longitudinal support is not necessarily new but has been lost over time. While individual practitioners may take this approach in their work, a developmental approach is not structurally embedded in how most colleges and universities offer support services to students. Instead, colleges and universities often target their developmental support in discrete, relatively brief, first-year initiatives like summer bridge programs, student transition programs, extended orientations, developmental courses, and first-year seminars, for instance. The support in these programs is typically disconnected and siloed off from the rest of the campus, creating "sub-environments" within the larger campus to support students' development and success rather than shifting the larger campus. Moreover, when most of this first-year programming ends, the support they offered to foster student development ends – regardless of where a student stands in their developmental trajectory at that point. This may be particularly problematic considering that students often follow different developmental paths and develop at different rates given their past experiences and experiences during college (Bronfenbrenner & Morris, 2006; Chickering, 1969; Patton et al., 2016). Moreover, students' developmental needs in their second, third, fourth, or fifth years will likely look different than what their needs were in their first year.

A developmental approach is not a new concept and continues to undergird the student affairs profession. Decades ago, Arthur Chickering (1969) proposed seven vectors of development and the environmental conditions that help foster those domains of student development. He suggests that student development and success is best understood holistically, in terms of progression along a trajectory, and that students develop at different rates over time given their educational conditions, support, and experiences (Chickering & Reisser, 1993; Patton et al., 2016). Other scholars have similarly argued for the need to think about student development as something that unfolds with time and on different timelines given a student's past experiences and engagement with the world around them (Bronfenbrenner & Morris, 2006).

Some colleges and universities have recognized the need to take a developmental approach to student support and have experimented with integrating additional support beyond the first year, such as sophomore year programming (Young et al., 2015). However, this approach is not widely used. Instead, colleges and universities typically offer a litany of many other kinds of support to foster student development in identity centers, career and advising offices, financial counseling offices, disability services, and the like. However, these support offices typically operate in silos. This siloed approach to student support requires students to independently monitor their developmental needs. Consistent with what scholars have argued in terms of student developmental trajectory over time, colleges and universities need to be re-designed with a developmental approach in mind to avoid exacerbating inequities in at-promise student success and to avoid the pitfalls of disconnected, disjointed support in students' developmental trajectory.

Need for a New Structural Approach to Alter Work Norms

For several decades, researchers have concluded that siloed structures must be bridged or broken down in order to best support student success. Scholars have variously referred to these new ways of organizing work as horizontal functioning (Keeling et al., 2007), guided pathways (Bailey et al., 2015), programmatic alignment (Tinto, 2012), and integrative learning (Peet et al., 2011). The problem has not been alleviated by restructuring efforts. More recently, efforts have intensified around providing guidance for restructuring efforts and the work of teams – The Council for the Advancement of Standards in Higher Education released a report about the need for cross-functional teams and ways to structure such teams. Many campuses are structured and organized in ways that inhibit collaboration and focus on a fixed set of student services, mired in bureaucracy, disconnected, managerial subcultures, with little evidence of a shared commitment to student success (Kezar & Lester, 2009; Kuh et al., 2006; Manning et al., 2014).

In these kinds of environments, the institutional norm suggests that it is up to the student to seek support to achieve success. Siloed approaches to student support assume that students are aware of how to navigate campus and what resources are available to them. The siloed work culture and lack of coordination and collaboration across fragmented student supports further prevent student learning and success (Buultjens & Robinson, 2011; Kezar & Lester, 2009; Kuh et al., 2006). Ehrmann (2021) highlights postsecondary institutions that have created coordinated and collaborative approaches that are distinctly different from the siloed structures that frequently exist in higher education. His work illustrates the significant impact these shifts can have on at-promise students' academic and psychosocial outcomes.

We need to consider new norms for how we work, which are reinforced by institutional structures and processes that can help frame the daily practices of educators – essentially, we are talking about a new campus culture. Our research identified how structures reflect values and norms, so we need to re-examine our underlying approaches to our work that focus on being proactive, identity-conscious, strengths-oriented, holistic, and developmental. These norms lead to different approaches to daily work such as advising, teaching, mentoring, and student support and services. Shifting institutional culture by creating new norms and adjusting structures and processes to support the new norms will enable all students to consistently experience validation by building trusting relationships with educators across campus.

One might be inclined to say that it is up to the student to adapt to the way institutions are currently designed as well as the current cultural values and norms. However, we counter that logic with the question: what is the purpose of these institutions if not to address the educational needs and success of the students they serve? If the way systems are designed does not fully accomplish the goal of the system – in this case, at-promise student success – then we argue that those support systems need to be changed. Similarly, if the cultural norms of an institution continue to marginalize at-promise students, then new approaches are needed instead of creating supplemental programs designed to teach students how to adapt to traditional institutional cultures that were designed to exclude them. As Chapter 2 illustrated, there is substantial evidence to suggest that the systems and cultural norms as currently designed in higher education do not meet the needs of the increasingly diverse students they purport to serve.

Next Step: Shifting Institutional Culture

Postsecondary institutions need new norms of student support and working together as educators that are supported by campus processes and structures, which create a new institutional culture. Attempting to create a new culture without the structures in place to support it will not be effective in the long run. Similarly, structures can be shifted to create a different way of organizing the institution without significantly changing the cultural norms that frame how policies are created and practices are enacted. In order to improve academic and psychosocial outcomes for at-promise students, postsecondary institutions need to consider how to build new structures and processes that are holistic, identity-conscious, proactive, strengths-oriented, and developmental. In addition, institutions should explore how to create reflective and collaborative norms related to educators working across the institutional structures to break down the silos that undermine at-promise student success. While focusing on all these norms at the same time may seem overwhelming, we have found that they reinforce each other in ways that positively influence at-promise student experiences.

In this chapter, we focused on aspects of higher educational culture that inhibit postsecondary institutions from moving the needle on at-promise students' academic and psychosocial outcomes. As more at-promise students enter our campuses, the time has come to explore ways to reorient the institutional culture to meet their needs and unleash their potential. While adding technology and developing new structures with clear pathways for students are important, educators are a fundamental component of supporting at-promise students.

To date, supplemental programming has not had a significant impact on the transition, success, and completion rates of at-promise students. While these programs assist some students in successfully navigating college, they generally do little to shift the overall culture of the postsecondary institution. As a result, at-promise students may continue to experience challenges and face barriers outside of the protective context of the supplemental program. Instead of creating supplemental programs to help at-promise students navigate postsecondary institutions designed for privileged students, the time has come to explore how to shift institutional culture.

Reflection Questions

- How have you seen silos influence the experiences of at-promise students at your institution?
- Identify a structure or policy that reflects identity-neutral, fragmented, reactive, deficit-oriented, and nondevelopmental norms at your institution. How do these structures and policies influence at-promise student experiences and outcomes?

4

PROGRAM OF STUDY, RESEARCH DESIGN, AND STUDENT OUTCOMES

Throughout this book, we encourage institutions to explore how to shift institutional structures and culture in order to serve at-promise students. We argue that developing disjointed programs of support will not fully capture the needs of at-promise students. Campuses may develop comprehensive college transition programs (CCTPs) as a first step toward shifting institutional culture, and these programs could serve as hubs of innovation for campuses to develop and test promising practices. This book draws significantly from a longitudinal mixed-methods study of three CCTPs. The Promoting At-promise Student Success (PASS) Project was a foundation-funded study that included both research and evaluation elements. The goal of the study was to understand if, why, and how the CCTPs influenced the academic and psychosocial outcomes of a diverse group of at-promise students. Given the limited descriptive information about CCTPs, we include a description of the programs, which may serve as a reference point for campuses interested in creating a similar program.

We begin by discussing the Thompson Scholars Learning Community (TSLC) programs, which served as the context of the study. In particular, we describe the program elements of these CCTPs. We then provide an overview of the PASS Project study design and methodology. The study is one of the largest and most comprehensive studies of how at-promise students experience the transition to college and what types of support positively influence their experiences and outcomes. The final section of the chapter presents findings that emerged from our quantitative examination empirically documenting the positive outcomes resulting from participation in the TSLC programs and promising practices we identified from the

DOI: 10.4324/9781003443711-5

programs, as well as insights related to program design and implementation that may be helpful for campuses interested in creating a CCTP. These findings provide the impetus for understanding *how* and *why* the TSLC programs support positive college outcomes for at-promise students, which offers insights to educators about creating institutional change that can similarly foster positive college outcomes for at-promise students.

Thompson Scholars Learning Community

The Susan Thompson Buffett Foundation selected approximately a thousand students each year to receive a scholarship. These students could attend any public postsecondary college or university in Nebraska, including community colleges. The majority of the students chose to attend one of three University of Nebraska campuses where students were required to participate in the Thompson Scholars Learning Community (TSLC), which began in 2008 and was financially supported by the foundation.

The three University of Nebraska campuses differ in structure, size, and student population. The Kearney campus was an emerging Hispanic Serving Institution situated in a relatively small city in central Nebraska and primarily served students from the rural communities across the state. The Lincoln campus was located in the state capital and was a large research-oriented land grant university that attracted students from across the state, nation, and world. The Omaha campus was located in a metropolitan area and served the most racially, ethnically, and linguistically diverse group of students of the three campuses. Approximately 700 students entered one of the three TSLC programs each year. And about 700 second-year students were supported by TSLC across the three campuses. In addition to the 1,400 first- and second-year students supported by TSLC, the programs also remained connected with students who exited the formal program but continued working on their undergraduate degrees at the campus.

TSLC – a comprehensive college transition program – offered opportunities and supports beyond a typical learning community. The programs offered two years of concentrated support for at-promise students that included multiple different elements (see Figure 4.1). In the sections that follow, we provide an overview of the program elements that were generally included as part of the program; there was some differentiation in implementation due to campus context and student populations served by a specific program.

Staff Care and Support

TSLC staff members worked closely with students during the two years of formal programming and continued to serve as a resource until the students

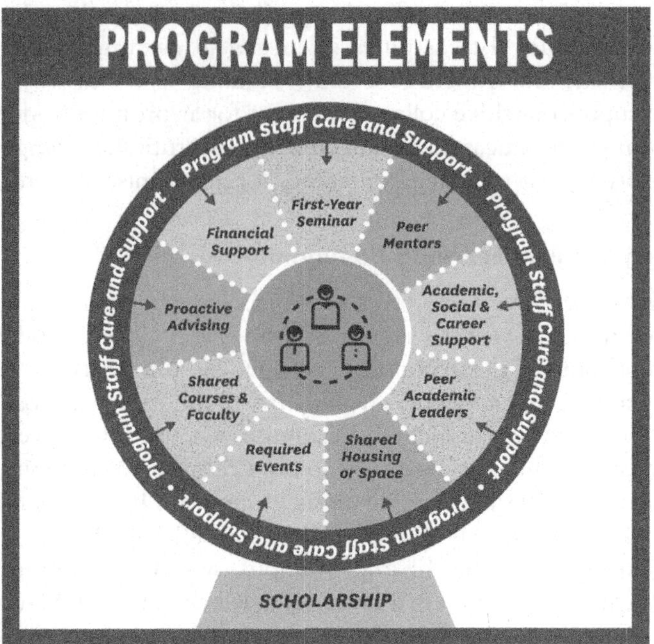

FIGURE 4.1 TSLC Program Elements.

graduated. The staff formally coordinated the program elements (e.g., proactive advising and first-year seminar) as well as providing informal support. Students were encouraged to stop by the office space even if they did not have a specific question. These informal connections allowed staff to celebrate individual successes with students, connected them with opportunities, and identified when a student might be experiencing challenges before their grades were affected. Each student had a designated staff member who served as their point of contact if they had questions, needed support, or just wanted to connect with someone on campus.

Scholarship

Students in the TSLC program received scholarship funding from the Susan Thompson Buffett Foundation that was approximately the cost of tuition and fees for up to five years of undergraduate education (see end of the chapter for more details). The scholarship provided support up to the cost of attendance and was designed to be added to students' financial aid packages after other forms of funding (e.g., grants and scholarships) were included.

First-Year Seminar

Each TSLC program required students to participate in a seminar the first semester of college. The seminar was taught by TSLC staff members and focused on college knowledge and building community. Each campus program developed a common syllabus for the seminar that all staff members used to guide instruction while also leaving room to individualize lessons based on student needs.

Peer Mentors

For the first year, students were assigned a peer mentor. The staff members selected mentors who represented the diversity of TSLC, which included high-achieving students as well as those who struggled the first year but took advantage of resources. The staff also considered the compositional diversity (e.g., race and gender) of the students in the program when choosing mentors. Mentors completed extensive training that focused on how to provide guidance and support to at-promise students. They regularly connected with staff about potential student issues. Mentors provided informal academic and social support to students to help them navigate college.

Academic, Social, and Career Support

Staff coordinated multiple forms of academic, social, and career programming for students during their first two years. This support included social activities designed to build community, such as yoga, movies, and picnics. Academic support included developing study skills and selecting a major. Career support included how to find an internship and research opportunities as well as professional etiquette and mock interviews. Staff members also provided individualized academic, social, and career support in the proactive advising sessions.

Shared Housing and Space

Two of the programs required students to live in shared on-campus housing the first year unless they were living with their parents/guardians or had another approved accommodation. The third campus primarily served commuter students; for the relatively small number of TSLC students who chose to live in a residence hall at this campus, the staff connected them with other TSLC students so they could share a room. All of the programs had additional spaces designated specifically for TSLC students to spend time socializing or studying. These spaces included murals, pictures, and language that demonstrated the values of TSLC and encouraged students' success. They also had resources for students, such as computers and printers, to support academic success. For postsecondary institutions creating a comprehensive college transition program, housing may or may not be possible. While students living in shared housing developed closer relationships with peers and felt a stronger connection to the campus, a successful program could be developed that does not require shared housing but has another designated space for students to connect with each other and educators working with the program.

Recognition and Celebration Events

TSLC created opportunities to celebrate students' successes. The programs had events to acknowledge students who made dean's list or achieved above a 3.5 GPA. They also had a graduation celebration where students were encouraged to bring their family and loved ones. While many postsecondary institutions send out certificates and emails acknowledging student achievement, the public event with family, staff, instructors, and administrators mattered to at-promise students even if they were unable to attend. The recognition ceremonies served as validating experiences because these events included messages about how the students belonged on campus and mattered to the program.

Shared Academic Courses and Instructors

Students were required to take 5–6 shared academic courses with other TSLC students over their first two years of school. These courses typically fulfilled general education requirements. The foundation provided supplemental funding in order to designate the class as only for TSLC students and keep the enrollment at 25 students or fewer. Each program had a faculty coordinator who worked closely with the instructors teaching TSLC classes. The faculty coordinator served as a point of contact for instructors, which included assisting the instructors who identified students who needed additional support. The faculty coordinator worked with TSLC staff to connect with these students and develop a support plan. Some learning communities require students to take the exact same classes together. This approach can be logistically difficult when students are in different majors or for students who completed college credit in high school; they may be resistant to retake a class they already completed. Even though students did not have the same peers in each class, they frequently spoke about feeling a sense of connection because they were in the same program.

Proactive Advising

Staff members met individually with students at least once a semester for the first two years to discuss the student's goals and review their academic progress. About halfway through the semester, students submitted a summary of their mid-semester grades for each class. At two of the campuses, students connected with each of their instructors to get an estimate of their grade while the other campus asked students to estimate grades. For those who might be struggling, the proactive advising conversation focused on exploring what was happening and identifying potential resources, tools, or strategies that the student could utilize. For the students experiencing success, the conversation focused on identifying additional opportunities (e.g., clubs, internships, and research) that the student could engage in to extend their learning and prepare for their future careers. Students consistently spoke about how these meetings were a safe and validating space.

Financial Support

TSLC provided formal and informal financial support for students. Students had an opportunity to attend budgeting workshops that focused on money management, including a discussion of credit cards and loans. The programs also shared information about the difference between scholarships, loans, and grants to help students make decisions about their financial aid packages. During the proactive advising meetings, staff members had individual conversations with students about their financial situation. For students experiencing financial struggles, the staff member explored different opportunities available on campus; at times, they assisted the student in contacting the financial aid office to have their financial aid package reevaluated.

Academic Probation

In addition to the required aspects of the program, TSLC provided targeted support and continued proactive advising for students who entered academic probation. Staff members received training related to developing academic recovery plans so they could guide students through the probation process. The staff individualized the probation plans depending upon each student's situation. Many campus probation programs include meetings with an advisor who creates an academic recovery plan for students. One important distinction was that the TSLC students on probation already had a trusting relationship with the staff member, which made it easier to develop a plan based on the staff member's knowledge of the student's background, goals, challenges, and resources. While being on probation was still difficult for students, the trusting relationship appeared to reduce the level of shame students felt as they collaborated with a staff member in developing and implementing their plan.

PASS Project Methodology and Study Design

The Susan Thompson Buffett Foundation funded the Promoting At-promise Student Success Project with the intent of understanding if, how, and why the TSLC program worked. We summarize the methodology briefly in this section, and more details about the methodology can be found here: https://pass.pullias.usc.edu/methodology. The six-year (2015–2021) mixed-methods study focused on academic and psychosocial outcomes. The quantitative portion involved surveying two cohorts of students five times starting in 2015 and 2016 (Cole et al., 2019). The first survey was conducted during the first month of college, with follow-up surveys each spring until the end of the students' fourth year of college. Surveys focused on understanding students' TSLC and general college experiences with a focus on psychosocial outcomes (e.g., belonging, mattering, validation, and academic, social, and career self-efficacy). The study design enabled us to compare student experiences based on if they received TSLC and a scholarship, just a scholarship without TSLC, or no scholarship or TSLC. For readers who may be curious about the role of scholarships, a complementary study looked specifically at the positive influence of receiving the five-year scholarship (see MIT website at the end of the chapter). In this chapter, we focus specifically on the role of the TSLC program in achieving desired academic and psychosocial outcomes. We also point to the key research publications that provide a more in-depth analysis of each finding.

The qualitative aspects of the study included multiple forms of data: documents, observations, student digital diaries, and interviews with staff, instructors, and stakeholders (Hallett et al., 2020). We gathered documents to understand the historical context and mission of each program (e.g., syllabi for first-year seminars, instructor orientation materials, lists of shared academic courses, and annual reports submitted to the foundation each year). The annual reports summarized what the program accomplished each year as well as goals for the next year. We conducted over 200 hours of observation at each campus for a total of approximately 600 hours. We met with program directors, staff, faculty coordinators, and students to identify key events and program elements to observe (e.g., staff meetings, classrooms, program spaces, mentor and staff training, instructor orientation, and events/workshops). We also observed the websites and public social media pages for the programs.

Students participated in digital diaries, which is a longitudinal method involving a combination of short video reflections and in-depth interviews.

We recruited students during their first semester of college, and they continued through their third year of college. We had 83 students complete digital diaries, which involved 938 interviews and 958 video entries. We had a diverse group of students participate:

- 55 women, 26 men, and 2 trans/nonbinary individuals
- 10 African American/Black, 5 Asian/Pacific Islander, 27 Latinx/Chicanx, 32 White, and 7 multiracial students; 2 individuals did not disclose racial identity
- A wide range of academic majors was represented, including those who began college undeclared and those who changed majors
- All participants graduated from a Nebraska high school; some attended small rural schools while others attended large urban schools in Omaha
- 23 students identified a language other than English as their primary language
- Parent education level ranged from never attending college (26), attending college without graduating (15), earning an associate's degree (16), and earning a bachelor's degree or higher (25); 1 student did not provide parent education level

Interviews with staff, instructors, and campus stakeholders gave us the opportunity to understand how TSLC functioned (see Tables 4.1 to 4.3). Interviews with staff members included the directors and faculty coordinators. They discussed program implementation, challenges they experienced, and goals for the program. Instructor interviews focused on their experiences teaching the TSLC classes. Stakeholder interviews involved individuals across campus who worked closely with TSLC (e.g., financial aid, counseling, residence hall). These individuals focused on the partnership they developed as well as how they perceived the programs supported students.

The remaining chapters are based on data from this study. Rather than extensive quotes and raw data, we provide case studies and narratives. This approach supports our goal of making the information accessible to and

TABLE 4.1 TSLC Staff Members

	# of People	# of Interviews	Man	Woman	Trans or Nonbinary	White	Racially Minoritized	Unsure
UNK	4	9	2	2	0	3	1	0
UNL	9	15	2	7	0	5	4	0
UNO	13	18	4	8	1	7	6	0
Total	26	42	8	17	1	15	11	0

TABLE 4.2 TSLC Instructors

	# of People	*# of Interviews*	*Man*	*Woman*	*Trans or Nonbinary*	*White*	*Racially Minoritized*	*Unsure*
					TSLC Instructors			
UNK	8	9	5	3	0	8	0	0
UNL	10	10	2	8	0	8	2	0
UNO	10	10	6	4	0	7	2	1
Total	28	29	13	15	0	23	4	1

TABLE 4.3 TSLC Stakeholders

	# of People	*# of Interviews*	*Man*	*Woman*	*Trans or Nonbinary*	*White*	*Racially Minoritized*	*Unsure*
					TSLC Stakeholders			
UNK	12	14	8	4	0	9	3	0
UNL	9	9	3	6	0	8	1	0
UNO	7	7	4	3	0	5	2	0
NU	1	2	0	1	0	1	0	0
Total	29	32	15	14	0	23	6	0

useful forcampus leaders and practitioners. In order to protect the confidentiality of our participants, we present some of the staff, faculty, and student data using a combination of direct data and composite data to illustrate the ideas throughout this book. At times, we have made minor adjustments to some details about individuals that are not consequential to the idea presented, but help to remove identifiable information. The goal is to provide detailed examples to support our ideas without violating the confidentiality of our research participants.

Program Outcomes

As noted above, our mixed-methods study examined if, how, and why program participation and exposure to TSLC program practices and approaches increased at-promise students' college success. While the purpose of this book is to offer educators insights into fostering a student support culture that effectively increases at-promise student success, it is instructive to first note how we know the TSLC program and its practices effectively increased student outcomes prior to describing the mechanisms and lessons learned about how the program achieved those outcomes.

Our study focused on psychosocial outcomes that are consistently linked with academic success (e.g., GPA, retention, and graduation) including a college sense of belonging, students' feelings of mattering, major and career self-efficacy, and academic self-efficacy. A focus on psychosocial outcomes in college is warranted for at least three reasons. First, employers have recognized and acknowledged the importance of developing psychosocial skills among college students and in the workforce (Aspen Institute, 2019; Hart Research Associates, 2013). Second, while discussions about the purpose of higher education are often focused narrowly on increased income as a result of earning a college degree (and evidence suggests a college degree does indeed result in higher earnings), positive psychosocial development during college can also contribute to individuals' growth and well-being, and develop citizens who thrive and contribute to a better, stronger society (Mayhew et al., 2016; Schreiner, 2010; Swanson et al., 2021). Third, a substantial body of research links psychosocial outcomes to students' academic success and college persistence (Mayhew et al., 2016). For instance, our study found that at-promise students who reported higher levels of psychosocial outcomes such as sense of belonging, mattering, and academic self-efficacy earned higher grades and were significantly more likely to persist in college (Swanson et al., 2021). Thus, academic outcomes (GPA, retention) and psychosocial outcomes (e.g., belonging, self-efficacy) are not at odds with one another but, rather, are complementary aims of a well-rounded college education. Moreover, focusing on psychosocial outcomes also moves the conversation beyond finding ways for at-promise students to survive college and looks to how to enable them to thrive. In the sections that follow, we provide an overview to illustrate the impact of the TSLC's practices and approaches on several psychosocial outcomes associated with students' persistence and academic success.

Sense of Belonging

It is well documented that developing a sense of belonging in college influences student persistence and success (Strayhorn, 2019). Sense of belonging explores the extent to which students feel part of the campus community, of being connected to a group, and accepted by peers. At-promise students face numerous potential threats to their belonging, including microaggressions, isolation, and lack of representation in the student body. Our study looked at the effect of TSLC participation on at-promise students' sense of belonging compared with students who did not participate in the program. Quasi-experimental findings showed that TSLC participation led to sizable increases in students' overall sense of belonging in college compared with students who did not experience the TSLC's support (Melguizo et al., 2021). We also explored the role of TSLC program components in fostering belonging and found evidence that staff care and support, engagement with peer mentors, peer social and academic interactions, and participation in shared courses, for instance, were positively linked to building TSLC students' sense of belonging in college (Cole et al., 2019; Swanson et al., 2021). In other words, program participation helped students to feel connected to others on campus, that they were a part of a community of learners in college, and that they were accepted by their peers.

Feelings of Mattering

Students feeling like they and their success matters to others is associated with students' academic and social success in college and their well-being (Rayle & Chung, 2007; Schlossberg, 1989; Tovar et al., 2009). Mattering focuses on if students feel that people at their campus care about them as individuals and if others are invested in their personal well-being and success. Our study explored whether participation in the TSLC program increased at-promise students' feelings that they mattered to others compared with at-promise students who did not participate in the program. Our quasi-experimental study indicates that TSLC participation leads to particularly large increases in students' feelings of mattering to others (Melguizo et al., 2021). When we explored the role of particular facets of TSLC programming and their link to students' feelings of mattering, we found evidence that students had stronger feelings of mattering when they received higher levels of care and support from program staff as well as when they had higher levels of social and academic-related peer interactions with their TSLC peers, such as discussing class concerns, academic work, group projects, and studying together, for instance (Cole et al., 2019; Swanson et al., 2021). These findings suggest that when other individuals express interest about students' accomplishments, disappointments, exams, or projects, the students believe that they matter and their success matters to others.

Academic Self-Efficacy

Students' confidence in their academic capabilities is linked to students' college experiences and academic success (Pajares, 1996). A number of factors can influence students' academic self-efficacy, such as exposure to role models who are academically successful, successfully doing an academic-related task, or earning a good grade, as well as academic encouragement and feedback from educators. While we did not find that at-promise students in the TSLC program reported higher levels of academic self-efficacy than students who did not participate in the program (Melguizo et al., 2021), we did discover some promising TSLC program practices that significantly increased academic self-efficacy within the program. For instance, we found that support from program staff significantly boosted students' confidence in their academic capabilities with a sizeable effect on their academic self-efficacy (Rivera et al., 2022; Swanson et al., 2021). We also found a positive link between students' academic self-efficacy and their participation in TSLC's shared academic courses (Swanson et al., 2021).

Major and Career Self-Efficacy

Major and career self-efficacy (MCSE) refers to students' belief in their capabilities to successfully explore, choose, and pursue a particular major and degree path (Betz & Luzzo, 1996). Most postsecondary institutions invest resources in supporting students' major and career development to increase their confidence in selecting and pursuing a major and career path that is a good fit for their goals. Similar to academic self-efficacy, MCSE is influenced by factors such as verbal encouragement from educators (e.g., telling a student they would do well in a career field), mastery experiences (e.g., successfully completing a project related to their major), and exposure to role models in their major or career with whom they can relate. MCSE linked to students' college persistence and success (Bullock-Yowell et al., 2014; Peterson & DelMas, 2001). We found that the major and career programming offered by the TSLC program significantly increased students' MCSE compared with at-promise students who did not participate in the program (Hypolite et al., 2020; Kezar et al., 2020). Qualitative evidence suggests that the program played an integral role in connecting students with an ecology of major and career-related experiences and resources (e.g., mock job interviews, career exploration assignments, meetings with staff advisors) that exposed students to sources of MCSE that helped students feel more confident in making decisions about their career and major path (Kezar et al., 2020; Kitchen et al., 2021b).

Validation

Our study identified validation as a process or lever that leads to psychosocial outcomes in our study. Validation is a holistic, proactive process of affirming and recognizing at-promise students' assets, experiences, and capabilities for success in college (Rendón, 1994). Our study examined the link between validation and several psychosocial outcomes among at-promise students. We found that validation significantly, positively shapes at-promise students' major and career self-efficacy (Kitchen, 2021), their sense of belonging (Kitchen, 2023), feelings of mattering, and academic success as measured by GPA (Swanson & Cole, 2022). The link between validation and these psychosocial and academic outcomes is critical to note because finding that the process of validation increases at-promise student success further supports our exploration of how and why the TSLC program works.

Program Design and Implementation

This section describes the mechanisms, practices, and approaches that helped foster conditions that led to the aforementioned positive psychosocial outcomes for at-promise students. Based upon our analysis of the TSLC program, we identified several findings related to the program design and implementation that may be useful for other campuses interested in developing a comprehensive college transition program. In addition, we provide some reflections on the importance of the scholarship funding component of the TSLC program.

How Programs Are Implemented Matters More than What Elements Are Included

Our initial design included exploring which program elements improved students' academic and psychosocial outcomes and which ones were less impactful. What emerged from our study was the critical importance of the underlying approach to support used by educators and peers; the approach was more important than any specific program element. Specifically, it was the affirming, validating approach that educators took to support student success across the various program elements that mattered and was infused across the program's proactive advising sessions, shared academic classes, informal interactions with staff, and academic and social interactions with peers (Hallett et al., 2020b; Kitchen et al., 2021d; Kitchen et al., 2021e). Students consistently spoke about how educators reassured them of their capabilities for success; provided space for students to be vulnerable and take risks; and served as a safety net where they could seek support to reach their goals – which students found validating (Hallett et al., 2020b). Many of the program elements are also high-impact practices (HIPs; e.g., first-year seminars, proactive advising), which previous literature suggests are important for student success. However, it was the validating approach to implementing these HIPs that helped support at-promise students (Kezar et al., 2022a; Kitchen et al., 2020). This suggests that educators seeking to support at-promise students should focus not only on what support they offer, but also on *how* they are delivering support to students. In later chapters, we discuss ecological validation as a key aspect of how the programs were implemented.

Multiple Interventions Were Key Levers for Promoting Student Success

While the way that the program elements were implemented mattered for student success, having multiple coordinated, structured spaces for engagement also influenced student success. Generally speaking, when students were more engaged with the TSLC program elements, they tended to have higher psychosocial success outcomes (Swanson et al., 2021). For example, staff care and support was positively linked to students' sense of mattering, belonging, and their academic and social self-efficacy; engagement in shared courses was linked to mattering, belonging, and academic and social self-efficacy; and peer mentoring was linked to students' feelings of mattering and belonging (Swanson et al., 2021). Having multiple coordinated opportunities to engage with TSLC promoted student success by creating multidimensional wraparound support. While subgroups of students had similar levels of engagement and experiences in TSLC, different program elements led to those outcomes for different subgroups of students. For example, staff care and support was associated with women feeling a sense of mattering while faculty interactions were associated with mattering for men. Having a variety of program elements was necessary for a diverse group of students to achieve similar psychosocial outcomes.

Flexibility in Program Design and Implementation Allowed for Similar Outcomes across Campuses

There are many kinds of college transition programs that vary in terms of the student needs they seek to meet, their focus, and timing and duration (Hallett et al., 2020a). For TSLC (a 2-year comprehensive college transition program), each campus was given guidelines about what needed to be included: seminar the first semester; shared academic courses during the first two years; peer mentoring; proactive advising; and academic, social, and career programming. However, each campus was given flexibility to determine how to implement the guidelines based upon the specific student needs in each program and institutional context (Swanson et al., 2021). The ability for campuses to make slight modifications in order to be responsive to student needs led to similar outcomes across the campuses. This finding challenges the idea that strict program fidelity is needed. Our findings suggest that requiring strict-implementation of the programs may undermine the success of programs because they cannot be responsive to student needs and tailor support that reflects the student population and context.

Shared Academic Courses as a Loose Cohort Model

Many small learning communities have shared academic courses where all students take the same classes together. Given the size of the TSLC program and diversity of majors that students were pursuing, it was difficult to force students to take exactly the same classes with the same group of students over a two-year period. TSLC coordinated a number of shared academic courses that students took in a loose cohort model. Each semester, students were provided a list of TSLC classes that were capped at approximately 25 students and taught by an instructor who had been selected based on their demonstrated success as an instructor.

Students engaged in these courses in similar ways across social identities, family backgrounds, and prior academic achievement, and their engagement in these courses promoted their sense of belonging, feelings of mattering, confidence, and academic achievement (Culver et al., 2021). The shared courses are designed in such a way that they provide opportunities for students to connect with one another and develop a community of supportive peers in the classroom. Course instructors embed in the curriculum coursework that reflected the diverse identities of the students, they used active learning experiences to encourage students to participate, and when they worked with the students, they employed asset and strengths-oriented approaches and messaging when soliciting input in the class and providing feedback to students. One prominent example of these shared courses is called an autobiographical reading and writing course that is offered to first-year students (Perez et al., 2021). The course provided students with opportunities to reflect on who they are, write about who they are, learn about who they are in the context of culturally relevant texts, share their stories about who they are and their life experiences with peers and the instructor, and ultimately to have their stories validated and affirmed. Ultimately, participation in this shared "autobio" course led students to enhance their writing skills, to feel a stronger connection to peers and instructors and a greater sense of belonging, to have a deeper appreciation for their peers and their life stories, and ultimately, to feel more confident in their capabilities for success in college.

Importance of Scholarship Funding

While our study focused specifically on the comprehensive college support program, we want to acknowledge the importance of the scholarship funding that students received. TSLC students frequently indicated that receiving the Buffett scholarship influenced their college-choice process and their collegiate experiences. For example, several participants indicated that if they had not received the scholarship, they might not have attended a four-year university and would have opted to attend a community college that was more affordable or would have delayed starting college for a year or two while they worked to save money for college. Other students indicated that without financial support, they might not have attended college at all since it did not seem financially feasible for them. The scholarship for many students not only allowed them to feel confident attending a four-year institution, but also enabled them to more fully engage in college.

Students spoke about benefitting from having five years of scholarship support because it afforded them flexibility to spend time exploring their passions and career interests in college, which provided the opportunity to switch majors better aligned with their interests and toward a more fulfilling career path. For some TSLC students, alleviating some financial stress associated with paying for a bachelor's degree created new possibilities for pursuing postgraduate education. As institutions provide financial support to at-promise students, the messages that are sent in relation to financial aid matter. Specifically, they can be intentional about directly conveying to students that financial awards are given because they recognize students' constraints and their potential to succeed at the institution. When at-promise students have access to financial support and trusted educators who validate their potential to succeed, their scope of possibilities may expand and their financial stress may decrease.

Transferability and Limitations

While our study involved a comprehensive methodological design, we recognize a few limitations exist that frame the transferability of our findings. In particular, we discuss the institutional type and cost of the programs.

Considering Institutional Type

Our study was conducted at three very different four-year campuses: a suburban research university, a metropolitan commuter campus, and a rural regional college. While they represent different campus contexts, higher education is extremely diverse. As we discuss in other chapters, our findings relate to other types of postsecondary institutions. For example, community colleges such as Amarillo College have developed a model – a culture of love – that is similar to ecological validation and demonstrates that the ecological validation model is likely transferable to community colleges (Lowery, 2022). Career and technical higher education certificate programs may also find that ecological validation could encourage success for their students, who often are low-income, racially minoritized, and first-generation college students. While these findings are likely transferable to most predominately White four-year institutions, we believe our frameworks and ideas may operate differently at minority-serving campuses, which may already have validating environments. Therefore, future research should continue to explore ecological validation at more institutions in order to better understand its transferability.

Considering the Cost of the Program

TSLC was funded through an external foundation. Expecting each postsecondary institution to get similar financial support is unrealistic. However, comprehensive college support programs have varying costs; for example, an ASAP light program that had more streamlined support achieved the same outcomes as the original ASAP program. Various experiments are currently happening to understand the costs associated with offering comprehensive programs and still maintaining outcomes. There are campuses such as University of North Carolina Greensboro and Amarillo College that have moved to cultures of ecological validation (they do not use this specific term, but their transformations mirror what we argue for) without an infusion of significant funds (Lowery, 2022). Culture changes can be done through professional development and without the creation of new programs by re-imaging how current staff do their work. Thus, the question about needed funding to support ecological validation is still an open inquiry, with data suggesting that it can be supported with moderate or very limited additional funds. Our book is not advocating for securing additional funding to support ecological validation but instead asking academic leaders to explore how to embed these ideas into the existing work of faculty and staff, since the continuous adding on of new supplemental programs and services is too costly to be a sustainable model.

Digital Resources

- The Promoting At-promise Student Success (PASS) Project has a website with additional information about findings and research design (https://pass.pullias.usc.edu/). The website includes links to academic articles as well as research briefs specifically designed for practitioners and policymakers, which will continue to be updated.
- For more information about the Susan Thompson Buffett Foundation Scholarship, visit: https://buffettscholarships.org/

- A team of researchers at the Massachusetts Institute of Technology evaluated the impact of the scholarship on student outcomes such as enrollment, persistence, degree completion, and college debt: https://evaluatingcollegesupport.mit.edu/

Reflection Questions:

- What programs and services do you currently offer for at-promise students? Are these programs and services comprehensive in their approach to providing support to students? How are these programs delivered?
- How do you assess the individual and collective success of the programs and services currently providing support for at-promise students attending your campus?

SECTION 2

Introducing a Culture of Ecological Validation

Section 2 presents an alternative approach to supporting at-promise college students – creating a culture of ecological validation. Chapter 5 discusses the theoretical underpinnings of our work: validation theory, ecological systems, identity-consciousness, and student success cultures. Each of these theoretical approaches allows educators to understand the experiences of at-promise students; however, each approach in isolation paints an incomplete picture. We argue for creating a culture anchored in all four of these frameworks. Chapter 6 presents a culture of ecological validation, which builds upon validation theory, ecological systems, identity-consciousness, and student success cultures. We define and describe the seven norms that frame a culture of ecological validation: holistic, strengths-oriented, proactive, identity-conscious, developmental, reflective practice, and collaborative. A culture of ecological validation can help address the inequities, challenges, and barriers to at-promise student success described in Section 1 This culture we describe is ecological in nature and validates at-promise students' multiple identities, assets, strengths, and capabilities for success in a coordinated web of student support contexts over time. As noted in the theory chapter, cultures of student support are instrumental in creating and sustaining student success. A culture ensures that practices are widespread and deeply understood.

We then shift to how educators and students experience a culture of ecological validation. Chapter 7 explores how the TSLC educators enacted a culture of ecological validation with specific attention to leveraging the seven norms to support a large and diverse group of at-promise students. Chapter 8 highlights several of the promising practices related to a culture of ecological validation, which educators utilized across the institutions we

DOI: 10.4324/9781003443711-6

studied. Chapter 9 focuses on how students experienced the culture of ecological validation in order to help readers better understand why altering their approach is important. We highlight how students experienced the culture of ecological validation at three distinctly different institutions: a rural comprehensive university that is an emerging Hispanic-Serving Institution, a large research-focused university that recruits students nationally and internationally, and a metropolitan university primarily serving commuter students.

5

THEORETICAL UNDERPINNINGS

Several key concepts guided and informed our understanding of at-promise student support, including ecological systems theory, identity-consciousness, validation theory, and cultures of student success. This chapter details each of these key concepts individually to provide the necessary context and information for you to understand how they each contributed to our new approach to student support described in the chapters that follow. We created scenarios that are informed by our research findings to illustrate how each could be applied in a higher education setting.

We did not begin our study with these four concepts in mind. Rather, we turned to the literature after engaging in data analysis in search of explanations for what we observed about how and why TSLC promoted at-promise student success. For instance, we began with theories that took a more or less singular view of "campus environment" (e.g., Tinto's student integration theory, Astin's I-E-O) and later sought out a theory that provided a more complex ecological view of campus environments based on our observations of how the program operated. Ultimately, we found that no single explanation fully captured the nuance of what drove the program's success. While each concept described in this chapter has been studied independently, they have not yet been brought together to understand at-promise student success.

Ecological Systems Theory

Brief definition: Ecological systems theory explains that student development and success results from the synergistic effects of student interactions with

DOI: 10.4324/9781003443711-7

individuals and groups in an interconnected web of educational environments over time.

(Bronfenbrenner, 1994)

Ecological systems theory (EST) is a person-environment theory that explains student development and success (Bronfenbrenner, 1994; Bronfenbrenner & Morris, 2006; Renn, 2003) by exploring how the environment shapes student outcomes. However, unlike other person-environment theories, like Tinto's (1988) student departure theory, EST explains student development and success in terms of student interactions over time with a dynamic web of contexts that foster development beyond what any one context contributes alone and the effects are cumulative. EST argues for a systems-based perspective of student success that draws attention to who the students are and the multiple educational, family, and community contexts they come into contact with over time, such as classrooms, places of worship, and friend groups. Considering student success and development within an ecology or network contrasts with singular understandings of student interactions that attempt to artificially isolate contexts, which does not reflect the reality of student experiences (Renn, 2003).

Bronfenbrenner and colleagues (1994; 2006) expanded on the original theory to create a more mature version of EST with four dimensions: person-process-context-time (PPCT). PPCT was most useful in framing our understanding of how students experienced the multiple, coordinated support contexts provided by TSLC. PPCT holistically approaches understanding student development by centering both the multifaceted environments students come into contact with and diverse student identities and characteristics (Patton et al., 2016).

In the PPCT, *person* represents who students are and the characteristics they bring with them into multiple contexts. Person includes personality, motivations, interests, past experiences, and emotional, social, and material resources as well as identities such as race, gender, and age (Tudge et al., 2009). *Context* refers to the multiple environments that shape and influence student development and success. Bronfenbrenner (1994) outlines four levels of contexts:

- Microsystems are those that students interact with directly and have the largest influence on student development and success (e.g., friend groups, workplace, residence hall, classrooms, home, advising, financial aid, career services, office hours, and student organizations).
- Mesosystems represent the interactions between the multiple microsystems where the student is directly involved. For instance, the

communication between an advisor and faculty member about the student's success would represent a mesosystem. In the mesosystem, microsystems can work in tandem to promote student success (e.g., engaging classroom environment and academically oriented peer group), or they may conflict with one another to hinder student success (e.g., demanding academic schedule and demanding job schedule).

- Exosystem refers to social contexts that do not directly involve the student but may indirectly shape their development and success (e.g., media, parent workplaces, federal work-study policies).
- Macrosystem reflects broad societal contexts like gender norms, belief systems, society's culture, social ideologies, and systems of oppression.

Process links the person and context elements (Bronfenbrenner, 1994). Process reflects the interaction between the person and the web of contexts with which they directly interact. Students with different identities and backgrounds can experience the same environments in different ways, and the interaction of the student's characteristics and characteristics of their environments influence development and success (Renn, 2003).

Finally, development and success occur over *time* and are influenced by broad sociohistorical events (e.g., elections, civil rights movements) and individual-level events and markers of time (e.g., divorce, graduation, death in the family, birth of child). The time element often receives less attention than the other parts of the model; however, it is key to understanding how development and success unfold. Student characteristics change over time; environments change over time. As such, the interactions between students and environments change over time.

While some scholars have applied ecological systems to postsecondary contexts (Renn, 2003; Renn & Arnold, 2003), it is underutilized to examine college student success. Higher education research tends to focus on examining one environment at a time, like the impact of a summer bridge program or a first-year seminar, rather than studying how student interactions with an interconnected system of environments over time may propel or inhibit students' development and success. The comprehensive and longitudinal nature of our study allowed for using the full complexity of the PPCT model to understand how TSLC promotes student success. Finally, campus ecology literature rarely centers the perceptions and experiences of at-promise students (Cabrera et al., 2016). We incorporate an asset-based perspective when applying EST that elevates the perceptions and experiences of at-promise students, informed by scholars like Museus (2014) and Rendón (1994). We now turn to an applied example to illustrate the PPCT model in action.

Person-Process-Context-Time Model Applied

Susanna, a third-year student, is a first-generation White woman from a working-class family who came to college because she has a drive to make a difference in the lives of children in her home community. Susanna had a difficult time choosing a major her first few years of college. She initially wanted to become a pediatric doctor, but did not enjoy her science classes. She felt lost. Her advisor recommended that she take a career exploratory seminar and called the Career Center to help her register. As part of that seminar, Susanna visited with several departmental advisors to discuss her interests and goals, which enabled her to explore different major and career options aligned with her interests and goals. Susanna realized there were multiple ways for her to achieve her goals to make a difference in her home community beyond becoming a pediatric doctor, including becoming a social worker, psychologist, or school counselor.

During the career exploratory seminar, Susanna was encouraged to attend discipline-oriented student club meetings on campus to get a feel for what her peers might be like in these different majors and career paths. She felt the strongest connection to students at the Counseling Student Organization hosted by the psychology department. Those students and the club advisor had similar values to her and shared a commitment to serving people. One of the students recommended that Susanna take a course in school counseling, which she did. The applied nature of the class work and the prospect of providing counseling services to children excited her. She decided to major in school counseling.

Applying the PPCT to this example, Susanna's love of children and goal to make a difference in the lives of children in her home community are some examples of "person" characteristics. The advisor meeting, the career exploration seminar, student clubs, and courses are examples of "contexts" – and microsystems in particular. The communication between Susanna's advisor and the career center advisor on campus to arrange for her to take a career exploratory course is an example of a context in the mesosystem. The interactions between Susanna and the web of multiple contexts where she was involved are examples of "process." The cumulative and synergistic effects of Susanna's negative interactions with her science coursework, and positive interactions with the career exploration seminar, advisors, the Counseling Student Organization, and school counseling course combined with her "person" characteristics (i.e., love of children and desire to make a difference in her home community) came together to shape her developmental trajectory and success over time. These interactions cumulatively led Susanna to successfully identify a major and career path in school counseling that she felt excited about and comfortable with. The series of processes she engaged in across these multiple contexts occurred over the course of "time."

Validation Theory

Brief definition: Validation theory explains that student development and success results from student interactions with educators who proactively enable and affirm the student's innate capacities for academic and interpersonal success.

(Rendón, 1994)

We noticed early in our study that TSLC educators expressed deep, genuine care for students and often communicated beliefs that all students had the ability to be successful if they were given the right support. This led us to validation theory. Validation theory explains that student development and success are a result of "intentional, proactive affirmation of students by in- and out-of-class agents" intended to "validate students as creators of knowledge" and "foster personal development and social adjustment" (Rendón & Muñoz, 2011, p. 12). The theory was developed to explain the success of college students from diverse backgrounds such as low-income, first-generation college, and racially minoritized groups (Rendón & Muñoz, 2011). Validation elevates the background, assets, knowledge, and experiences of at-promise students and acknowledges that postsecondary education systems are inherently sociopolitical spaces that tend to privilege White middle-class ways of knowing, values, and capital in ways that often hinder the success of at-promise students (Colyer, 2011; Rendón, 1994). The theory argues that at-promise students find it difficult to succeed in traditional college environments that tend to be competitive, individualistic, and invalidating (Rendón, 1994; Rendón, 2002).

In validation theory, institutional agents (e.g., faculty, staff, program directors, counselors, coaches, and student mentors and leaders) are responsible for proactively reaching out to students to communicate a belief in the students' innate capabilities for success and to connect students to the appropriate supports to help them realize their innate capabilities for success (Rendón & Muñoz, 2011). Validation theory argues that at-promise students' development and success is best served by institutional agents who recognize and affirm students' knowledge and capabilities for success, and when provided with the right kind of support tailored to their needs. Moreover, at-promise students have often experienced *in*validation, such as a family member or teacher communicating their belief that a student like them will not be successful in college. As such, institutional agents taking the initiative to validate at-promise students can challenge those past messages and give students a sense of self-worth, impart a belief that they can succeed, and make them feel it is acceptable to seek help navigating college (Rendón, 2002). Validation must occur early and consistently over time to achieve the intended goals of student success (Rendón, 1994).

Rendón (1994) theorized two domains of validation: academic and interpersonal. Academic validation is characterized by educators encouraging students to "trust their innate capacity to learn and to acquire confidence in being a college student" (Rendón, 1994, p. 40). Interpersonal validation entails efforts on the part of educators to acknowledge and affirm that college students are individuals with lives and experiences that extend beyond academics (Rendón & Muñoz, 2011). An example of academic validation would be a faculty member engaging students in readings produced by people from minoritized backgrounds and acknowledging the contributions of those people to the field. An example of interpersonal validation would be a campus counselor engaging a first-generation college student in a conversation about the role of family support in their success. The combination of educators affirming students academically and interpersonally propels their academic, personal, and social development and empowers them to be successful in college. The structures and culture of higher education often serve to academically and interpersonally invalidate students from at-promise backgrounds and treat their academic and interpersonal domains separately rather than holistically. Intentional proactive efforts by institutional agents to validate at-promise students' backgrounds, experiences, and assets contributes to their success in college (Rendón et al., 2000; Rendón & Muñoz, 2011). In practical terms, students feel validated when educators:

- Learn their names and use them;
- Incorporate the diversity of student backgrounds into the curriculum and educational activities to create inclusive learning environments;
- Collaborate with students on their learning and recognize the knowledge that students bring with them into the classroom and other learning spaces;
- Work with students to plan a course of action to accomplish their goals; encourage students to draw on their peers and others to form a network of support;
- Meet with students outside of regular classroom or formal settings to connect to students personally and to get to know who students are as people; and
- Communicate to students their genuinely held belief that the students are capable of succeeding in college and that they will help them successfully accomplish their goals.

Validation is more than communicating a belief in students' capabilities. Validation is the action of connecting students to resources that enable them to achieve the success educators say they believe the student is capable of achieving. As students continue to experience validation, they feel a greater sense of comfort engaging in college. The external validation and affirmation then lead students to internal beliefs about their own capabilities that further enables students to succeed (Rendón & Muñoz, 2011). We now provide an example of validation theory applied with an illustrative scenario.

Validation Theory Applied

Kira, a Black woman from a lower middle-income community, loved numbers growing up and excelled in math. She decided to pursue a degree and career in engineering. She applied to a local university so that she could visit frequently with her mother and two young sisters. She was admitted to the university and received a tuition scholarship. She felt good about the scholarship, and her mother was very proud. Kira was the first in her family to go to college.

Partway through her first year, Kira's mother became ill and lost mobility. Kira's mother was going to need on-going care as well as assistance with her two young daughters who still lived at home. Kira started making more frequent trips home to help her mother and siblings. She took a part-time job to assist with the family bills. Her grades began to slip as she could not find the time to study for her math and engineering classes. She also had no time to socialize and felt isolated on campus. She thought about leaving college, but remembered how hard she worked to get where she was. She wanted to make her family proud. She felt lost, hopeless, and confused.

Kira's engineering instructor noticed that her demeanor changed over the course of the semester. The first several weeks of class, the instructor got to know Kira because of her eagerness to answer and ask questions in class and contributions to class discussions. Later, Kira stared out the window during class and sat in the back texting on her phone – the instructor could see the worry in her face. She was often late for class, and her grades dipped. One day, the class ended. Kira remained and was at the back frantically texting her mother on her phone. The instructor asked if Kira was OK. Kira apologized profusely for being on her phone during class; her mother was having issues at home, and she was trying to figure out who was going to pick up her sister from school. The instructor said he understood and reassured her that she was not in trouble. He asked if there was anything she wanted to talk about. Kira welled up and told the instructor he was the first person to ask how she was doing. He asked if she would come to his office so they could talk.

In his office, the instructor began by saying he noticed how involved she was in class and her input enriched class discussions. He especially appreciated the time when she brought up the lack of diversity in engineering and how that hampers innovative solutions to pressing societal problems. He felt it helped drive class conversation and got other students thinking. Kira felt heartened to hear her perspective and contributions in class were valued. She started to feel more relaxed and could tell that the instructor was genuinely interested in her. Kira shared about her mother's illness and need to care for her younger siblings. The instructor thanked her for sharing. He explained how he saw a lot of potential in her and wanted to help her reach her goals. As the conversation unfolded, the instructor could see that Kira's family situation not only affected her grades, but also took a toll on her mental health. He offered to connect Kira to counseling services on campus to help her get additional personal wellness support and offered to meet with her via video during class office hours so she could access additional academic support to help her meet her goals for the class while also remaining at home to care for her mother and younger siblings.

In this example, the instructor affirmed Kira's capabilities for success and proactively reached out to her when he noticed something seemed off. He validated her meaningful contributions in class and offered to connect her to support. This is one example of validation by an institutional agent who took into account a student's holistic well-being, affirmed the assets and strengths the student brought into class, and tailored support to the student's needs.

Identity-Consciousness

> *Brief definition: Identity-consciousness explains that student development and success results from college support systems designed with students' diverse identities in mind.*
>
> (Pendakur, 2016)

TSLC educators were cognizant of students' backgrounds, identities, goals, and experiences when providing support. Educators created space for and acknowledged the multiple identities and experiences at-promise students brought with them to college. TSLC educators tailored the support they offered in a way that was conscious of at-promise students' diverse backgrounds and multiple identities (Kezar et al., 2021). In our effort to find concepts and theories to capture this observation, we explored funds of knowledge (Kiyama & Rios-Aguilar, 2017) and community cultural wealth (Yosso, 2005). Each of these concepts sensitized us to the cultural skills, resources, knowledge, strengths, and assets that at-promise students brought with them to college that are often not recognized or leveraged by institutions to promote their success.

TSLC's approach to supporting student development and success took a broad view of students' diverse, multiple identities. Identity-conscious approaches promote student retention and success by intentionally designing support with students' multiple identities in mind – with acute attention to the identities of those students from underserved and underrepresented backgrounds (Pendakur, 2016). Identity-consciousness acknowledges that higher education systems were often set up to offer the same support to all students without regard to the needs of low-income, first-generation college, racially minoritized, and other underserved students (Harper, 2009; Pendakur, 2016). Identity-consciousness calls for policies and practices that attend to the needs and experiences of at-promise students to address structural disadvantages and systems of privilege. An identity-conscious approach is asset-based rather than deficit-oriented, and calls attention to the potential, possibilities, and capabilities of at-promise students (Harper, 2009).

Identity-conscious support is not restricted to creating identity- and culture-based centers on campus (Pendakur, 2016). While these centers and services offer important support and resources that speak to the identity and cultural needs of students from diverse backgrounds, identity-conscious support seeks to broadly transform postsecondary systems. Pendakur (2016) argues that at-promise students' academic needs and success are best served by support that acknowledges that students' identities shape how they experience the entire campus environment and how their environments affect them. Identity-conscious approaches do not take a one-size-fits-all lens to student success; the support must be tailored to students' identities in order to engage students as whole people and leverage their full range of assets toward enabling their success in college.

Identity-conscious approaches to support are intended to shift postsecondary environments. Failure to design student success initiatives and services with students' identities in mind will inevitably lead to students from certain identity groups – typically those most marginalized – to be underserved by those initiatives and services and thereby undercut their success. Identity-conscious student support is a shared institutional responsibility and cannot be the sole purview of any one siloed office or campus committee if it is to transform higher education systems in a way that will meaningfully increase at-promise students' academic success and retention (Pendakur, 2016). Next, we illustrate how identity-consciousness could be applied with a scenario from the perspective of an institution.

Identity-Consciousness Applied

Leadership at Coral College worked with the Institutional Research Office on campus to conduct yearly surveys of their students for the past two decades to assess student engagement and satisfaction, and to analyze student GPAs and retention trends. The college historically had success in serving their students. However, leadership noticed some troubling trends. Students seemed to be less engaged and less satisfied, and GPA/retention numbers were trending downward. Leadership asked the institutional research office to do some further investigation into these trends. The office discovered that, when they broke down the numbers by race/ethnicity, reported income levels, and college generational status, there were clear differences in the experiences and success of students from racially minoritized, low-income, and first-generation college backgrounds. Leadership knew Coral College was increasingly serving a more diverse population, and they wanted to address matters affecting these students' success immediately. They offered a number of student support services on campus and were puzzled as to why they did not seem to be working.

Coral College worked with the institutional research office to conduct focus groups with at-promise students. They wanted to understand students' perceptions of the college, how effective they felt the campus services were, and what other kinds of support they might benefit from to be successful in college. A key finding emerged: many of the supports they offered on campus were simply not known or, when they were used, were not particularly helpful to many of the groups (e.g., racially minoritized, first-generation college, low-income). Focus group participants who used the services commonly shared that the campus services just "didn't speak to their needs" and they "didn't feel welcome" or see themselves represented in those spaces.

Coral College leadership was alarmed to hear that the services they dedicated so many resources to were not serving the needs of a large segment of their student body – at-promise students. A member of the leadership team suggested that if the students were not using the services, they should just stop offering them. Another member vehemently disagreed. She said that if the students were not using these services because they do not know about them or because they did not speak to their needs, the college should retool those services to better meet students' needs. The majority of the leadership team agreed and moved forward with a plan to retool the services to meet at-promise student needs.

Coral College leadership embarked on a process to change the nature of the services and supports offered on campus to be more proactive in meeting the needs of at-promise students. Leadership had a retreat where they discussed what it means to be identity-conscious in their work and where the gaps existed on campus. They discussed strategies for implementing a more identity-conscious approach, including (a) hiring more educators who shared identities with the students they served, (b) training for educators who directly interacted with students to think more holistically about the support they offered and the multiple identities students brought with them into those support spaces, and (c) workshops each semester to educate the educators about the at-promise identity groups they increasingly served, the systemic barriers to their success, and how educators could connect students to resources that supported their multiple identities.

Leadership piloted their new approach with the academic advising center. They changed job advertisements for advisors to reflect a call for diverse applicants to help address the structural diversity of their advising team going forward. Next, they developed a workshop each semester to help current advisors learn identity-conscious approaches to student advising support, where advisors learned different student identities and backgrounds as well as the other offices on campus that they could collaborate with to meet the needs of at-promise students. These advisors also participated in training sessions with other student affairs offices on campus about what it means to take a holistic approach to advising support that is responsive to multiple identities. For example, one of the trainings focused on how advisors could get to know students' backgrounds and identities in order to bring those into conversation with helping students access relevant support on campus. The leadership evaluated the success of this identity-conscious academic advising approach and considered expanding to other areas of campus support to create broader systemic change at the college.

College Success Cultures

Brief definition: College success culture scholarship explains that student development and success results from student experiences on campuses with missions, values, practices, norms, and beliefs that reflect a shared commitment to student success through collaboration, cultural responsiveness, equity-oriented support, and proactive, holistic engagement.
(McNair et al., 2016; Museus, 2011; 2014)

Culture in higher education refers to the overall campus environment shaped by an institution's history, mission, policies, symbols, underlying assumptions, values, practices, norms, traditions, and beliefs (Kuh & Hall, 1993; Kuh & Whitt, 1988; Museus & Jayakumar, 2012). Faculty, staff, and students are socialized into the institutional culture, and they in turn collectively shape the culture of the institution. Culture reflects expectations for what work is done, who should do it, and how it should be done. It also directs socially acceptable behavior in a given college context and is an underlying organizational force that influences how educators, administrators, and students behave and make meaning of their experiences (Kuh & Love, 2000; Kuh, 2002; Kuh & Whitt, 1988). Fostering a culture that reflects and affirms at-promise students is a promising way to boost their success (Kezar et al., 2022b; Kuh, 2002). However, the culture of higher education institutions tends to be one that is ingrained with White, middle-class values, beliefs, norms, and ways of knowing that influence practices, policies, and structures (Kezar, 2011; Museus, 2011; Schiele, 1994).

Privileged students can navigate traditional college cultures seamlessly while at-promise students often face the added challenge of learning a new culture as well as locating subcultures on campus that resonate with their identity and experiences, such as in culturally based organizations or fighting against the system (Kezar, 2011; Museus & Jayakumar, 2012; Pendakur, 2016). Institutional culture is an invisible force guiding actions, norms, expectations, and practice that most educators possess only a passive or intuitive awareness of, yet it remains a powerful force in what decisions are made and how things get done. Some argue that at-promise students need to acculturate to an institutional system's culture in order to assimilate and succeed in college (e.g., Tinto, 1988). However, we align with scholars like Hurtado and Carter (1997), Harper and Quaye (2009), Museus and Jayakumar (2012), and McNair et al. (2016) who argue for a shift toward institutional responsibility for fostering educational environments and cultures that reflect the needs, values, opportunities, and cultures of at-promise students.

The dominant culture of many U.S. colleges and universities creates barriers to implementing transformational changes, which leaves it up to the student to adjust and figure out how to succeed (Jayakumar & Museus, 2012; Kezar, 2011). These prevailing institutional cultures include siloed and bureaucratic units focused on a discrete set of tasks, such as academic departments, academic affairs, student services, financial aid offices, and other administrative units (Kezar & Lester, 2009; Manning et al., 2014). These structures contribute to the development of subcultures within each of the silos that incentivize task and goal completion rather than a shared commitment to holistic student success across campus units (Jayakumar & Museus, 2012; Kezar & Lester, 2009; Kuh et al., 2005). The siloed organization of campuses and resulting fragmented culture creates a learning environment where it is difficult for students to succeed – particularly at-promise students (Buultjens & Robinson, 2011; Kezar & Lester, 2009; Kuh et al., 2005; Tinto, 2012).

Siloed offices and associated campus cultures commonly reflect a deficit-oriented perspective when serving at-promise students – with educators seeing students as problems to resolve (McNair et al., 2016). Student support is often transactional and impersonal in this kind of culture. The disconnect in support may also contribute to a campus culture where educators assume it is someone else's responsibility to address student issues and students are responsible to figure out how to get support (Jayakumar & Museus, 2012). This approach stands in contrast to cultures of student success that reflect an asset-based perspective that focuses on student potential and seeks to build upon students' assets by organizing support in a way that reflects a shared campus commitment to the success of each student.

Rather than address underlying issues with campus organization and culture to better support at-promise student success, a common response is to introduce myriad unaligned and disconnected interventions and services that often focus on single aspects of students' identities or needs (Tinto, 2012). The list of interventions and services that have been implemented to support at-promise student success include culture centers, identity-based centers, mentoring, proactive advising, and summer bridge programs. While these interventions offer support to at-promise students and often reflect a student-success-centered subculture separate from the broader campus culture, they have not significantly increased at-promise student success overall. Tinkering at the margins of student success with culturally based or identity-based programs and interventions on the side does not achieve the deep systemic change that an overall culture shift would accomplish (Jayakumar & Museus, 2012; Kuh et al., 2005).

Institutions need to address tensions and discomfort at-promise students feel navigating culturally alienating environments in an effort to meaningfully boost their success (Museus & Quaye, 2009). Cultures of student success should be characterized by holistic support, campus coordination, alignment, and integration across silos that reflect a shared commitment to at-promise student success (Bailey et al., 2015; Jayakumar & Museus, 2012; Museus, 2014; Tinto, 2012). For campus cultures to have student success cultures, they must support all students. To fully support at-promise students, the overall culture of the institution needs to shift toward becoming culturally conscious and equity-oriented (Jayakumar & Museus, 2012). The journey to institutional transformation requires moving from disconnected subcultures toward broader campus cultural change that is shaped by the needs and experiences of diverse educators and students (McNair et al., 2016; Museus, 2012).

Campus cultures that promote at-promise student success are committed to humanizing education, collaboration across student support contexts, promoting a shared responsibility for the success of at-promise students, a collectivist orientation, proactive targeted student support, and offering meaningful opportunities for students to learn about and engage with cultures of their own and of others (Museus, 2012; 2014). Such cultures also are characterized by campus environments that resonate with at-promise students' backgrounds, identities, and cultures; incorporate opportunities to connect with peers and educators with whom at-promise students identify; and engage students in opportunities to work across differences to solve sociopolitical issues (Museus, 2014; Museus et al., 2016). Equity-oriented cultures should address cultural values, assumptions, and practices that perpetuate discrimination, exclusion, and Eurocentrism by explicitly acknowledging and changing the campus culture (Jayakumar & Museus, 2012). These efforts should not be siloed, but rather infused into the broader campus culture. Assessment, data-informed action, and feedback are critical aspects of moving toward college success cultures that better serve students (Kuh, 2002). We provide an example scenario of how an institution could foster a college success culture for illustration.

College Success Cultures Applied

Camarillo University, a predominantly White institution, began enrolling more at-promise students. Annual campus assessment reports showed that they had lower graduation and retention rates compared with their peer institutions, which was not the case in the past. Leadership noticed differences in outcomes for student subgroups, including race/ethnicity, socioeconomic status, and first-generation college. The leadership partnered with the institutional research office to conduct a "campus audit" to determine what factors could be contributing to their lack of success in serving at-promise students. The campus audit entailed targeted student focus groups; faculty and staff interviews; observations of workplace and class environments; a review of campus documents (e.g., strategic plans, mission statement, job descriptions); and a review of email communications and newsletters from leadership sent out to faculty, staff, and students on campus.

The institutional researchers noticed an emerging theme across their campus audit analyses. While Camarillo had many key structures in place for a functioning university, there was a deeply embedded culture that was individualistic with unilateral top-down decision-making, isolated office work cultures, and student services guided by the idea that students should – as one campus office director put it in an interview – "pull themselves up by their bootstraps" to be successful. They also identified that faculty and staff had deficit views of students. It was common for educators during interviews and in observations to deflect responsibility for students to other offices on campus. For example, faculty commonly said they were only responsible for academics and that students' personal well-being or success was "not their job" and it was someone else's problem to deal with, like student affairs. Others said the support they needed already existed on campus, like the multicultural center, and it was the students' fault for not seeking out that support themselves. Faculty were also reluctant to consider ways to incorporate readings from more diverse scholars in their curriculum in the name of academic freedom.

Campus leadership was both surprised and alarmed to hear these deeply embedded cultural problems. Leadership committed to making changes to improve their campus culture. Camarillo embarked on a campus culture campaign that involved several steps toward fostering a culture of student success. Campus leadership began with a town hall meeting to be open and transparent about the campus audit and to invite educators and students into the conversation about creating cultural change on campus. Several ideas emerged out of those conversations that the campus pursued to create a culture of student success.

They started by re-examining their institution's mission. A committee of faculty, staff, and student representatives was formed to revise the mission statement so that it centered social justice and equity as well as highlighted the important role of Camarillo University in educating and developing the whole student and fostering a more socially just society. Human resources and faculty affairs were directed to incorporate statements into their job advertisement templates to explicitly encourage applicants from racially minoritized, low-income, and first-generation college backgrounds in an effort to enhance the compositional diversity of the campus to more closely reflect the diverse student body they served. A series of workshops for faculty and staff were implemented that educated them about the systemic inequities and what it meant to take a proactive, holistic, asset-based approach to supporting students – particularly those from underrepresented and underserved backgrounds. These workshops included skits where faculty-student and staff-student scenarios were played out by faculty, staff, and student actors to illustrate how to be holistic and asset-based in their support. To pursue a culture of student success, a number of structural changes were also made to the campus. Campus support services were centralized, and staff members were re-trained to encourage collaboration across the different kinds of support they offered to students (e.g., multicultural office, advising support, writing center). The provost met with the academic deans and dean of students to have frank discussions about what kind of knowledge and ways of engagement they were centering and privileging on campus. They also discussed the assumptions each had about what it takes to be successful in college and who had what it takes to be successful in college. She challenged the deans to reflect on the culture of their respective colleges/departments and to devise ways they could de-center White, Eurocentric assumptions about what it takes to succeed and what success looks like in order to expand definitions of success and opportunities to achieve success that speak to the backgrounds and identities of their students. Camarillo leadership knew this was just the beginning of a journey and they still had a long way to go to shift toward a culture of student success, but it had taken several key steps forward on this journey.

Integrating Concepts to Formulate a New Approach to At-promise Student Success

We set out to study TSLC using student engagement (Astin, 1984; Kuh et al., 2007) and drew on literature regarding psychosocial factors such as sense of belonging and mattering. Many of these theories and explanations for at-promise student success did not fully capture how TSLC successfully supported at-promise students. We sought additional concepts and theoretical frameworks that provided a fuller explanation of key factors that seemed to promote at-promise student success. What emerged were several distinct concepts and theories that contributed to a more complex, multi-faceted, and holistic understanding of TSLC's approach to student success.

We drew on the aforementioned concepts to make sense of our data. For example, we drew on identity-consciousness, validation theory, and PPCT to inform our development of ecological validation. Together, these concepts sensitized us to the importance of validation as a driver of student success, the multiple contexts where students experienced validation over time, and why student interactions with educators in the multiple program contexts were experienced as validating. The college success culture literature drove our desire to understand the underlying assumptions, norms, and values that facilitated and sustained ecological validation to discover a durable, long-lasting approach at-promise student support based on our observations of TSLC. The concepts discussed in validation theory and identity-consciousness also helped inform the identification of norms and practices within the TSLC's culture ecological validation that fostered at-promise student success.

Reflection Questions:

• What specific changes can you make to the support you provide to at-promise students so that it better reflects the principles of identity-consciousness?

- Is the campus culture at your institution a culture of student success? What changes could you be a part of to contribute to a culture of student success?
- How could you embed validating practices into the work you currently do with students?
- What would be some of the benefits of taking an ecological view of supporting students with whom you work?

6

A CULTURE OF ECOLOGICAL VALIDATION THAT SUPPORTS AT-PROMISE STUDENT SUCCESS

As we described in Chapter 3, the siloed structures in higher education result in practices that are deficit-oriented, fragmented, reactive, identity-neutral, and nondevelopmental. In this chapter, we present a new approach to student success that can assist educators who are looking for research-based approaches to creating more equitable experiences and outcomes for at-promise students. A culture of ecological validation provides guidance for educators who want to move away from siloed postsecondary structures that undermine at-promise student success.

For decades, practitioners and researchers have noted the importance of campus culture in student success, learning, and development. Most higher education researchers define campus culture as the overall environment that involves a school's mission, enacted through norms (or values) that become embedded in practices and policies, and socialized into faculty, staff, and students (Kuh, 1991). Kuh and Hall (1993) defined culture as "the collective, mutually shaping patterns of institutional history, mission, physical settings, norms, traditions, values, practices, beliefs and assumptions that guide behavior of individuals and groups in an institution" (p. 3). As Kuh et al. (2005) noted, "Virtually every study of high-performing entities concludes that culture is the single most important element that must be altered and managed in order to change what an organization values and how it acts" (p. 50). For the past two decades, scholars called for additional research and theory to understand how to develop an institutional culture that supports at-promise student success.

In this chapter, we explore how to create institutional cultures that support a diverse group of at-promise students. Our research builds upon

DOI: 10.4324/9781003443711-8

the work of scholars like Pendakur (2016) and Museus (2014) who suggest the need for transforming overall campus environments and cultures to support at-promise students. A culture of ecological validation was found at three different campuses. While all three campuses are classified as predominantly White institutions, the programs we studied serve a racially diverse group of students who are all classified as low-income. Thus, the norms and practices seem transferable and applicable to many higher education contexts.

We begin this chapter by providing a conceptual overview of the culture of ecological validation. We discuss and illustrate how the TSLC program created a culture of ecological validation that included seven norms that resulted in structures and processes, which resulted in educator behaviors and practices that supported at-promise student success. In addition, Chapter 7 discusses how TSLC educators enacted a culture of ecological validation, and Chapter 9 provides detailed narratives of how students experienced the culture in ways that positively influenced their engagement and persistence.

Creating a Culture of Ecological Validation

Brief description: A culture of ecological validation is an approach to program, college, or institutional culture that centers the experiences, strengths, and needs of at-promise students through the implementation of seven norms (i.e., holistic, proactive, strengths-oriented, identity-conscious, developmental, collaborative, and reflexive practice). These norms shape the structures and processes (e.g., leadership, socialization, relations and working interactions, rituals and traditions, and language, spaces, and communication) in ways that result in ecologically validating behaviors and practices of the staff, faculty, administrators, and other educators.

A culture of ecological validation centers the experiences, strengths, and needs of at-promise students through institutional or program norms – holistic, proactive, strengths-oriented, identity-conscious, developmental, collaborative, and reflective practice (see Diagram 6.1). Through embedding the norms into key structures and processes, they become omnipresent and standard social and work practices. In other words, if leadership communicates the importance of the norms through communication and rituals to reinforce them, educators will begin to orient to these new ways of working. Unlike attempts to change students or only select students who appear to be ready for college, a culture of ecological validation focuses on norms that allow institutions to be student-ready – meaning the program or institution adjusts to serve at-promise students instead of primarily focusing on changing the students (McNair et al., 2016). In addition, the culture

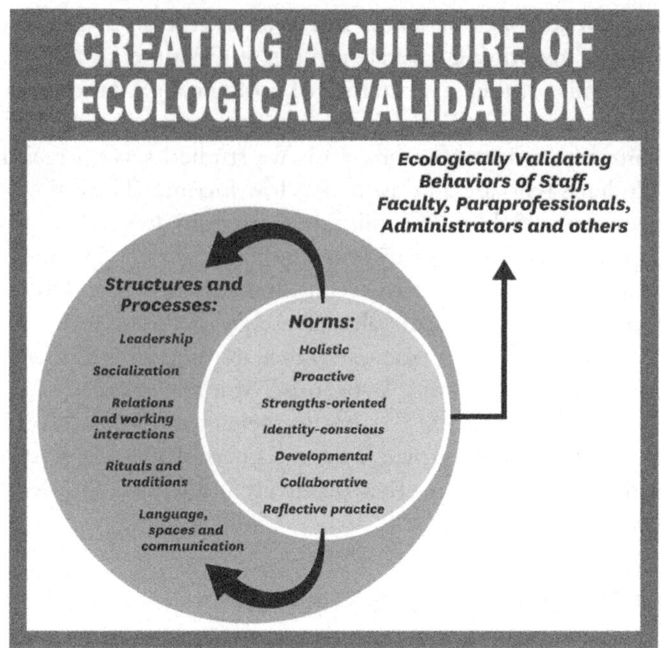

DIAGRAM 6.1 Creating a Culture of Ecological Validation.

encourages leadership, staff, and instructors to build relationships that reflect the norms instead of departmental silos that compete against each other and focus on bureaucratic aspects of the organization instead of holistically considering how to support students.

Ecologically Validating Norms

Norms are the standards or appropriate forms of social behavior that influence how people act within a situation. Work norms define how people execute their roles and responsibilities. TSLC disrupted the existing dominant White, middle-class, and generationally privileged institutional culture by creating and sustaining a culture of ecological validation that involved seven norms that influenced practice (see Diagram 6.2). Five of the norms focus on how educators interact with students (holistic, proactive, strengths-oriented, identity-conscious, and developmental), and two norms shape the interactions between educators (collaborative and reflective practice). In turn, these norms came to influence the structures and processes within the program that resulted in a culture that reflected the goals, experiences, and needs of at-promise students. Ecological validation requires all seven norms. These norms often are considered by researchers

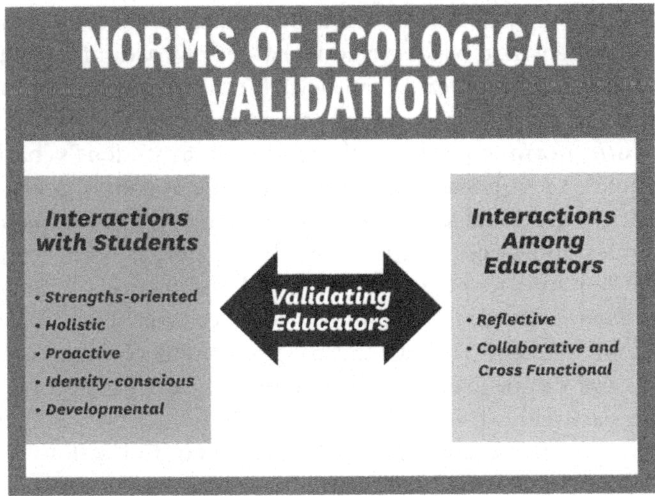

DIAGRAM 6.2 Norms That Support a Culture of Ecological Validation.

and practitioners in isolation, but they become more powerful in supporting at-promise student success when they are intentionally integrated and then enacted across campus contexts. In the remainder of this section, we provide an overview of each norm.

The *strengths-oriented* norm focused on the cultural assets, talents and skills, previous successes, and personality traits that students bring with them to campus – and not employing a deficit approach, which focuses primarily on the assumed challenges that at-promise college students may face. Within proactive advising sessions, the TSLC staff built relationships with individual students in order to learn about their goals, skills, and previous experiences. This created a context where the staff could build upon the strengths of each student. For example, a staff member discovered that a student wanted to pursue graphic design so they created an opportunity for her to design several fliers for TSLC events and showed the student how to put this experience on her résumé. The previously discussed autobiographical writing course helped students explore their personal stories and write a narrative that reflected the strengths they brought to higher education. The peer mentors were trained to not only identify potential challenges, but to also look for the strengths of each student, and then the staff would work with the mentor to connect each student with information about clubs, internships, and research opportunities. Even when a student experienced a challenge, such as a low grade in a course, the staff would begin by affirming the student's place in higher education and then look for ways to build upon the student's individual strengths in order to create a plan of action. Students frequently spoke about how they thought proactive advising would be focused on what they were doing wrong, but the strengths-oriented norm meant that they left the sessions feeling encouraged and equipped to succeed even if they had experienced a challenge.

The *holistic* norm considers all aspects of a student's background, identities (e.g., race, gender, and sexuality), personality, goals, and academic and interpersonal experiences in college when connecting them with resources and opportunities. The TSLC programs developed multiple social activities to help students build connections with other students and staff members. In addition, one campus hosted a breakfast during parent weekend to help the students build connections between their home and campus relationships. Staff and instructors took a holistic perspective each time they engaged with students. The students spoke about how they felt comfortable bringing their full self to the TSLC program, which meant they were more likely to come to the program staff and instructors when an issue emerged because they knew that all issues were relevant. For example, one of the students needed help navigating a situation where a landlord would not address bedbugs; without the holistic approach of the TSLC staff, she would not have known how to find support in resolving this issue.

The *proactive* norm places the onus on institutional agents to regularly reach out to students to build relationships, address challenges, and identify opportunities. The programs proactively engaged with students from the summer before they started college until they completed the two-year program. Each student got called by one of the professional staff members soon after the announcement went out in May about who got selected. In addition to congratulating the student, the staff member spoke with the student about their plans for college and any questions or concerns they had. Often students were unsure about housing contracts, financial aid, and orientation. The staff member ensured that students had their contact information, checked to see if they had any questions, and let the student know that they would also get to speak with staff at the campus orientation over the summer. An important aspect of this norm was the proactive advising that occurred about halfway through each semester. Each student would get grade estimates for each of their classes from their instructors and then have a conversation with a TSLC staff member. Even though these sessions were only about 20–30 minutes, the advising gave staff the ability to identify any areas of concern as well as opportunities to extend learning. Using the previously discussed holistic approach, the staff began by asking students to reflect on their semester, share their goals, and identify questions. This enabled staff to understand why issues existed instead of assuming that low grades always meant lack of ability or skills; in many cases, there were issues such as a student needing to work two jobs to support family or confusion about the assignment description.

The *identity-conscious* norm intentionally considers students' identities, with acute attention to the identities of those students from at-promise backgrounds. Students in TSLC brought a wide range of identities with them to campus (e.g., racial, gender, sexuality, family income, rural or urban, religious, and ethnic identities). The programs served a diverse group of students who brought multiple different identities that often get marginalized by society and in higher education. For example, the autobiographical writing class allowed students to explore and discuss their identities, which also allowed students to engage with people who possessed different identities and to learn from each other. The peer, staff, and instructor training included information about at-promise student identities and how to affirm students during individual, group, and classroom sessions.

The *developmental* norm involved supporting students throughout their educational journeys in a cohesive way. The TSLC staff designed a two-year program that created a coordinated approach to transitioning students into college, through first-year experience support, and then programming throughout the second year that helped students transition into their major. Although the official programming lasted two years, TSLC students knew that they could return to the program staff for additional support until they completed college. The program was intentionally designed to include supports that built upon each other in an aligned way that helped students navigate the first two years of college. In addition, the staff considered students' individual development when providing guidance and support. For example, some students were ready for conversations about internships and careers the first semester of college, while others were still exploring majors and adjusting to the college context.

The *reflective practice* norm involved continually considering how students, staff, and leadership experienced the program in order to make shifts necessary to improve student success. The reflective process used both formal and informal data to inform decision-making. The TSLC staff met each week to reflect on how things were going and plan events. These discussions allowed the staff to identify patterns that might be emerging, including when subgroups of students had similar issues. For example, the staff recognized that parenting students did not feel comfortable at most social events, so they created a few family-friendly events that enabled students to bring their children. As a result of this reflective practice, the staff and faculty often tailor the program to fit the specific needs of subgroups of students, including racially minoritized, first-generation college, commuter, and working students (Kezar et al., 2023). The programs also built trusting relationships with students, which meant the students also felt comfortable sharing ideas with the staff about how to improve support.

The *collaborative* and *cross-functional* norm explores building connections across various campus services and programs to create integrated and reinforcing validating experiences across a student's ecology of experience. The TSLC staff, mentors, and instructors were not expected to have all the answers to every question that students brought to them, especially when the concern extended beyond their area of expertise. However, they were expected to get enough information from the student in order to connect them with a person who could provide support. For example, a student with issues paying for housing was introduced to a specific person in the financial aid office or a student wanting to find a summer internship was introduced to a specific person in career services. Connected with the identity-conscious norm, the programs built relationships with other programs and services on campus that provide support in order to look for opportunities for collaboration or cross-functional work. For example, one program discovered that racially minoritized students felt uncomfortable going to the counseling center, so they collaborated with the counseling center and multicultural center to have counseling services offered one day a week in a private conference room in the multicultural center, which was identified as a more comfortable space on campus. The collaboration allowed TSLC to holistically support students because the staff were consistently building relationships with specific people in each office across campus.

Structures and Processes That Embed the Norms

The norms that characterize a culture of ecological validation were operationalized throughout the TSLC program structure and processes; however, these norms have the potential to inform how departments, colleges, and universities create cultures that support at-promise students' experiences and outcomes. Our research identified areas that were most commonly noted both through observation and interview data as locations for embedding the norms. The leadership set the expectation that ecological validation was a central tenet of the program. Program directors played a key role, but leadership opportunities were distributed throughout the program, including instructors, faculty coordinators, staff, paraprofessionals, and peer mentors. We describe below how leaders set expectations, provided direction, modeled, coached, and held individuals accountable for appropriate behavior that moved the community toward ecological validation.

Hiring and socialization was another process for embedding norms. For example, TSLC mentors, instructors, and staff were hired based upon their potential to fit within the culture and then socialized on how to enact the validating culture in their practice. The language, space, and communication used within TSLC sent validating messages to students. The rituals and practices sustained the culture. And the relationships enabled TSLC leadership and staff to identify additional resources and opportunities to support at-promise student success. The sections that follow illustrate how the norms were threaded throughout the program culture across three different college campuses (e.g., rural, metropolitan, and research-oriented), and we include the norms in italics throughout the sections to highlight how they were enacted. While many programs speak about the importance of being student-centered, the TSLC program used the norms embedded within practices to illustrate and operationalize these processes that build a culture of ecological validation that supports at-promise student success.

Leadership

Although the director set the tone for the program, responsibility for creating validating experiences was decentralized so that all felt they needed to lead and support ecological validation. Staff, instructors, and peer mentors were expected to engage in holistic, proactive, identity-conscious, developmental, and strengths-oriented practices that affirmed students' academic potential. Program leadership had several key roles that supported ecological validation: they set expectations and provided direction, modeled and coached, and held individuals accountable for appropriate behavior.

Directors created the expectation that validation started soon after students got awarded the scholarship and continued until they completed the two-year support program (*developmental*). Students received a phone call soon after earning the scholarship from one of the staff members in order for the staff member to individually congratulate the student for earning the scholarship, to learn more about the student, and to see if there were any questions or concerns as the students prepared for college (*proactive*). TSLC had its own orientation the day before classes started to make sure students knew the people, resources, and opportunities available. One of the directors began the event with a mantra that she often repeated, "Who are you, what are you doing, and why are you doing it?" (*holistic*). She explained how all aspects of the student mattered to the program staff, instructors, and mentors. All three programs engaged in similar activities related to early contact with individual students (*developmental*).

The directors expected the staff to engage with data to make informed decisions about how to support students. At one campus, the director recognized that students placed in the entry-level college math course were completing at low rates and the staff were consistently hearing from students that they needed more support in order to successfully complete the course (*reflective practice*). The director met with the math department on campus (*collaborative*) to explore potential solutions that could offer additional support for students while also creating a validating experience. Within the shared academic courses, the TSLC staff worked with the math department to pilot expanding the math course to include an additional unit that offered supplemental instruction and tutoring. After running the course a few times, the program and math department determined that students in this format consistently performed at a higher rate than those without supplemental support. As a result, the entire campus shifted to that format. TSLC consistently considered what was working and was open to letting go of things that did not prove successful. As another program director explained, "We have a lot of varied perspectives, but we all have experience with the community, so nobody gets offended about tweaking things." Across the three campuses, the directors set the expectation that instructors and staff should consistently explore ways to improve the program and ensure that all students have validating experiences in every aspect of the program (*reflective practice*).

After expectations were set, then leaders modeled appropriate behavior so others could see the norms in action. Modeling entailed interacting with students in a validating way so that other staff and faculty could see what this looks like. The leaders then provided a space for staff to ask questions about what they saw during the observation and make decisions about how that might influence their work with students (*reflective practice*). Additionally, the directors encouraged the staff to connect with other departments and programs on campus in order to identify opportunities and resources for students as well as to reduce the need to replicate effective practices that already existed (*collaborative*). Often, the director would coach the staff member on why building the relationship with a specific department mattered and then participated in the initial meeting in order to broker the connection – especially for newer staff who had not engaged in developing partnerships across campus before.

Next, leaders held staff accountable for acting in accordance with the modeled behavior. TSLC directors used multiple tools to keep themselves and their staff accountable to the norms that guided the programs. First, the staff met each week to both look back at what had happened the previous week (*reflective practice*) and plan for the short- and long-term. These meetings were key to monitoring and reinforcing TSLC cultural norms. Everyone – staff members, faculty coordinator, administrative assistants, and director – was responsible for identifying both successes and failures associated with the cultural norms. For example, at one meeting, a staff member noted students did not always use preferred pronouns, which created discomfort for others in the community. This led to a discussion about how to integrate a conversation about pronouns within the first-year seminar, and staff members began listing their preferred pronouns and modeling for students how to ask for preferred pronouns instead of making assumptions (*identity-conscious*). Since everyone working for TSLC program was committed to creating a culture of ecological validation, the conversations about improving were welcomed. Instead of considering these issues as shortcomings of a particular person, everyone actively engaged in conversations about how they could collectively identify opportunities to improve work (*reflective practice*).

In addition to the weekly meetings, the directors met regularly with staff members for individual meetings. These conversations provided opportunities for directors to learn about successes, challenges, and ideas from each staff member as well as to provide individuals professional development related to the program goals (*reflective practice*). At one meeting, the director thanked a staff member for building connections with the study abroad program, which had led to a larger percentage of TSLC students participating in study abroad than the overall student population. The director reminded them to make sure to have a note on the door whenever not in the office so that students knew when they would be back and whom to contact in the meantime if an urgent issue existed. The directors also modeled the importance of being open to feedback. As directors explored ways of improving the program, they solicited and used feedback from students, staff members, and relevant stakeholders to guide future practice. One director also used feedback from the staff members about their leadership style to shift their approach to working with others in ways that collectively enhanced each staff member's ability to use their strengths and contribute to the decision-making process.

At the end of each year, the directors coordinated an annual report that summarized what had been accomplished during the year and identified goals for the next academic year (*reflective practice*). The process of developing the report included reviewing both formal and informal data. The formal data included grade point averages, course-taking patterns, retention, and graduation rates. The programs also collected student surveys, and the staff kept notes from their proactive advising meetings, which allowed them to identify patterns. The informal data included the directors' and staff members' observations of students and programming. They also had feedback provided by the TSLC instructors and the professional staff members with whom they collaborated across campus. The annual reports provided an opportunity to carefully consider what was working. Since TSLC valued experimenting with new ideas, the reports allowed for reflection on which initiatives had been successful and which had not. For example, they might share that they had tried a new career activity for students in their first semester that had limited success – the student evaluations consistently noted that they were not ready for an in-depth career conversation in the first semester – so the program planned to explore moving this activity to the end of second-year programming (*developmental*).

Directors addressed times when norms were violated. For example, at the program orientation for one of the campuses, mentors were expected to briefly introduce themselves including their name, hometown, major, and one activity (which included clubs, work, community service, or hobby.) A White female mentor from a suburban community ended by throwing her hands in the air and saying, "I've been living the thug life." The director met with the mentor right after the event to explain why this culturally inappropriate language did not fit with the culture of TSLC and may be offensive to some of the racially minoritized students (*identity-conscious*). The goal of this conversation was not to punish the student, but to help them learn from this experience and gain a deeper understanding of how the culture worked. The next mentor training included a discussion of culturally sensitive language. The staff also discussed how this information probably should have been included in the mentor training that happens the summer before they met their mentees, so they decided to add a culturally sensitive language workshop to the mentor training for the next academic year (*reflective practice*).

Another way to support staff in enacting the norms was to create learning opportunities. One program director had staff members read research articles in order to remain informed about promising practices. When discussing an article about validation theory at one of the staff meetings, the director stated, "Validation is all we do." The director then asked the staff members to spend 15 minutes considering how the program could create more affirming experiences for students as well as identifying any students who might be slipping through the cracks (*reflective practice*). Staff members identified areas they wanted to tailor support: LGBTQ+ students raised in conservative families who might benefit from discussions about how to access counseling on campus; exploring how to support Black students who felt uncomfortable on campus after a few racial incidents occurred; and examining the subgroup of first-generation college students who ended up on academic probation each year to understand how to support them (*identity-conscious*). The remainder of the meeting involved sharing successes and challenges in working with students as well as brainstorming all the ways to support students who were struggling and connect students experiencing success with opportunities to extend their learning (*holistic*).

In addition to the directors, the programs had another key leadership role – a faculty coordinator. The faculty coordinator received a course release each semester to help coordinate the shared academic courses for TSLC, including working with the academic departments to identify instructors. The faculty coordinator served as a point of contact for faculty members in order to be a bridge between the classroom and resources available on campus. An instructor could contact the faculty coordinator with any question or concern they had about students in their classes. If the instructor had questions about pedagogy, the coordinator might provide advice, suggest resources, or offer to observe the classroom. If a student was having academic challenges, the coordinator would connect with the TSLC staff to have a conversation about what might be happening and then reach out to the student for additional information. Based upon the information gathered, the faculty coordinator and staff would connect students with resources they might need within the program and on campus (*collaborative*). Instructors valued the role of faculty coordinator because they knew there was one person they could contact who understood the experiences of instructors and could develop a plan of support for any issue. As a result, the instructors felt more comfortable engaging with their students because they were less concerned that an issue would emerge that they did not know how to handle.

TSLC took a distributed approach to leadership that enabled staff members to identify areas to lead and assisted in the decision-making process. For example, the staff at one campus each identified an area of specialization (e.g., study abroad, counseling, career development) and served in a leadership role for that aspect of the program. The staff member developed relationships with other individuals and offices on campus who did similar work in order to communicate the norms of TSLC with other educators as well as look for opportunities to collaborate on initiatives designed to support at-promise student success. For example, one staff member coordinated with the counseling center to identify counselors and services for racially minoritized students who reported challenges including a discomfort with the counseling center (*identity-conscious, proactive,* and *collaborative*). In partnership with the multicultural center and the counseling office, the staff member identified a racially minoritized counselor who provided appointments in the multicultural center once a week, which resulted in more students taking advantage of that resource.

Socialization

Faculty and staff were provided ongoing opportunities to learn about and contribute to ecological validation. At the beginning of each term, training sessions were offered where faculty engaged in dialogue about the assets and needs of low-income, racially minoritized, and first-generation college students (*strengths-oriented* and *identity-conscious*). The faculty coordinators consistently mentioned that not all at-promise students are the same;

the purpose of the training was to provide information to inform practice, not that the instructors should perceive all students the same. Some instructors had not previously engaged with the research about at-promise students because all of their training had focused on acquiring disciplinary expertise. Ideas like first-generation college students not being familiar with a syllabus or some at-promise students needing to work to support family were new to them. For example, faculty were encouraged to be flexible with students because of these obligations (*holistic* and *identity-conscious*). A few instructors who taught TSLC classes in a range of disciplines spoke about their experiences working with the students. These instructors highlighted how engaged students were in class and provided some suggestions about how to adjust pedagogy within their specific discipline to help students achieve their potential. For example, one instructor moved a portion of her optional pre-exam study hours to one of the TSLC spaces on campus where students felt more comfortable, and a math instructor reflected on how he adjusted that examples he gave in class because many of the students were unfamiliar with the White middle-class contexts that he previously used (*identity-conscious*). Then regular breakfasts were established where faculty could talk throughout the semester about issues that emerged in classes and brainstorm solutions (*reflective practice*), which often included connecting with other resources on campus (*collaboration*). Many of the sessions provided data and research about key topics ranging from the needs of first-generation college students to teaching in culturally responsive ways (*identity-conscious*).

One of the faculty coordinators created a tip sheet for new instructors that explained how to create validation for students, including knowing their names, starting classes with questions and updates, encouraging active learning, and suggesting instructors linger after class in order to speak with students (*holistic, identity-conscious,* and *proactive*). Instructors were encouraged to explain why assignments, activities, and readings were important. In addition, the faculty coordinator explained how students benefitted from the instructor pulling back the curtain and explaining how to study, providing clear guidelines for assignments, discussing how to read the syllabus, and sharing any tips about how to be successful in class.

The coordinator also reviewed feedback from students. If an instructor did not demonstrate the ability to meet the expectations of the program, the coordinator would not invite them back to teach again (*reflective practice*). For example, several students shared with TSLC staff that an instructor provided discouraging feedback and had not been available when they stopped by during office hours to ask for support. The faculty coordinator reached out to the instructor who stated that they believed students needed tough feedback and to be independent in order to prepare for future careers.

After discussing this with the director, they made the decision to recruit another instructor and let the academic department chair know that that instructor would not be permitted to teach a TSLC class in the future.

Directors created training for staff members to orient them to multiple resources and opportunities within TSLC and on campus as well as socialization related to enacting the program culture. Training and development took place in individual meetings that occurred monthly with the program director as well as in weekly group meetings where they shared their work experiences and received feedback about the ways they could have been more validating or connected students to more support. At one of the campuses, we observed new staff training since five staff members were hired during the four years of data collection. The director utilized a coaching approach that involved new staff members observing her interacting with a student and then engaging in a conversation with the staff members after the student left (*reflective practice*). She began by asking what the staff members saw, and then she explained why she made the specific decisions for this student. In one situation, the staff observed two student meetings, and one of the staff members asked why the director pushed one student more than the other. The director explained how staff need to approach a student experiencing anxiety related to a potentially serious issue with a boyfriend differently than a high-achieving student who is feeling stress related to taking on a leadership position (*identity-conscious*). After a couple of weeks, the director then switched roles and observed the staff member interacting with students before engaging in a debrief. The director consistently affirmed the importance of considering all aspects of a student's experiences (*holistic*), acknowledging their successes and goals (*strengths-oriented*), understanding all aspects of their identity (*identity-conscious*), exploring how to provide coordinated support over the two-year period of the program (*developmental*), and considering multiple options for support that may be offered by TSLC or across campus (*collaborative*). In addition, the entire staff attended the diversity conference hosted by the university each year that focused on how to support students with differing identities and backgrounds. The staff then collectively discussed what they learned (*reflective practice*). For example, they decided to incorporate more discussions about race in their events after one of the conferences (*identity-conscious*).

Peer mentor training at each campus began over the summer and continued throughout the academic year. Peer mentors were assigned to a staff member who served as their point of contact for individual development (*reflective practice*). At one of the campuses, the staff and peer mentors went to a retreat center for four days to engage in extensive training related to the program culture and expectations. While peer mentors received information related to resources and program structures, the majority of the time was spent role playing how to engage with students in ways that addressed the multiple issues students might face (*holistic*), understanding how to work with students with different backgrounds and identities (*identity-conscious*), how to build upon their mentees' successes (*strengths-oriented*), and the importance of establishing a trusting relationship with students. During their fall training at one campus, peer mentors participated in diversity and inclusion training facilitated by a faculty member with expertise in multicultural education and later spent time meeting with staff in multicultural affairs (*identity-conscious, holistic,* and *collaborative*). These sessions were followed by workshops led by the staff where mentors explored their socially constructed identities (*identity-conscious*) and considered how they inform their work with mentees (*reflective practice*). A significant amount of time focused on helping mentors understand the varied strengths that students bring with them to college as well as common challenges that exist (*strengths-oriented*). Mentors learned the importance of valuing cultural backgrounds that may differ from how they were raised. Professional staff from campus were invited to help build the mentors' knowledge based on the support available for their mentees (*collaborative*). A counselor from campus presented on how to identify potential issues related to mental health concerns and the importance of connecting students with support (*collaborative*). These combined efforts were designed to enhance mentors' knowledge and skills to support a diverse group of at-promise peers.

Peer mentors were held accountable for enacting a culture of ecological validation. At one of the mentor trainings early the spring semester, the director started by saying, "I have been receiving reports than not all mentors have been doing 1:1s [individual student meetings] or the 1:1s are quick and cold." She paused. "We need to clean that up. That is not what we do." She then affirmed the importance of these individual meetings by sharing examples of students reporting how they had been supported by their peer mentor and then asking the mentors to share how they had been organizing the meetings to support students who might have a wide range of experiences on campus. To help facilitate a deeper connection between the mentors and mentees, the director gave the mentors a quiz of 20 basic things they should know about all their mentees (e.g., full name, major, career goals, hometown, languages spoken, favorite activities, best part of college, hardest part of college). If the mentor could not answer all of the quiz items, they had a week to connect with each mentee and have a conversation to get to know them better.

Faculty, staff, and peer mentor trainings emphasized cultural responsiveness, including having uncomfortable conversations. One director would consistently say to students that it was imperative to "get comfortable with being uncomfortable" if TSLC was to truly be an inclusive community (*identity-conscious*). Subsequently, the program provided opportunities for students to learn more about social identities in the context of power, privilege, and oppression in a first-year seminar. They also provided opportunities to students to process sociopolitical issues that might have affected students differently based on their identities (*identity-conscious* and *holistic*). When an issue emerged, such as a racial incident on campus or a divisive national political event, TSLC leaned on the culture they had created to help students have difficult conversations. They consistently sent the message that the compositional diversity of TSLC was a strength, which meant that students, staff, and instructors had an obligation to support each other, even if they did not agree.

TSLC intentionally selected staff members, instructors, and peer mentors based on their potential to fit within the culture of ecological validation. Staff members were hired based upon their ability and/or potential to enact the norms, instructors were selected to teach classes based upon their commitment to support at-promise students, and peer mentors were chosen based upon their potential to support other students. For example, each of the programs included peer mentors who had been on academic probation and utilized support provided by staff members in order to broaden the idea of academic success (*holistic*). In addition, one of the programs made the decision to select math graduate students who were studying math pedagogy to teach entry-level courses because they could more easily explain basic concepts than professors who researched sophisticated and abstract ideas. TSLC programs were conscious of selecting individuals who represented the diversity of the students in the program, including race/ethnicity, urban and rural, gender identity, and sexuality (*identity-conscious*). The directors wanted the students to see themselves represented within the staff, instructors, and/or peer mentors.

Language, Space, and Communication

TSLC staff and directors carefully considered how the program engaged with students in terms of messaging and language. Across the three campuses, the term *scholars* was used to identify the students (*strengths-oriented*). In addition, TSLC was associated with a public figure (Warren Buffett) who achieved local and international success. Being a "Buffett Scholar" was consistently associated with academic success. TSLC ensured this was more than just semantics as they structured the program to support students' academic potential. Staff, directors, instructors, and mentors sent the message that students had earned the right to be in college and the role of TSLC was to help them achieve their potential. The term *scholar* was used at all of the events. For example, speakers at dinners with professionals were often heard using the term *scholar,* and staff recounted examples, such as one local leader saying: "You are scholars. I believe in speaking life into all that was and all that will be."

Directors required staff, mentors, and instructors to know students by name and build trusting relationships with the students they served. One director explained: "Our staff, we try hard to let the students know they're important, they're noticed. We know their names. We care about their stories, and again, trying to constantly communicate that fact so they don't feel like they're not noticed as they continue to move through the year." Ways to do this included the director studying student profiles so she could greet students by name and recite a fact or two about their backgrounds at orientation. This form of communication sent the message that students were known and mattered. Students spoke about how they rarely heard their name used outside of the TSLC space because they were most often referred to by their student identification number when going to other offices on campus and many of their instructors did not know their names. During the mentor training at one campus, the director spoke about the importance of making sure the mentors and staff correctly pronounced the first and last names of each student they worked with in the program (*identity-conscious*). They practiced how to ask for correct pronunciation and how to apologize if they said someone's name incorrectly.

TSLC consistently used language associated with care. Students often spoke about TSLC as their "family" at the campuses. The directors made comments like "you are my heart," "I love you," and "we are here for you" when speaking to the students at group events. At one campus, the program commissioned a TSLC student to design a large mural for the program space that featured the TSLC logo and used words such as "family," "inclusive," "community," "friendship," "opportunities," "resources," and "succeed" – terms intended to communicate that this is everyone's "home" and students from all backgrounds can be successful. TSLC emailed newsletters and posted on social media as additional ways to send validating messages to students. When talking with students individually, the directors encouraged staff to send the message that they were invested in supporting the student's individual success. The directors believed this language of care that exceeded simply focusing on grades (*holistic*) was an important aspect of creating a culture of ecological validation for at-promise students.

Validating language was consistently used and reinforced over time – from when they got their first letter and phone calls from TSLC to orientation, welcome breakfasts, monthly dinners, advising sessions, and in each programmatic activity (*developmental*). Staff identified student accomplishments each week that could be acknowledged in the TSLC newsletter and key events. Leadership incorporated validating language into all program materials from T-shirts to planning binders to recognition pins that were given to students at the "halfway to graduation" event at the end of year two. One director chose a quote for TSLC T-shirts that featured Malcolm X – an African American historical figure who had been born and raised in Omaha. The intentional selection of this individual allowed for both formal and informal conversations about issues of race and class in the local context. When the shirts were passed out to students, the director explained how this famous individual had navigated challenges (e.g., low-income background, foster care, racism) on his path to becoming an influential national figure. After pausing, the director emphasized that as "scholars" in TSLC, each student had the potential to do the same.

Social media was also used to reinforce validating messages. Each program made different decisions about which social media platforms were appropriate based upon their student usage. One of the campuses used multiple platforms – Facebook, SnapChat, Instagram, WhatsApp – to connect with students. Mentors often provided feedback to the staff about the platforms that students used. These platforms provided a way for TSLC to send information to students in a space where they were comfortable and frequently visited. For example, they would send announcements about upcoming events or reminders about university deadlines. As one staff member noted, "So, I share [on social media] information about financial aid, about opportunities on campus, about offices on campus … we try to make efforts to get people to add the social media group, because we post a lot of opportunities there." Staff used these spaces to celebrate the achievements of individual students, such as when students had an art exhibit, were on the dean's list, got an internship, and completed a research project with a faculty member. These recognitions of individual students' success got the most "likes" and were reposted more than announcements about resources. Directors and staff posted encouraging notes throughout the week and semester. One director posted the following social media message at the beginning of spring semester:

> As you start this term, I encourage you to consider what steps you are going to take to grow beyond your comfort zone. The Spring term is full of opportunities for students! Take positive risks, pursue opportunities to develop your skills, and don't let fear/doubt stop you from seeking leadership roles.

Physical space was used to communicate that students belonged on campus and to highlight their successes. One program had nearly an entire floor of a building dedicated to TSLC. In addition to the staff and faculty coordinator offices, TSLC had a quiet study room, computer room with free printing, hangout room, and lounge in the front office (*holistic*). Throughout the space were validating messages related to opportunities and previous successes. The hallways included multiple boards with chalk, Legos, and magnetic words so students could post their feelings, messages, and ideas. This campus served a large number of commuter students. The space sent a message that they had a place that was theirs to occupy and connect with staff, instructors, mentors, and peers. Another campus had the office located on the first floor of the residence hall where the first-year TSLC students lived. Students knew they could stop by anytime to ask questions or just to connect with a staff member, including the days that they gave out free popcorn to encourage students to come by. Outside of the office was a lounge area where students could study or socialize. On one of the campuses, there was a study café in the residence hall where first-year TSLC students lived, and staff made sure that food and beverages were available. Instructors were encouraged to use a private room adjacent to the study café when they did optional review sessions for exams, and they also partnered with the writing center to move a portion of their support to this space once a week (*collaborative*). TSLC hired peer-tutors who were available four days a week in the evenings to assist in key general education courses where students needed assistance, including English, math, and sciences. Staff noted how having the snacks present demonstrated care so that they had energy for study.

Rituals and Traditions

The director, staff, and faculty created rituals and traditions to cultivate and maintain TSLC's culture. They created multiple environments where validating practices regularly occurred so that they became normalized and were built into the fabric of how TSLC operated. These rituals and traditions spanned from the first semester though graduation (*developmental*). For example, first-year seminar meetings opened with "happies and crappies" or "highs and lows" where all members of the course, including the instructor, shared an academic or personal success and a challenge they had experienced over the past week (*holistic*). By co-creating space to share information about oneself, staff normalized celebrating successes and struggling during college. Furthermore, they created opportunities to help students realize they were not alone and affirmed their abilities to achieve their goals and negotiate challenges.

One campus created community dinners for first-year and second-year students a few times each semester that met distinct needs for these students (*holistic* and *developmental*). Dinners for first-year students primarily focused on community building; students ate dinner with their peer mentor and the students in their seminar class. The unstructured time allowed for students to connect with their peers and for the mentors to informally check in with each student. If questions arose, the mentor could ask a staff member to come over and provide an answer. After dinner, students engaged in a fun activity intended to build social connections and a sense of collective support. The dinners for second-year students were designed to support major and career exploration with activities that allowed them to cultivate interviewing skills, expand their professional networks, and build relationships with peers and faculty in their major.

TSLC staff used rituals and traditions to publicly recognize students' achievements and validate their abilities to succeed from the first semester through graduation (*developmental*). One campus had a recognition reception each semester that acknowledged students' academic achievements (e.g., Chancellor's list, securing internships), leadership positions, and campus awards (*strengths-oriented*). Notably, students were encouraged to bring family or others in their support systems to this reception to celebrate alongside them (*holistic*). Two campuses hosted events to recognize students' completion of their first two years of college. One campus called this event the Second Year Experience Launch with the idea that they were "launching" students out of their formal time in TSLC and into their academic major (*developmental*). To facilitate these connections to academic departments, the faculty coordinator and staff worked with deans and department chairs to ensure that instructors and academic leaders were present to meet with students in small groups and welcome them into their college and major (*collaboration*). At the launch, students received a campus insignia pin and were told the pin was symbolic of "the journey that you are on, that you belong here, and that you'll complete your degrees." This message affirming students' capacities to succeed (*strengths-oriented*) was reinforced at the TSLC graduation ceremonies where students were individually recognized in front of their families and guests (*holistic*) and they received a medal to wear to university-wide graduation as a reminder of their accomplishments and connection to TSLC.

One of the annual events that meant a lot at one of the campuses was the autobiographical readings. During their first semester, each TSLC student took a writing course where they engage in autobiographical writing. In addition to writing about their own experiences, the faculty identified readings for the students that they think would resonate with their experience. For example, one year they assigned the book *The Distance Between Us* by Reyna Grande (2013), who writes about crossing borders (U.S./Mexico; cultural borders, and higher education as a first-generation student). At the end of the course, students were selected by their instructor to read a portion of their own autobiography. Another program did something similar in a speech class that included a culminating assignment where students shared their stories, which fostered connections between students and helped to humanize each other across differences they might possess. Students who shared were affirmed by the faculty, staff, and peers in attendance. Such events validated students both academically and inter-personally (*holistic*). By bringing together faculty, staff, administrators, and students, the programs were able to reinforce ecological validation with different groups all participating in an event together.

Relationships and Working Interactions

The culture of ecological validation was supported by TSLC building relationships that reflected the norms in working with each other, across campus, and in all their working interactions. Directors set the expectation that staff and instructors needed to collaborate within the program and across the broader campus to maximize their efforts to support student success and fully address student needs – acknowledging that students are capable of success when educators work together toward that goal (*collaborative*). As one director noted, "Just the culture of our office … we have a very collaborative nature as a team." Staff met with other offices on campus throughout the year to identify opportunities to work together as well as challenges students might face. There was a clear understanding among staff that student success relied on strong working relationships with other offices.

Staff proactively built relationships with students and learned about their multiple identities/cultures, needs, and goals, which allowed the staff to collectively reflect on any trends that emerged (*reflective practice*) and then to utilize the relationships they had built with other student support offices on campus to create lines of communication, facilitate addressing students' needs, and connect students to opportunities in the broader campus community (*proactive*). At one campus, the program recognized that many of their Latinx students had distinctive needs based on work commitments and family dynamics. In response, the director connected to the office of diversity and inclusion on campus to coordinate support for the program's Latinx students in a way that met their multiple needs and was culturally responsive (*identity-conscious*). At another campus, they recognized that students whose initial language was not English often needed additional support and that this needed to happen as soon as possible before challenges emerged: "So, really for us, we try to target in the summer with new student enrollment, we have students that say I come from a home where English is not the primary language … We try to connect them with other programs on campus, sometimes we reach out to the International Education Office to talk with them about resources" (*identity-conscious*).

Staff consistently worked with partners to share information about students, their needs, and learning opportunities to create an environment where students could readily access support services. As one staff member noted, their intention was to "encourage [students] to build bridges" (*collaborative*). This staff member went on to comment how working with other offices on campus allowed them to connect students "with the different pieces that are on campus that can [enrich their lives] according to their individual needs and experiences" (*holistic*), so students saw "that we really care about them and their success. It's not just them getting the degree." They connected students in order to transition them to the campus supports after they completed the two-year program and maximize their success in college (*developmental*).

Proactive efforts to work across domains of student support enabled the culture of ecological validation to permeate multiple spaces where students were supported, ranging from classes, multicultural center, TRIO, writing center, academic services, honors program, financial aid, LGBTQ+ programs, and counseling center on campus – creating a collaborative network of holistic support that the staff utilized in order to meet the students' multiple needs and support their success (*holistic* and *identity-conscious*). For instance, TSLC at one campus collaborated with TRIO and several other student support offices that served low-income and racially minoritized students in order to proactively connect at-promise students to a holistic range of resources, including the study abroad office, graduate school, and pre-professional opportunities, career advising support, and the undergraduate research office (*holistic* and *identity-conscious*). One undergirding motivation for this effort to work across offices was that at-promise students were just as interested in many of the same learning opportunities as their more privileged peers (*strengths-oriented*), and it was a matter of proactively connecting students to these opportunities and removing barriers to their success, such as lack of adequate institutional communication about the existence of these opportunities for all students (*proactive*).

Staff emphasized the need for maintaining open lines of communication between faculty, director, and staff in order to coordinate proactive support working from the assumption that students are capable of success (*collaborative*). And they did not just meet around specific student needs but also expanded outreach to include changing more broadly the way they did their work – enacting new practices they believed would better suit students.

Reflection Questions:

- Does your campus reflect and encourage the seven norms necessary for creating and sustaining ecological validation?
- How does your campus leadership; socialization; language, spaces, and communication; rituals and traditions; and relationships and working interactions encourage and reflect the norms? How might you improve in areas where support does not exist?
- Are there certain norms that are prevalent but not others? Does this represent a way that the culture might not be strong or sustained over time?

7

EDUCATOR ENACTMENT OF ECOLOGICAL VALIDATION TO CENTER AT-PROMISE STUDENTS

As Chapter 6 explained, a culture of ecological validation involves norms that influence how educators engage in work practice to support at-promise students. In this chapter, we provide an illustration of how educators enact the seven norms. We begin by discussing how a culture of ecological validation enabled TSLC educators to center at-promise students. Researchers and practitioners often speak about the importance of centering student needs, experiences, and identities – the TSLC program culture and practices provide an illustration of how to be student-centered. Drawing from our data, we then highlight the experiences of a TSLC faculty member and a staff member to demonstrate how the seven norms influenced how they engaged in their work. We illustrate how they enacted each of the norms that support a culture of ecological validation. To connect the work of educators to student experiences and outcomes, the final section focuses on how educators in TSLC engaged in ecologically validating practices that supported academic and career development of at-promise students.

Centering At-promise Students in a Culture of Ecological Validation

Unlike the siloed models presented in Chapter 3, a culture of ecological validation centers the at-promise student (see Diagram 7.1). Educators start with the assumption that each student brings a set of multiple identities, experiences, and characteristics that are assets that a validating educator can build upon and leverage to support the student's college success. These assets include an at-promise student's cultural background, race/ethnicity, first-generation college status, personality, motivations, family support, social

DOI: 10.4324/9781003443711-9

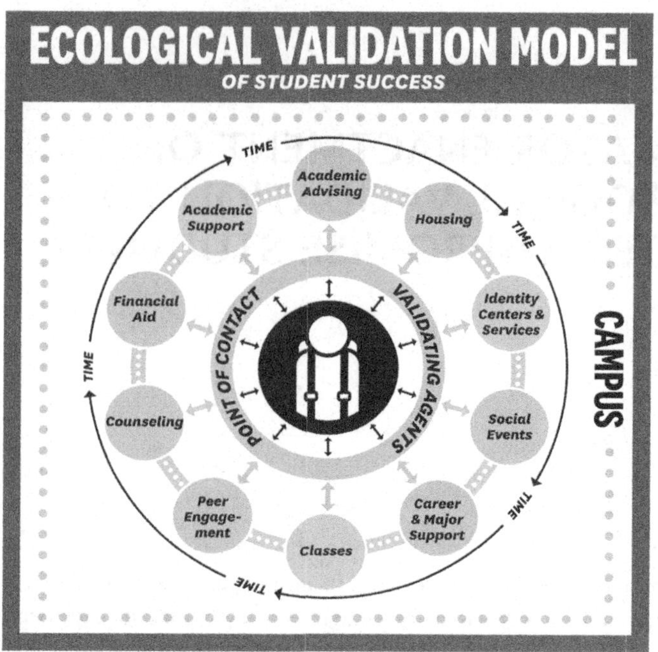

DIAGRAM 7.1 Centering At-promise Students in a Culture of Ecological Validation.

capital, feelings/emotions, work status, health conditions, career aspirations, life experiences, gender identity, academic preparation, immigration background, and personal interests and goals.

In our observations of the TSLC program, educators served as a point of contact who proactively built a relationship with the student to discover and learn about the student's identities, experiences, and characteristics. In Diagram 7.1, the arrows between the point of contact and student represent how the point of contact initiated the relationship and proactively provided support as well as serving as the person whom the student trusted to provide support if they had a question, concern, or challenge. In turn, the educator connected the student to coordinated support to meet that student's unique set of assets, needs, and goals. The point of contact took a holistic approach to student support and considered students' personal and academic assets, strengths, and challenges when connecting students to campus support contexts. The point of contact did not create individualized programming for each student; rather, they coordinated and connected students to existing support contexts that were relevant given the student's assets and goals. The educator acted as a validating campus navigator who helped students find the support they needed. The process of discovering students' assets and proactively connecting students to other offices was an act of validation that communicated to the student that the educator genuinely cared about their success as individuals.

Connecting a student to a coordinated set of support contexts is represented in the image by the arrows from the student to the support contexts in the outer ring. The arrows are bidirectional because the goal is both to connect the student with other educators and to create a context where the other educators can provide ecologically validating support for the student. Educators in the students' support ecology shared relevant and appropriate information across contexts in order to help meet the needs of the student, reflecting a shared commitment to student success rather than siloed support efforts. The web of coordinated support contexts that the point of contact connected students to is represented by the multiple contexts in the outer ring of the image, which includes academic or career advising, financial aid, counseling, peer engagement opportunities, identity centers and services, and many other support contexts and offices on and off campus. The coordinated set of support contexts enabled students to build upon their assets toward achieving success by addressing their needs and taking advantage of opportunities.

Through the relationship the point of contact had proactively built with the student, they collaborated with the student to identify what kind of support and opportunities would best suit the student's needs and goals. Not every context included in the image was part of every student's support ecology, and there could be others not represented in the image that could be included given a specific student's needs, assets, and goals. Consider the coordinated ecology for a student with a racially minoritized identity who is interested in pursuing a career where they can give back to their community and is challenged by a specific course, but willing to put in the work to succeed. Their racially minoritized identity, interest in pursuing a career to give back to their community, and willingness to put in the work to succeed academically would be assets that the educator could proactively discover through the relationship they built with the student. An educator could coordinate an ecology of support that might include a campus identity center, career services office, a service learning opportunity, and tutoring in order to build on the student's assets and connect them to support needed to achieve their goals.

In addition to the point of contact, we argue that all educators that the student interacts with should function as a "validating agent" (see Diagram 7.1). With ecological validation, *all* educators create validating experiences during *all* interactions with *all* students. It is not truly ecological validation until students receive affirmation of their assets and capabilities from educators across their web of multiple support contexts over time, including student affairs educators, advisors, instructors, faculty, administrators, student services professionals, peer mentors, tutors, and student leaders. Everyone who interacts with students should be a validating agent. This point is crucial to creating systemic change and fully enacting ecological validation. Acts of validation consist of proactive recognition, affirmation, and enabling of students' capacities for learning and college success in and out of the classroom, both academically and interpersonally (Rendón, 1994). Validating educators remove barriers to student success in the college environment and build bridges to enable student access to opportunities that enrich their college learning experience.

Channels of communication are kept open between support contexts in order to promote collaboration. The connection, collaboration, and communication across students' coordinated ecology is represented by the lines linking each of the context circles in the outer ring of the image (e.g., financial aid, counseling, classes). These lines of communication are what Bronfenbrenner (1994) called the mesosystem and do not typically directly involve the student – yet still have an impact on a student's experiences in the contexts where they directly engage with those educators who are communicating with each other about the student's success. Information sharing allows educators to make informed decisions about the kind of support the student needs given their assets and goals, which is experienced as validating by the student. The effort on the part of educators to know each student's assets and needs and communicate those across contexts also conveys broader institutional affirmation that the student and their success matters. This process also allows educators across campus to assess potential gaps in support that may exist as well as providing an opportunity to collaboratively provide support for students' multiple identities in a more coordinated way.

A final factor that is important to consider in ecological validation is the matter of time. Time is represented by the outer ring of the image. Time is an important facet of students' development and success (Bronfenbrenner, 1994), and in ecological validation, time operates at a few different levels. First, educators are proactive and reach out early to students to discover their assets, connect them to support contexts, and engage them in validating experiences. Second, the act of affirming students' assets and building from them to help a student achieve their goals is something that occurs consistently over time from multiple educators across contexts. This ongoing affirming support over time serves to build and maintain students' trajectory to college success that results from validation (Rendón, 1994). Third, different needs, opportunities, and challenges related to students' assets may emerge at different points in time over the course of their development during college. Thus, one-time validation is unlikely to fully address students' needs and ultimately improve their likelihood of academic success; validation needs to happen consistently as new needs and opportunities emerge.

Norms in Practice: Highlighting a Faculty and Staff Member

The norms that frame a culture of ecological validation reinforce each other in practice. Seeing how the seven norms work together in practice makes it easier to understand how they are all needed to build and sustain ecological validation. In this section, we draw from our research to build a composite example of how an instructor used the norms to support their students. The information shared below was not based on exceptional faculty members; rather, the illustration represents common practices among the instructors who taught courses within TSLC.

A Faculty Member's Perspective

Duane taught an introduction to communications general education course for the TSLC program. He was excited to be selected by his communications department chair to teach in the program. The faculty coordinator emailed him about a required workshop for new TSLC faculty the week before classes began. During the workshop, the faculty coordinator drew from previous research and information gathered from the program about at-promise students. She began by sharing how at-promise students have many different identities, backgrounds, and experiences to draw from when engaging in class (*strengths-oriented* and *identity-conscious*). She engaged in a discussion about how she used this information to explore her curriculum to see if there were opportunities to include these different backgrounds within her curriculum and encouraged the new faculty to do the same (*reflective practice*). Duane took note of how he might want to think about how he could shift some of his assignments in ways that continued to meet course objectives, but might better reflect the diversity of the students' backgrounds and interests.

The faculty coordinator also shared information about how some subgroups of students experience challenges in higher education (*identity-conscious*). For example, she shared how the program serves some students with refugee, immigration, and undocumented experiences that frame how they navigate college and some of the challenges they have accessing resources. She shared some background about the varied experiences that they may bring from high school, some of their continued work obligations during college, and the skillsets they have learned through caring for siblings and elders (*strengths-oriented* and *holistic*). The faculty coordinator provided information about some of the challenges that at-promise students might experience and recommended a short video – from the office of community outreach – for Duane to watch about the experiences of certain immigrant groups in the local area (*identity-conscious* and *collaborative*). The faculty coordinator also provided Duane with information about all of the key resources and support available on campus to first-year students (*collaborative*). Duane reflected that he was really surprised he had not heard about these services before. After Duane reviewed the materials and video, he decided to make changes to some of the course materials to make them more relevant for his students. Duane reviewed the pictures provided in the learning management system of all the students and memorized their names so that on the first day he could greet them individually.

After bringing in a panel of current TSLC instructors who shared how they approached their instruction and spoke about how they found the TSLC students to be highly motivated, the faculty coordinator concluded the instructor workshop by encouraging the new instructors to set up meetings with students in order to get to know them as individuals. The faculty coordinator underscored how the general information was useful for instructors to reflect on their practice, but it was important to know the specific students in their classes in order to avoid making assumptions that might not be accurate (*holistic* and *proactive*).

The first day of class came, and students were surprised that Duane already knew their names (*proactive*). He told them that he was really interested in learning more about them and their backgrounds and wanted to set up a meeting with each of them (*holistic* and *proactive*). He started the class by asking each of them to share a moment they were proud of how they communicated a key idea well and they thought they made a difference (*strengths-oriented*). He was surprised by how quickly students engage on the first day because most classes take several weeks to start talking – he thought back to the new instructor workshop where previous faculty shared how this happens because the students feel safe and connected in the TSLC classes. The class seemed off to a great start. The initial meetings with students went really well. What a rich array of backgrounds they had, and he found that he could enrich the examples that he provided in class because of understanding more about their experiences (*holistic, proactive,* and *identity-conscious*). He now wished that he had used this strategy with the previous classes he taught.

After a couple weeks of class, he noticed that a couple of students were not engaging as much as the others. As he reflected on their individual meetings, these two students discussed how English was not their primary language growing up and they sometimes got nervous speaking in public (*reflective practice*). The university had an online system where he could post a red flag if students had an issue, but the students' grades were fine so this did not make sense. Duane remembered how the faculty coordinator mentioned that she was a resource, so he sent an email requesting a meeting. The next day they spoke on the phone, and the faculty coordinator recommended that he reach out to the students and connected him with some resources from the English as a Second Language center. Duane set up individual meetings with these students and made sure to let them know that there was not a problem but that he wanted to chat with them about some possible resources that might be helpful. Duane noted that he could see that they understood the material but sometimes were not feeling confident in communicating (*strengths-oriented*). He recommended that they consider some additional tutoring with language skills to enhance their confidence. The students were appreciative that he did not single them out in class and instead emphasized what good ideas they had, which he wanted them to share with the entire class.

As Duane reached the mid-point of the semester, he contemplated how different this class was from others he had taught, through the support of the faculty coordinator, department chair, and others who helped him to better understand how to support students in this course (*reflective practice*). He also considered how this experience might influence how he approached other classes.

The previous example illustrates the culture of ecological validation from an instructor perspective. Drawing from our research, we also present an example of how professional staff can enact the norms to demonstrate the concepts from another perspective.

A Staff Member's Perspective

Angel joined the TSLC program as an assistant program coordinator two years ago. One thing that excited them about working for the TSLC was that it provided the type of student support that they themselves would have benefited from as a low-income first-generation college student 10 years earlier. Angel also identified as a Latinx queer person who struggled expressing their identities because they grew up in a nonaffirming family and home community. They wanted to be part of a program that worked with a diverse group of at-promise students while affirming and supporting the individual needs, experiences, and challenges of each student.

Part of Angel's role was assisting with the TSLC summer orientation program, which involved partnering with the campus orientation director to allow TSLC staff to meet with their students during the campus-wide orientation program (*collaborative*). The afternoon before each orientation day, Angel reviewed the information about the students who would be attending the next day so they could greet students by name and know some basic information about each student (*identity-conscious* and *holistic*). The next morning, Angel or another TSLC staff member greeted each student by name and welcomed the guests participating in orientation. Then students and guests get a chance to have an individual conversation with a staff member before going to the campus orientation welcome session in order to make sure they have all their questions about their academic and personal concerns answered before the day begins (*proactive* and *holistic*).

During one of these individual conversations with a student as part of TSLC summer orientation, Angel sat down with Tiffany and her mother, who accompanied her to orientation. Tiffany was an African American woman and had not declared a major. She was nervous that she would be the only student who did not know what they wanted to do in college. Angel assured Tiffany that many students start college undeclared, and Angel promised to connect Tiffany with one of the advisors in the exploratory program for undeclared students on campus (*collaborative*). Tiffany's mom also mentioned that they were both concerned about a racial incident that happened on campus last year, and she wanted to make sure that Tiffany could build connections with other African American students, faculty, and staff on campus. Angel affirmed the concerns about the previous incident and explained the steps the university was taking to ensure similar issues would not happen. In addition, they gave Tiffany and her mother a list of student groups as well as the contact information for the African American advisor in the exploratory studies program (*identity-conscious*). Angel told Tiffany that they would introduce her to one of the orientation leaders who is a member of an African American group for women during lunch (*collaborative*). It was important to Tiffany that Angel created space for both her concerns about choosing a major and desire to build connections with other students (*holistic*). Angel ended every meeting with new students by letting the student know that they were chosen for the program because they had the potential to succeed (*strengths-oriented*) and the TSLC staff would be available to support them along the way (*proactive*).

After students completed the advising sessions in the afternoon, Angel met with each TSLC student individually to review the class schedule. Angel was not an academic advisor, so they did not focus on academic requirements. Their goal was to make sure students understood the information and answer questions that emerged before the students left orientation (*proactive*). They met with a student who was confused about how to complete the requirements for both the TSLC and the honors program while also making adequate progress with his major. The student mentioned how he was thinking about dropping out of the honors program. This had been an issue with students in the past. Angel explained how they worked with the honors program director to make it possible for students to do an extra project in a TSLC class to get credit for an honors class (*collaborative*). The student thanked Angel and said he was looking forward to being in both programs.

As the semester began, Angel worked with other staff members to develop social, academic, and career development opportunities for students (*holistic*). Angel volunteered to coordinate three TSLC events the first month of class: a yoga event around the time when math classes have the first exams to help students relax, a picnic for parenting students, and a résumé workshop for second-year students who want to begin preparing for internships (*developmental*). These three events were developed in response to program assessment results and student focus groups the prior year. For example, during the last TSLC staff meeting, the team reviewed student survey data from the previous year, and several of the students with children expressed frustration that there were not events for families (*reflective practice*). Angel was excited to pilot the family picnic this year and had coordinated with a few students to come up with a plan for the event.

Around mid-semester, Angel and the entire TSLC team blocked out their schedules to hold mid-term meetings with students. Students met with each of the instructors to get a grade estimate and any feedback about their participation in class before meeting individually with a TSLC staff member to review the information they had gathered (*proactive*). Each meeting differed because Angel wanted to be responsive to each student's situation (*holistic* and *identity-conscious*). Lisa, a student who had gotten above a 3.5 GPA the first year, came into the meeting without the smile that Angel had gotten used to seeing (*developmental*). She handed over a list of grades that showed she was on track for a 2.5 GPA. Before addressing the grades, Angel asked how the student was doing. Lisa's brother found out that she had joined a LGBTQ+ group and told their conservative mother, who had decided she could not come home for winter break. Angel validated Lisa's experience and asked if she had anyone to speak to about this. Lisa shook her head no. Angel explained how important counseling had been for them when they navigated their own identity disclosure and offered to connect Lisa with a counselor on campus who had expertise with LBGTQ+ experiences (*identity-conscious* and *collaborative*). Angel helped Lisa call to set up an appointment and then made a phone call to housing to get more information about winter break housing (*holistic* and *collaborative*). Angel also gave Lisa information about applying for an emergency grant to cover extended housing costs that could be submitted to the financial aid office. Before the meeting ended, Angel reminded Lisa of her previous successes and explained how they believed in Lisa's potential to succeed. Lisa agreed to stop by the following week to check in. Angel made a note that the team should explore how to create additional support for LGBTQ+ students because they had noticed a pattern of issues (*reflective practice*).

Norms in Practice: Academic and Career/Major Support

The Thompson Scholars Learning Community (TSLC) offers examples of ecological validation in action around key outcomes for students. Recall from previous chapters that TSLC is a comprehensive college transition program serving low-income students, many of whom are first-generation college and racially minoritized, at three University of Nebraska campuses. TSLC offers a full range of coordinated support contexts including proactive advising, major and career activities and support, shared courses, a first-year seminar, social activities, and shared space. The program leverages existing services on campus (e.g., counseling center, career advising office, study abroad office, financial aid) to coordinate support for the at-promise students it serves. The goals of TSLC are to promote at-promise student success, and it does so by creating a validating system of support that addresses many of the challenges and inequities described in Chapters 2 and 3. As we review this case study, we encourage you to think about how the process of ecological validation is unfolding within TSLC as well as how ecological validation could unfold in other postsecondary contexts, including your campus. We suggest that you focus on *how* ecological validation occurs in TSLC rather than *what* discrete services or personnel are enacting ecological validation.

To provide a deeper understanding of how the programs engaged ecological validation, the following sections focuses on two challenges and inequities that at-promise students face that TSLC addressed through ecological validation: (a) academic challenges and opportunities, and (b) major and career path navigation. Our focus in the examples below is on how TSLC educators enacted ecological validation to address challenges and inequities faced by at-promise students. Chapter 9 focuses on student voice to illustrate how ecological validation affected TSLC students' experiences and success in college.

Academic Challenges and Opportunities

In Chapter 2, we discussed how at-promise students often have differing pre-college academic experiences and preparation. Depending on the student's pre-college experiences, some at-promise students may face challenges such as navigating academic support services on campus, applying for academic enrichment opportunities, or understanding the real-world relevance of what they are learning to maintain their academic motivation. TSLC serves a diverse group of at-promise students; some are highly involved in class and maintain solid GPAs, others grapple with managing college-level work or study skills, and still others excel and desire to pursue additional learning enrichment opportunities like study abroad. At-promise students benefit from having validating educators who holistically know them and can coordinate support in TSLC and on the broader campus (*holistic, identity-conscious,* and *collaborative*). For instance, a student named Emma commented how the TSLC staff and instructors coordinate to identify students who may be struggling academically at mid-semester because they "really want to check up with us and give us opportunities to raise those grades, they're very good at customizing their advising to each student."

In terms of addressing students' academic challenges, the program coordinates a set of contexts that provide space for program staff and instructors to connect with students, uncover their academic challenges, strengths, and goals, and offer validating support to address those challenges, affirm those strengths, and achieve those goals. TSLC staff connect students early on in coordinated contexts such as a first-year orientation, a first-year seminar, shared courses, and mentor meetings (*proactive* and *collaborative*). Staff, instructors, and mentors use these contexts as a forum for building connections with students and getting to know their academic challenges, strengths, and goals. Take, for example, the first-year seminar, a support context coordinated by the program and taught by staff instructors who ask students to share academic and personal "highs" and "lows" each week to give them a sense of how students are doing and to get a sense of their academic challenges, strengths, and goals (*holistic*). First-year seminar instructors then acknowledge and affirm each student's academic "high" or "low," provide encouragement to the students, and communicate their belief in their individual capabilities to overcome challenges and achieve academic success (*strengths-oriented*). They follow up with the students in TSLC staff meetings (or communicate to TSLC peer mentors to follow up with them on the topic during TSLC mentor meetings) about the academic challenges or opportunities to receive additional support and encouragement.

For instance, a student expressed during the first-year seminar that their high school did not offer rigorous chemistry classes and they were struggling to keep up with coursework in college and the lecture-style delivery makes learning difficult for him. He recently got a B- on a chemistry exam, but he was used to getting As in high school. The student had a strong desire to do well academically in the course because he enjoyed chemistry and was considering pursuing it as his major. The first-year instructor acknowledged the challenge the student felt, briefly offered some ideas to address the challenge (such as making use of study hours or tutoring resources as a normal and expected way to succeed in college), and then made note of the challenge in order to follow up with the student (*proactive*). That note was communicated to the staff member with whom the student met regularly so that the staff member could follow up with the student (*collaborative*). During that follow-up meeting with the student, the point of contact asked how things were going academically and explained that they heard the student expressed some concerns about chemistry specifically. As the conversation unfolded, the point of contact acknowledged the fact that the student felt they did not have rigorous chemistry courses at their high school, confirmed that college chemistry coursework is challenging, and communicated that a B- is quite a good grade for challenging college-level chemistry work (*identity-conscious* and *holistic*). The point of contact also acknowledged that the student's willingness to share their challenge and desire to do better in chemistry was a strength that they can work from to help the student achieve their academic goals for chemistry (*strengths-oriented*).

As a result of what they learned through the first-year seminar and follow-up meetings with the student, the point of contact then connected the student to additional support contexts to build from his assets – in this case, the student's desire to excel in chemistry, his interest in the field, willingness to share challenges, desire to learn, and his solid academic achievement to date (*collaborative, holistic,* and *strengths-oriented*). Given the challenge the student noted with the lecture style of his chemistry professor as an inhibitor of his learning, the point of contact connected the student to another faculty member's chemistry course and encouraged the student to attend that course alongside the chemistry course he was already enrolled in so that he could be exposed to a different kind of teaching style. The point of contact knew that this other chemistry faculty member took a more validating approach to instruction that benefitted many at-promise students, where students were encouraged to contribute to their learning in the classroom and engage in lively, enriching conversations, and that the faculty member tended to give practical illustrations of real-world applications of chemistry that resonated with many at-promise students. The instructor had allowed students who where experiencing challenges to sit in on lectures in the past, but the point of contact made sure to send a quick email to let the instructor know the situation (*collaborative*). This new chemistry class helped the student understand the chemistry course material and helped him believe that chemistry was something he could pursue successfully academically and for a major/career path.

The point of contact, recognizing that the student's desire to do well in chemistry class and interest in the field of chemistry were assets, connected the student to additional support contexts on campus, including an undergraduate research session and a chemistry instructor who does research with undergraduates (*strengths-oriented* and *collaborative*). During the undergraduate research session, the campus undergraduate research director encouraged students to consider undergraduate research as an academic enrichment opportunity and communicated to them that these kinds of opportunities were meant for students like them. Later, the student worked with the chemistry faculty member whom the point of contact put him in touch with. The chemistry faculty member with whom he was doing undergraduate research took a real interest in the student, mentored him, and supported his interest in and pursuit of chemistry as a major. That experience helped affirm for the student that his interests in the field were well founded and that he was capable of not only pursuing this major but also excelling in chemistry field work, which also helped him better understand the application of what he was learning in his courses.

Major and Career Path Navigation

As noted in Chapter 2, at-promise students often benefit from support navigating their major and career decisions. They may not have the kind of privileged capital and knowledge that would enable them to know all the major and career opportunities that are available in college, what kind of career paths exist, how to explore options, how to achieve those major and career goals in difficult-to-navigate siloed campuses, or how to access major and career support. TSLC educators recognized at-promise students may face these challenges, and they reached out early to ensure that students were connected to support tailored to their unique set of assets and needs in order to proactively address potential challenges and inequities (*proactive* and *identity-conscious*). Moreover, they connected students to validating major and career support contexts across campus where their capabilities for success in identifying and pursuing a major and career path are affirmed by educators to increase their major and career confidence (*collaboration*). The act of connecting students to tailored major and career support to enable their success is also an act of validation.

TSLC educators acknowledged that at-promise students' family backgrounds, their past job experiences, high school coursework, personal interests, and motivations are all potential assets that they could build on in order to help students navigate their major and career choices and pursuits (*strengths-oriented*). As one staff member explained, "the experiences they're bringing can make them really, really good students ... we need to be valuing every experience ... no matter if it's 'I come from a low socioeconomic background or I'm first-generation,' or whatever." Educators took time to discover those assets by building a relationship with each student and seeking to understand who students are through various activities including a first-year seminar, orientation, proactive advising meetings, and major and career activities (*holistic* and *developmental*).

For instance, each TSLC point of contact worked with a group of students early their second year to help students assess, based on their past experiences, opportunities, and their interests, whether they have made an informed decision about their major and career path or whether they are still exploring potential options (*holistic, identity-conscious,* and *developmental*). Staff did this through major and career assessment tools and follow-up conversations with students (*proactive*). In those major and career-related conversations, staff acknowledged that each student had their own major and career motivations, experiences, and beliefs, that each student would have their own path to a major and career, and the staff would connect them to support along the way to reaching their goals. Following the initial assessment and discovering students' major/career interests and motivations, students were then connected to an appropriate set of contexts responsive to their assets and their major and career development needs (*collaborative*). The staff coordinated a web of major and career support for students based on their needs and assets that provided opportunities for staff, advisors, and faculty to connect with students, engaged with their major and career assets, and provided validating support to help them attain their goals. For instance, staff coordinated mock job interviews, résumé writing sessions, major and career exploration activities, a campus career fair, and a business etiquette dinner.

Within the coordinated major and career support contexts, students had multiple additional opportunities to connect with advisors, faculty, staff, instructors, and mentors who delivered validating major and career support (*collaborative*). For instance, as students participated in mock job interviews with staff advisors in the program, each staff advisor took the time to acknowledge the student's work that went into preparing for the interview, to note what was strong about what the student shared during the interview, and to offer additional areas for improvement and direction for how they could build on their interview skills (*strengths-oriented*). In another example, students participated in a coordinated résumé review where they brought in their résumé for TSLC staff advisors to review. Staff used these meetings as an additional opportunity to get to know students' major and career experiences, knowledge, and goals (*holistic* and *strengths-oriented*). They used this information about students' assets to inform their résumé review, to point out the strengths in the résumé, to offer constructive critique, and to give meaningful direction and resources to enhance their résumé so they can reach their major and career goals. Staff similarly leveraged these résumé review sessions as opportunities to communicate to the student their belief that with additional enhancements, their résumé will put them in a strong position for success in pursuing their major and career goals. At times, the staff also communicated with career advisors on campus to connect students to an additional layer of résumé development (*collaborative*).

Staff also coordinated support that connected students to broader campus staff and advisors who are trusted campus partners that adopt validating approaches to their major and career support (*collaborative*). For instance, TSLC coordinated a session for students to learn about how to prepare for and find internships, which was facilitated by the campus academic advising center. TSLC staff was aware of the validating nature of the campus partner's approach to support because of the relationships they had built with this office over time, and because of positive experiences their students have had visiting this campus partner's office for support. During the internship preparation session, the campus partner communicated to the students his belief in their ability to successfully prepare for and find an internship that would suit their needs and meet their career goals and that his advising team would give them tips, tricks, and resources.

Over the course of the program, staff proactively reached out to students to check about their major and career needs and experiences with major and career activities. The point of contact coordinated support and served as a campus navigator. The point of contact carefully considered whom they could connect the student with on campus to bridge the student to an additional layer of major and career support, considering factors such as whether the educators in the prospective office were known to be validating and supportive of at-promise students' major and career aspirations and understood at-promise students' unique set of needs and experiences (*reflective practice* and *collaborative*). They did this over time because confidence in a major and career path is not stagnant and can fluctuate as students have new experiences (*developmental*).

There are several examples of when a student continued to experience challenges determining their major/career or they grappled between multiple choices. The students' point of contact would become aware of these challenges through on-going meetings with the student or conversations with other educators in the program. The educator would reach out to trusted, caring faculty, advisors, or departments to connect the student to in order for them to have a conversation about their major and career options (*collaborative*). The faculty advisors and department chairs would then express genuine care about helping the student find a major/career path by explaining the day-to-day work, nature and goals of different jobs, and the kind of preparation that would be necessary to achieve their career goals in order to help students make an informed decision about their major and career path. The relationships the point of contact had established with other offices on campus were critical for them to know whom they could connect students to that would be experienced as validating.

Reflection Questions

- Who could be the validating agents for at-promise students at your campus?
- How could educators be more informed about the nature and kinds of support contexts available to students on campus to better direct students to the resources they need?
- What role will campus leadership play in promoting ecological validation on campus, and how can you advocate for this approach to be adopted?
- What kind of barriers will you need to address in order to fully realize ecological validation on campus?

8

PROMISING PRACTICES USED TO SUPPORT ECOLOGICAL VALIDATION

We identified several promising practices that emerged from the Promoting At-promise Student Success (PASS) Project. We highlighted practices that could be integrated within the work of postsecondary institutions more broadly to support the success of all at-promise students. In our study, we found that the educators who created a culture of ecological validation used these promising practices; however, we imagine that there are other promising practices that leverage the norms, structures, and practices of ecological validation.

Here we focus specifically on four promising practices: proactive advising, tailoring, career and major support, and faculty coordinators. With each promising practice, we begin with a definition of the practice before explaining why the strategy is important and how to enact it. We provide additional resources (e.g., briefs and videos) on our website (https://pass.pullias.usc.edu) that could be useful for practitioners who want to implement these promising practices at their institutions.

Proactive Advising

What Is Proactive Advising?

Traditional forms of advising typically entail short meetings with advisors to register for classes, select a major, and determine whether degree requirements have been met. Proactive advising is an increasingly popular alternative approach that promotes early and ongoing advisor outreach to students to engage them in conversations about their academic and personal challenges

DOI: 10.4324/9781003443711-10

and opportunities, as well as connecting students to resources and support related to their college goals. Proactive advising meetings engage students in a holistic range of topics including personal issues, emotional needs and wellness, time management, academic planning, career ambitions, and academic skills, to name a few.

Our study identified a proactive advising model that promotes at-promise student success and includes several key aspects that are instructive for educators and institutions considering implementation of proactive advising. Proactive advising involves advisors proactively reaching out to build relationships with students, discover their assets, understand their academic needs and goals, and connect students to opportunities and resources to achieve college success. The onus is on advisors to discover students' assets, goals, and challenges and to create an environment where students feel open to discussing each of these during proactive advising meetings to make informed decisions about resources and support students' needs. Our study identified a proactive advising model characterized by three intertwined features: (a) structured opportunities for students to engage in reflection and self-assessment regarding their college success, (b) proactive planning and instrumental guidance with an advisor to chart a path to success, and (c) emotional and interpersonal support from advisors (Kitchen et al., 2021a, 2021d). Moreover, educators adopted a validating and affirming approach to proactive advising that empowered at-promise students to succeed.

Why Is Proactive Advising Important?

Proactive advising propels student success by connecting students to holistic support tailored to their individual assets, needs, and goals and addresses institutional barriers to increase student success. Our study showed that proactive advising promotes at-promise students' confidence in their capabilities for college success and empowers them to draw on resources that advisors coordinated and tailored to their needs to achieve that success. The proactive nature of this style of advising enables advisors to address student challenges early – before they emerge or worsen – and to empower students to take advantage of opportunities and resources that might otherwise go missed by the student during college without the proactive support. Students experienced the proactive advising process in TSLC as validating, affirming, and supportive whether they were excelling or experiencing challenges, which in turn contributed to students' confidence in their individual capabilities for success given their unique circumstances, experiences, and backgrounds. Other studies of proactive advising have also linked it to student retention, reduction in probation/withdrawals, and increased academic achievement and GPA (e.g., Abelman & Molina, 2002; Rodgers et al., 2014; Schee, 2007).

How Do You Proactively Advise?

There are several steps we identified in our study to guide proactive advising. First, the onus is on the advisor to proactively reach out to students early to build a connection with the student. Second, during the first proactive advising meeting and meetings that follow, the advisor works collaboratively with the student to identify their academic and personal assets, needs, challenges, and short- and long-range goals for college. They do so in a way that is conscious of students' multiple identities and accompanying experiences. Third, the advisor identifies the potential barriers and challenges to the student's success and the resources, opportunities, and student assets that could be leveraged to empower and enable students to succeed. The student and advisor work together to chart a plan to achieve college success and realize the student's goals. Fourth, the advisor works with others on campus to connect the student to resources tailored to their individual needs, assets, and goals. Fifth, advisors proactively follow up with students to discuss progress toward their college goals, to reassess and recalibrate plans as needed, and to connect students to additional resources as new needs, assets, challenges, and goals emerge over time.

A final aspect of proactive advising that we identified as key in our study that was embedded throughout the process was that educators took a validating approach to supporting at-promise students (Kitchen et al., 2021d). *How* proactive advising took place mattered in terms of enabling at-promise student success and convincing students they had what it took to succeed in college. Proactive advising could easily be done in a deficit-oriented or remedial manner that would detract from student success; for instance, chiding a student for low grades during an advising session or telling a student they cannot be successful in their major because of challenges they are having in a required course. However, we found that TSLC advisors' approach to proactive advising was affirming, uplifting, and empowering for at-promise students. The advisors expressed genuine, holistic care and concern for the students and communicated their desire to know who students were, their unique combination of experiences, backgrounds, identities, and assets. They consistently told students that they believed in their individual capacity for success and that they would connect them to the right resources they needed to accomplish their personal and academic college goals. Those seeking to implement proactive advising to support at-promise students should closely attend to how advisors engage students in the process to ensure it is a validating experience for students. Ensuring advisors take a validating approach to proactive advising may require additional training opportunities and professional socialization.

Tailoring Support for Subgroups of Students

What Is Tailoring?

Tailoring is a process in which program staff work to understand individual student needs while simultaneously exploring whether these needs reflect a broader trend among the students they serve in the program (Kezar et al., 2020; 2021b). Tailoring and customization differ. Customization focuses on creating individualized supports for individual students based on their unique needs. Creating a customized program for each student would not be possible for most postsecondary institutions. While customization may be needed in situations when a student has a specific circumstance that warrants an individualized plan to meet their needs, tailoring is a more scalable and sustainable approach to supporting at-promise students. Tailoring focuses on identifying trends or patterns for a subgroup of students. Staff members then explore and develop modifications within the overall program for groups of students to address their multiple needs and complex identities.

Our study identified dozens of examples of programmatic tailoring, including supporting students with learning disabilities, mental health needs, undocumented students, refugee and immigrant students, undecided majors versus decided, academically less prepared, honors students, racially minoritized students, students changing majors, first-generation, commuter students, transfer students, and financially insecure students. We have a short video on our website that describes the tailoring process (see https://pass.pullias.usc.edu/).

Why Is Tailoring Important?

Students experience cognitive overload trying to navigate complex bureaucracies. Several descriptive studies of college students' experiences describe how negotiating the college landscape where different functional offices and services target specific parts of their identities can impose significant cognitive burdens in terms of time and energy (Harper, Wardell & McGuire, 2011; Purnell & Blank, 2004). Tailoring can reduce cognitive load and help support at-promise students' success at scale (Kezar et al., 2021). Tailored interventions can be embedded within a single program or department, rather than having students visit dozens of offices trying to piece together the support they need. The program curates and brings together all the resources for students under one student support umbrella.

Our research findings indicate that staff best serve students' multiple needs and reduce their cognitive load when they work at two levels simultaneously: interacting with students to understand their multiple individual needs, while exploring how some of the needs they have identified might be shared among larger groups of students. Then after identifying that these needs are broader and thus amenable to allocating resources, they create interventions calibrated to address these multifaceted student needs or concerns at scale.

How Do You Tailor?

TSLC educators were sensitive to students' multiple identities, backgrounds, and needs. Some students needed to access multiple offices and services to meet their needs. For instance, a low-income gay student experiencing academic challenges may benefit from visiting the LGBTQ+ center, financial aid office, and the tutoring commons on campus to meet their multiple needs. Rather than leaving it to the student to piece together campus support, TSLC tailored program interventions to meet student needs (Kezar et al., 2021). Drawing on elements of predictive analytics and case management, TSLC created tailored interventions for subgroups of students based on formal data (e.g., assessments) and informal data (e.g., observations from student meetings) with the goal of reducing cognitive load and increasing the success of the students by being attuned to students' multiple identities and needs. For instance, one program created a tailored intervention called PERSYST in response to observations that students who came in with low ACT scores, who worked many hours, and who were student parents were experiencing academic challenges and often ended up on probation (Kezar et al., 2021). There were dozens of other student subgroups for whom the TSLC tailored programming to increase their success and reduce their cognitive load.

We identified a five-step process for tailoring (Kezar et al., 2021). First, staff and instructors develop relationships with students so the staff and instructors can help understand their needs and be a trusted person to help the student in tailoring the experience. Second, students can support this process by better understanding their own needs and strengths. Staff and instructors develop mechanisms that support students in this learning so that students are better able to articulate and understand their unique needs. Third, staff collect a variety of forms of information (e.g., assessments, faculty, and peer input) in order to build a comprehensive understanding of students' needs – starting at the individual level, but then exploring whether similar students in the program may have the same needs. And finally, staff reflect on all the information in order to develop the best solution to tailoring individually and then scale to groups with similar identities or experiences.

We identified principles for tailoring that result in an approach that is not deficit-oriented, which has sometimes happened historically in efforts to create supplemental support programs. The programs took an asset-based approach to explore how to build upon the students' various forms of capital they brought with them to campus. When providing support and encouragement, the programs took a holistic approach that included considering both academic and interpersonal aspects of the students' experiences. And the programs used a student-centered approach that involved considering how individual student experiences could be used to inform the development of future programming to support subgroups of students with similar identities and experiences. Being holistic and student-centered enabled the programs to consider how to support students' multiple and intersecting identities. The overarching goal of tailoring was to reduce students' cognitive load in order to empower the students to fully engage with and benefit from the educational process.

Career and Major Support

What Is Career and Major Support?

Major and career support refers to the guidance and resources students receive from advisors to navigate their choice and pursuit of a major and career path. In our study of the TSLC, we identified an approach to major and career advising that we call the major and career self-efficacy (MCSE) ecology model (Kitchen, Kezar, & Hypolite, 2021b, 2021c). In the MCSE ecology model, advisors recognize that at-promise students come into college at different developmental phases regarding their major and career choices and pathways – some at a phase where they are exploring majors and careers and others who come in with an established major and career path in mind. Students at different major and career development phases require different kinds of major and career support. Thus, advisors in the MCSE ecology model reach out early on to engage students in conversations about their major and career paths, to explore what students' past major and career-related experiences are, and to identify students' unique set of assets and experience relevant to their major and career paths. This conversation assists the advisor in understanding where the student is developmentally and, as a result, guides the kind of major and career support they decide to connect students to. In turn, the advisor curates a set (or ecology) of appropriate major/career experiences, such as job shadowing, departmental advisor meetings, or résumé reviews, that are relevant to students' major/career assets, experiences, and developmental phase. The MCSE ecology model empowers and enables students to access the tailored, curated set of major and career resources they need to be successful in their major/career paths.

Why Is Career and Major Support Important?

Major and career support is important for at-promise students because many do not have access to the same resources, socialization, capital, and opportunities that their more privileged counterparts have, such as high school internships, a professional or familial career network, college-preparatory experiences, or college-educated family members or friends who can give advice on job seeking or opportunities (Gloria & Hird, 1999; Tate et al., 2015). This is problematic because we know that students' confidence in their major and career path is linked to their college success and retention (Hackett et al., 1992; Komarraju et al., 2014; Lent et al., 2008). Moreover, the existence and purpose of career services on campus is not widely advertised or well-known to students at many campuses, further necessitating proactive action on the part of educators to engage students in conversations about their major and career paths and preparation – particularly among at-promise students who may not be as familiar with the kind of support available to them in college or have the same college navigational capital as their more privileged peers. Further, not all major and career experiences and activities may be appropriate for students at a given time in their career development trajectory. Opportunities to engage students in developmentally appropriate major and career support early on and to curate an ecology of major and career experiences tailored to their experiences and assets can help students gather the information they need to make informed decisions about their major/career path and receive appropriate preparation toward achieving their major and career goals. Being exposed to the experiences, resources, and information students need to make informed decisions about their major and career path, in turn, propels students' major and career self-efficacy (i.e., their confidence in their capabilities to identify and successfully pursue a major and career path). By promoting students' MCSE, advisors can also increase students' persistence and success (Bullock-Yowell et al., 2014; Hackett et al., 1992; Komarraju et al., 2014).

How Do You Create Career and Major Support?

There are several steps that major and career advisors can take to craft a major and career support ecology and promote at-promise students' college success. First, advisors should proactively engage students in conversations about their backgrounds, identities, and prior experiences that may be relevant to their major and career interests. Advisors should collaborate with the student to identify the students' major and career assets (e.g., past career development experiences, interests, aspirations, motivations), needs, challenges, and goals and to assess where students are developmentally.

Second, advisors should use the sum of this information to assess the kind of support the student would benefit from to continue exploring major and career options (exploring phase), or if they have already had the appropriate experiences and preparation to have made informed choices about their major and career path (established phase), and assess what kind of additional support or resources the student could use to leverage and maximize that major/career path momentum. Third, the advisor should curate a tailored ecology of major and career experiences and activities that are suited for each student's set of assets, goals, challenges, and needs and where students are developmentally (i.e., exploring major/career paths or established a major/career path). Such experiences might entail a combination of career exploration assignments, résumé writing, identification of job shadowing or internship opportunities, selecting a class or connecting with faculty in a major/career field of interest, for example. The types of major and career activities and experiences the advisor connects a student to should be developmentally appropriate and tailored to students' assets and needs. Fourth, the advisor should proactively follow up with the student to engage them in sensemaking and validating conversations around their experiences in the curated major and career ecology to help students connect their experiences to their major and career choices, preparation, and confidence in their capabilities for major/career path success and to identify further major and career opportunities to build their MCSE.

Faculty Coordinators or Staff Navigators

What Are Faculty Coordinators?

Our research demonstrates the importance of a faculty coordinator who can serve as a link between the classroom and supports/opportunities available on campus (Toccoli, 2021; Toccoli et al., 2022). The coordinator is a faculty member who dedicates a portion of their time to serve as coach, sounding board, and connecter for instructors. Instead of simply providing instructors with a long list of resources and offices that exist on campus at the start of each semester, the faculty coordinator becomes a single point of contact for instructors who have questions or concerns related to a specific student or teaching more broadly. When instructors contact the faculty coordinator with a student concern or a question about how to support students, the coordinator provides assistance in connecting the student and instructor to the ecology of support on campus. In addition, the coordinator builds relationships with the multiple offices, departments, and support services on campus in order to effectively enact their role.

Why Are Faculty Coordinators Important?

Connecting classroom instructors with the programs, services, and resources in academic affairs and student affairs has been challenging for many postsecondary institutions. Faculty are socialized to develop content expertise within their specific disciplines without much support related to at-promise student success or teaching pedagogy. Instructors often feel ill-equipped to address the complexity and sensitivity of student issues that occur outside of the classroom, so they may avoid having these conversations with students. Postsecondary institutions often distribute long lists of resources available on campus to all faculty members as a way to create a bridge between instructors and the support provided by the academic and student affairs programs on campus. These lists can be overwhelming to faculty who do not feel they have the time to figure out who is the right person/office for a specific issue, do not always know how to assess if an issue is serious enough to refer, and may not feel they have time to dedicate to figuring out how to proceed. As a result, current systems often discourage instructors from proactively and holistically engaging with students.

The faculty coordinator role positively influenced how instructors engaged with students in a number of ways, including:

- Instructors appreciated having a colleague to reach out to who also was a faculty member, especially when they had questions related to pedagogy. The conversations about how to adjust instructional approaches to support at-promise students shifted how instructors thought about their work, and they were more likely to take risks needed to improve their teaching.
- Instructors consistently discussed how they felt more comfortable encouraging students to bring their experiences into class and having more holistic conversations with students when they knew there was one person to contact. They felt the campus red flag systems were a bit confusing, and these systems seemed to be only for serious issues. However, there were times that instructors were unsure if an issue was really an issue or they just had a feeling that something might be going on; they appreciated having a person to reach out to who could help them assess how to proceed and who would assist in navigating any student issues that might exist.
- Faculty coordinators build relationships with professionals across campus who worked in a variety of different offices. They got a better understanding of the many resources, programs, and opportunities available for students and instructors. When a faculty coordinator got an email about a student issue, the coordinator knew a specific person to contact.

The coordinator could then help the instructor connect the student with an actual person. The process did not take a significant amount of time for the instructor, but they were able to connect the student in a personalized way that encouraged the student to utilize the support available.

- Faculty coordinator positions did not just address problems, but also created opportunities for instructors and students. Instructors could contact the coordinator when they wanted to address challenges they experienced with teaching – such as when students seem disengaged or an assignment went poorly. The instructors knew the coordinator role was to support, not evaluate. The coordinator could gather resources to share with the instructor and brainstorm potential ways to improve the classroom experience. The instructor could also contact the coordinator when they felt a student was doing well in order to get ideas of potential opportunities to share with the student.

- The faculty coordinator role became especially important for adjunct faculty and graduate student instructors. These individuals tend to be less connected to other instructors, programs, and resources than full-time faculty. In addition, they have less time dedicated to their roles because of how these positions are structured. The single point of contact made it easier for these instructors to connect students with resources.

How Do You Create Faculty Coordinators?

Creating a faculty coordinator role at your campus would require a couple of considerations. First, you would want to think about the size of both your faculty and student bodies. You may need to identify several people to serve in this role – ideally including instructors from different disciplinary backgrounds. You will want individuals who have demonstrated success in improving outcomes for at-promise students. Second, you will want to explore how to adjust their time to allow them to support their colleagues. While it is important for them to continue teaching in some capacity, their contract may include a course buyout once a semester. Coordinators will also need support in building connections across campus.

While our study focused on faculty members who served this role, some campuses are exploring the use of staff navigators who serve a similar function in terms of connecting instructors to the broader campus supports. These professional staff members could be situated within each college and collaborate with proactive advising staff who work directly with students. In this model, the staff navigators would likely not be the point of contact if faculty members had questions about pedagogy; a center of teaching and learning or another space on campus would serve that function.

Guiding Questions

- How could these promising practices be integrated into the student support efforts of your program, college, or institution?
- Looking at your institution's current student data, which of these promising practices could be integrated to address an specific student need on your campus?
- Given the importance of the norms that frame a culture of ecological validation, consider how you might implement these (and other promising practices) in ways that could support an overall culture shift for your program, college, or institution.

9
STUDENT EXPERIENCES WITH ECOLOGICAL VALIDATION

In previous chapters, we focused on describing the processes within TSLC that promote at-promise student success. In Chapters 6 and 7, we discussed how TSLC educators utilized ecological validation to support a large group of diverse students in a comprehensive college transition program. But how did students experience TSLC and the ecological validation that undergirds the program? How did at-promise students describe the role of TSLC in supporting them as they navigated the complexities of their lives?

In this chapter, we examine TSLC from students' perspectives and explore several students' pathways through the program to understand how ecological validation informed their experiences. We draw data from the PASS Project to chronicle how two students at each of the three campuses experienced their time in TSLC and their subsequent transition out of the program. In doing so, we highlight how ecological validation was used to serve a compositionally diverse group of at-promise students across three programs and campuses. Their stories are organized to highlight concepts from ecological validation – from whom, when, and where they felt validation over time. We start each section with a brief overview of each campus and then review the transition of two students on each campus into college and through their third year.

University of Nebraska, Kearney

The University of Nebraska, Kearney (UNK) is a regional comprehensive four-year university. The campus enrolls about 6,000 students, 22% of whom are racially minoritized, 31.8% of whom receive a Pell Grant, 34.4% of whom are first-generation college, and 3.7% of whom were not born in the United

DOI: 10.4324/9781003443711-11

States. The campus's mission is to increase access to postsecondary education, particularly in rural areas throughout the state. Although TSLC has shared components across the three campuses, the program at UNK's ecology is distinct in that it is highly residential, and students are required to live in a TSLC residence hall during their first year of college, which is also where the TSLC staff offices are located. Notably, peer mentors live in the residence halls with their mentees, which provides opportunities for frequent interactions. In addition, the TSLC faculty was strongly encouraged and received financial support to provide opportunities to engage with students outside of the classroom. Now, we share the experiences of Alberto and Lana.

Alberto's Story

Alberto was a Latinx man and first-generation college student whose home community was close to UNK. Although his brother was also a TSLC scholar at UNK, his mother's health strongly informed his college choice. He said, "I came to Kearney because I wanted to be a lot closer to home so, like, if she needs me or anything, I could go home."

First year of college. When Alberto arrived at UNK, a TSLC staff member knew how important his mother was to him and regularly reached out to convey their support. He recalled:

> [This staff member] knows how my mom's not really in good health and they sometimes ask me how she's doing whenever they can. They ask me how my family's doing and they'd always say, "If there – if you need any help just ask. We're here for you and everything," and I thought that was really cool. That's really comforting.

Alberto described immediately feeling cared for and supported by the TSLC staff, who took a proactive and holistic approach to expressing care and concern for him.

Living in the residence halls with his peers and mentor was pivotal in his transition to college. For example, proximity to his mentor helped him initially navigate college as a first-generation student:

> I did [talk to my mentor] a lot during the first couple of weeks here on campus because I was so stressed out. I did not know what to do. I was so confused … And when I applied to my work study job, I asked them if my résumé looked good and asked them about questions – I asked them questions regarding, like, how an interview would go like if I was applying to this job and stuff.

Rather than being made to feel as though his questions were silly, Alberto's mentor helped him learn his way around. Although Alberto joined a Greek organization and had other friends at UNK, TSLC was the place where he felt most connected to his peers.

Alberto's sense of connection to his TSLC peers was enhanced by experiences in his TSLC classes. His communications instructor helped facilitate connections to his peers and enhanced his confidence in interacting with new people. One assigned speech required describing a hero, which allowed him to talk about his values and "really helped me open up." He was initially nervous to talk about his hero – who was his mother – but his communications instructor created an environment where his experiences were valued. He explained how the instructor "said, 'It's OK … a lotta people do open up in the class and talk about certain touchy subjects.'" The instructor affirmed his feelings and normalized being nervous while further encouraging him to share his experiences. Reflecting on what he took away from the class, Alberto said, "I learn something more than what the class is supposed to teach, something about life and stuff. And we share experiences and everything in the class." By grounding the learning in students' experiences, the instructor's approach was validating, asset-based, and holistic. Alberto was keenly aware of how his TSLC instructors' approaches differed from his other instructors. He described this difference by saying, "I guess [TSLC instructors have] a genuine – a deep concern for each individual … and the curiosity about each individual's lives and stuff."

By the end of his first year, Alberto was achieving most of his goals for classes, was involved on campus, and had developed a network of friends in and outside of TSLC. He won an award on campus, and a staff member shared this news with the entire TSLC community. Furthermore, a TSLC community member nominated him for an award, and he was publicly recognized for his contributions to the program. Receiving recognition in TSLC validated and affirmed Alberto's presence, strengths, and ability to succeed.

That is not to say that Alberto did not struggle at times. He did not get the grade he wanted on an exam despite studying and was not elected for a position in his Greek organization. Alberto found reassurance in TSLC:

I felt down, like, "Geez." I'm like – but they reassured me and everything like, "Hey, you're just a freshman. You got all this time. It's all right." … I know some of the staff in TSLC, they want us to succeed. They want us to do great things on campus. So, I feel like my success does matter to them. And my friends, they do like seeing me succeed, too. But if I don't, they're always there to support me if I don't.

Regardless of whether he succeeded or stumbled, Alberto knew that he mattered in TSLC and that his presence was valued by staff, faculty, and his peers. Those around him inherently believed in his ability to succeed, and they made efforts to affirm his contributions to campus.

Second year of college. Alberto deepened his connections to TSLC during his second year by serving as a peer mentor. He was excited and nervous: "Oh, my gosh. We have to talk to all the strangers." Peer mentor training provided him an opportunity to hone his helping skills. After completing a training exercise where they pretended a mentee asked him on a date, Alberto recounted processing with a TSLC staff member:

> So, we focused on what I did good. [The staff member] noticed how my posture was open at the beginning and then once she was trying to ask me out on a date, I kind of closed and went back because it's like I'm showing her like I'm not interested. Then [the staff member] gave me a few tips.

Alberto received constructive feedback from the staff member. Attending to what he did well before shifting to areas of potential improvement affirmed that Alberto was capable of responding to difficult situations and had the skills to be a mentor. Alberto met regularly with this staff member, and he appreciated their approach to working with mentors:

> They always ask how things are going and everything like that, and ask how are classes going, and ask about our lives. That's how it usually starts out for me, and then we go in and talk about the mentees and how things are going with them. I feel like it's nice having them check up on us.

Rather than approaching supervision meetings in a transactional manner, the staff member invested time and energy in checking in with Alberto. The approach was holistic and reflected care for each mentor. As a result, Alberto structured his meeting with mentees in a similar way. He wanted to cultivate trusting, affirming, and holistic relationships with mentees.

Alberto looked to those in TSLC when making difficult decisions. In particular, Alberto turned to the staff member who supervised him when he started doubting his decision to pursue a career in a health field since his mother encouraged him to find a financially stable career:

> And the TSLC staff member asked me how I felt. Did I enjoy the classes I was taking for those, for my [STEM] minor and pre-health stuff? And I told them, "No. I absolutely strongly dislike every class that I took." And then they asked me like if I would, like, one day want to work in a hospital setting ... And like, "You know what? I don't know. I don't

think I'd like that too much." ... And then I told them about how when I talk to my friend about [my social science or humanities] major – especially with the social science portion – I get super excited and a bit happy ... And [the staff member] said, "Well, it looks like that's where your passion lies, and doesn't really lie with that [STEM] and the pre-health stuff." And I've had doubts about it. So I was like, "Yep. I guess I should probably drop it and just focus on my [social science and humanities] stuff."

Alberto's discussion with his TSLC supervisor was pivotal in helping him listen to his instincts. Rather than telling him what to do, the staff member asked questions that helped Alberto listen to his own voice and follow his interests. The staff member supported Alberto's career exploration by providing him an alternative assignment when he was unable to attend a career fair on campus, which was a programmatic requirement. Alberto interviewed two professionals in a potential field of interest. Alberto's interest was piqued, and he starting considering graduate school in the discipline. Alberto benefited from working with a staff member who used a holistic and validating approach as well as being willing to tailor opportunities for him.

Alberto also received affirming messages from TSLC faculty. For example, he had never taken an art class before and doubted his abilities. After being given a drawing assignment and saying, "Oh no, I can't do that," his instructor conveyed that he could succeed:

They told me that I probably could do it ... It doesn't matter if I go slow, as long as I get it done. It doesn't matter as long as I'm good with the end product. And that was on multiple occasions about several different drawings and about the collage and about our bird sculptures and about painting. So yeah, they kind of talked me through some of those, 'cause I was pretty nervous about 'em ... they had talked to me a whole bunch of times, [laughs] because I felt nervous about it. And they said that they were proud of me working hard and not giving up on it and not just slopping something together and then just turning it in ... So that's the difference from the other classes.

Alberto's instructor affirmed that he could succeed and reiterated this message on a regular basis over the course of the semester. Though there were moments when Alberto questioned his abilities, TSLC staff and faculty consistently affirmed that he could succeed. Their confidence in him fostered a newfound self-confidence and sense of direction.

Third year of college. Alberto felt more confident in his career pathway and explored new opportunities. He became a resident assistant, continued with

Greek life, and joined several student organizations related to his majors. Although he visited TSLC less frequently, he knew he could go to them for support. When asked where he would turn to if he needed help, Alberto said, "If it's more personal issues, I … would definitely bring it up to the TSLC office and then elaborate more on it. I feel like they're a little more compassionate I guess with those types of topics and are very understand[ing]."

TSLC was a formative component of Alberto's college experience. His doubt and fears seemed to have faded. He was succeeding academically and socially. Reflecting on his accomplishments during college, he said:

> I'm making progress towards my degree. I'm getting one step closer to what I wanna do, and I am loving the information that I'm learning in the class, and actually, I'm enjoying reading the books and making more connections with the guys in my Greek organization and making connections with other people in Greek life and also still building upon my relationships that I made with TSLC and how those relationships have grown and have been maintained.

Lana's Story

Lana was a White woman and first-generation college student who chose to attend college locally. She had complicated relationships with her parents who have not always been able to care for her given their own struggles; other family and mentors provided more stable homes for her when she needed them. Lana also had a longtime boyfriend who was also a Buffett scholarship recipient, but attended another institution.

First year of college. Lana was eager to establish herself on campus and build relationships with her peers. Living in a residence hall with other TSLC scholars and her peer mentor provided her with a support network:

> I like that I automatically have friends. So if I'm in a class I can automatically pick out the people who are Thompson Scholars and I know that they can be my study buddies or they can, if I have questions I can text them, or just that I know that I'm safe because they're there so it must be OK.

Being around other TSLC students provided Lana with friends and people to support her in classes. The community also provided her with a sense of safety. Lana reflected:

> My mentor … like they and I just really clicked and they just do a really good job at just listening to me when I need to talk about something silly that doesn't make any sense, or if I need to talk about something serious.

They understand my anal retentiveness when it comes to like grades and getting things done in a certain way, and they're just so carefree and flexible and they're always out in the hallway and looking for people to go do things. They're super involved with stuff and they're definitely someone I look up to.

Lana described her mentor as a resource and someone who created space for her to ask questions and talk about more serious issues. Her mentor's approach was holistic. She felt understood by her mentor, and her individual traits were validated rather than viewed as limiting or deficits.

Lana's feelings, perspectives, and concerns were validated by the TSLC staff. The staff were "really friendly and excited to see you" and their advice was "really helpful" and they "keep me at ease." This student-centered approach was validating and helped fuel Lana's desire to serve as a leader in the TSLC student organization.

During her first year of college, Lana noted how TSLC validated her experiences as a low-income, first-generation college student who did not consistently have familial support. The program's FAFSA workshop helped her better understand financial aid applications:

I think I felt a little better about it this year because I had seen it already in the session. I distinctly remember last year being like, "No one in my family has gone to college. No one knows how to do this. I'm just trying to figure it out," and it was very stressful ... but I definitely felt better about it this year than I did last year.

TSLC provided her with valuable information and the support she needed, which eased some of Lana's stress and helped her feel less alone. Similarly, attending a TSLC session on healthy relationships affirmed her lived experiences:

One girl was talking with someone else and I stepped in the room and was like, "Oh, I want to talk." And she was saying that her unhealthy relationship that she listed was her mother and I kind of understand that because I like saw – when we were looking at all of these characteristics, and like, "Yeah. I see a lot of those things in my mom too." ... So we just kind of talked about how, like, it's hard to find a way to fix that because friends you can just get rid of, but you can't just tell your mom, "I think we have an unhealthy relationship." Like it just doesn't ever work that way, so I don't know. It was just nice to talk to someone else and be like, "Yeah, other people have issues too and it's all right."

The healthy relationships workshop created an opportunity for Lana to explore the kinds of relationships she wanted and a space for her to make sense of current relationships. Lana's struggles were normalized and validated by her peers. The holistic approach taken by the program to attend to students' interpersonal well-being was a form of validation.

Second year of college. Between her first and second years of college, Lana engaged in research with a faculty member whom she met through TSLC. Her research experience continued into the fall and she got to share her learning at local and national conferences. Sharing her research was an affirming experience:

> It was the [Research] Symposium and I presented my research that I did over the summer. I did a 10-minute oral presentation and then I just stood by my poster for a few hours. I had lots of professors walk by, and lots of students walk by, and ask good questions. During my presentation, I had three pretty tough questions from professors. My [research] mentor said I did a really good job answering them, and lots of people came up to them after and told them that I did really well … There was a Thompson Scholar the next day who told me that I had the best presentation that they had attended, and I was, like, that's really awesome! So, I guess I'm a really good speaker. I don't always feel like it. To me, I was thinking about every time I said "um" and every time I couldn't think of what I wanted to say. But everybody else said that it went really well. I did feel pretty confident with the material.

Initially, Lana was unsure of her abilities to present her research. However, she received messages from her research mentor and a TSLC peer that she had done well. They validated Lana's knowledge and skills, which helped her recognize her strength as a public speaker. The support, engagement, and affirmation she experienced at the symposium was mirrored in her TSLC courses. Faculty were willing to talk after class to help her determine if "I'm on the right track with things and I'm understanding things all right." Her peers supported her learning through rich discussion: "I feel like Thompson Scholars do generally have deeper thoughts and are more comfortable in our Thompson Scholar classes with sharing ideas." Her non-TLSC courses had less discussion and were more "awkward."

Lana's second year of college also included interpersonal challenges. An unexpected shift in plans with her longtime boyfriend intensified her anxiety and depression. She joined a mental health advocacy student organization, and she advocated to get an emotional support animal. She described the response from the TSLC community:

I got a lot of support from people who live here and the staff when I got [my support animal], and I all of a sudden started talking about my anxiety more. A lot of staff had nice things to say and were happy that I had come up with this solution.

Rather than framing her anxiety as a deficit, the staff took a holistic approach and validated her decision to advocate for the support she needed. In turn, Lana trusted the staff and was receptive to feedback they provided. She described her interactions with her point of contact after participating in a mock interview:

I know that [my point of contact] understands me, like, as a person. So, I'm not as intimidated about doing this [mock interview] with them, because I know one, that they're not going to tell me anything that's going to make me cry. So, I feel like if I just went into the [career services offices] and then they started giving me all of this feedback, I feel like it would be overwhelming. But I think that [my point of contact] kind of understands where I'm at right now, and I think that's really helpful … Constructive criticism is great, but I don't feel like I'm at a point right now where I'm, like, super stable. So, I trust [my point of contact] and I trust that they're going to tell me helpful things.

Lana knew that her point of contact understood her and how she received feedback as a person with anxiety. Accordingly, her point of contact provided constructive feedback in ways that affirmed Lana's abilities. They also tailored opportunities for Lana to explore career options in education by having her interview professionals in her field since career fairs had limited information aligned with Lana's interests.

TSLC staff members provided Lana with support when she lost a close family member:

[This] TSLC staff member is magical. All Thompson Scholars will tell you that they know everything and nobody knows how. So [the staff member] told me they read the obituary. I don't know how they found my name amongst all of the obituaries in Nebraska.

Although she did not explicitly ask for support, the staff member conveyed that Lana was cared for and valued. Across her experiences during the second year of college, Lana received messages that her identities, knowledge, skills, and presence mattered in TSLC.

Third year of college. Lana moved into an off-campus apartment. She missed the daily connections with her TSLC peers, staff, and faculty but noted that a staff member maintained contact with her: "I've talked to [the staff member] a couple times this year. They'll send me emails every once in a while checking up on me." Though her formal time in TSLC had concluded, this staff member continued to proactively convey care and concern.

Lana felt prepared for the remainder of her collegiate career: "[it's] this bird pushing you out of the nest kind of thing." Lana knew the program was there for her, but it had prepared her by helping her establish relationships on campus, affirming her identities, and validating her interests and abilities to succeed:

> I think I've gotten a lot of support just from the staff that has made me excited about staying in school and working on my degree. I wouldn't say it's like super education-specific. But I definitely never heard one of them tell me that it was a waste of my time, or that I wouldn't make enough money. Because they're in education, and they get it, and get the reasons that I'm interested in it.

University of Nebraska-Lincoln

The University of Nebraska-Lincoln (UNL) is a research-focused university that serves about 26,000 students, 27% are racially minoritized, 27% receive a Pell grant, 26% are first-generation college, and 4% were born outside the United States. As a land-grant institution, it has a mission to have a positive impact throughout the state. The ecology of UNL's program is distinct since students have multiple peer supports during the first year of college. Specifically, students engage with peer mentors who facilitate social connections, and they also live in a designated residence hall during their first year of college, which has an area known as the Study Café – where students can study individually and in groups, and can access tutoring services. TSLC staff offices are located within the multicultural center, and it provides supplemental funds for counseling services. To understand the ecology, we explore the collegiate journeys of Nevaeh and Sadie.

Nevaeh's Story

Nevaeh was a Black woman from Omaha and was very close to her family. She entered college as a pre-health pharmacy major, and her intended career held personal meaning for her:

> Well, just my parents, since they have some health complications – since they take a lotta pills, I used to help them with their medicines, giving it to them. And it amazed me how a single pill could help stop or increase something and help them out so very much.

Nevaeh participated in a college preparation program for low-income students and took dual enrollment classes in high school. She decided to attend UNL after receiving the Buffett scholarship. Without the scholarship, Nevaeh would have attended "a less expensive college or maybe a two-year college and just get my associate's degree – something that would be more affordable."

First year of college. Nevaeh lived on campus and struggled with homesickness. She found it challenging to engage with people she did not know since she described herself as "trying to break out of that shyness." Although Nevaeh went to Omaha every weekend to see her family, living on campus and being in TSLC helped her feel more connected to campus:

> I like how nice and how helpful everything is; if you need help there's always someone to help you … They're just so nice and close-knit; I feel like I'm a part of something. Especially the mentor groups, and then we've got all our group events, and then the bigger group events that we go to. It's just all so welcoming and everything.

Nevaeh's sense of connection was enhanced by her interactions with Black women who were staff members in TSLC: "I literally maybe go to talk to them about once a week, and they're always helpful and very nice; helping, asking questions and – I don't know – they're just very great resources for me." These women also provided personal and academic guidance. For example, Nevaeh was concerned about finding a salon where she could get her nails and hair styled in a city that was predominately White. The staff members provided recommendations of Black women they knew and trusted in Lincoln. Reflecting further on her meetings with her point of contact, who was a Black woman, Nevaeh said:

> Well, I like to meet with her because she's always so positive, and she gives very good advice. Like, I go in there with all my problems, like, "Oh, I don't know what to do about this," and then she's just like, "Well, you can do this," and I'm like, "OK. That makes much more sense." *[Laughter.]* She's just so helpful and nice."

Nevaeh appreciated that her point of contact helped her think through solutions to her challenges. The staff member took a validating approach by normalizing challenges and requests for help when needed rather than framing difficulties as an individual deficiency.

Nevaeh appreciated the diversity of perspectives and the opportunity to learn from her TSLC peers. Her TSLC social science class was particularly interesting despite her original trepidation since "political science sounds boring." Nevaeh discussed the instructor's approach:

> The teacher makes it fun. Like, instead of just a boring lecture, we have like group talks. So they ask us questions to see our opinions about it. Instead of just talking at us, we have more discussions, we hear what the students have to say, instead of the teacher just talking and talking for the whole 50-minute lecture. So, I think that kinda makes it better.

Nevaeh's instructor used interactive pedagogy, but more importantly, they validated students' knowledge and contributions to the group's learning. This approach to learning resonated with Nevaeh, and she benefited from learning from her peers' perspectives and contributing her own.

Second year of college. At the start of the year, Nevaeh changed her major to family sciences. Her decision was driven in part by her concern about taking the various science classes needed to pursue a career in healthcare. Nonetheless, her new major and intended career still leveraged her desire to help others.

Throughout Nevaeh's second year, she discussed race, racism, and compositional diversity more explicitly than she did as a first-year student. One of her favorite classes was her TSLC social science course that centered race:

> It's interesting to me, and I like how it's not really, like, the teacher that I have, they're really open. Like, we talk about everything … and it's open to different conversations and discussions and respecting people's opinions and everything, instead of just, "Oh, here's a book and we're gonna just, this is what they say about racism or other stuff," you know, just giving us the definitions and then just moving on, instead of just talking about it.

The instructor created space to talk about racism and being racialized as a lived experience rather than as an abstract concept. In doing so, the instructor validated Nevaeh's experiences as a Black woman and created opportunities for students to collectively inform the learning in the course.

Nevaeh's experiences in her TSLC courses were very different from her experiences outside of the program. She was often the only racially min-oritized person in non-TSLC courses, and she did not feel as supported by faculty outside of the program. For example, Nevaeh struggled with a group project in her major where she was the only racially minoritized woman on her team and she felt as though her peers ignored her. When

Nevaeh went to talk to her instructor about her concerns, her instructor further dismissed her:

> [The instructor] was like, "Well, you're just such a nice person. You're so shy. You don't really talk that much. If I was in a group, I'm the one to take the lead. I would have done the same thing." They told me that they would have done the same thing and that it's because I'm such a shy and nice person, so basically nothing. So that kind of made me like – that bothered me. Kind of like they just disregarded the whole situation. I went to them to get advice or something, and they just blew me over. They basically told me, I would have did the same thing. You're just so quiet and soft-spoken. I don't know. Justified it and that's it.

Rather than validating Nevaeh's experiences, the non-TSLC instructor framed Nevaeh's shyness as a problem and deficit, which signaled lack of care about her or her experiences.

Given her experiences outside of TSLC, Nevaeh was grateful to have the support of the racially minoritized individuals who worked in the program:

> I cannot say that I have any – any – professors that are people of color, at all. And I don't think I've had one, maybe one throughout my whole two years so far. So, it's just nice to see some other, like, diversity in the staff.

Nevaeh appreciated seeing herself represented on the TSLC staff. Her connection with her point of contact continued to be an important source of support: "When I was really nervous about something, then I'd go to talk to her. Like, "Oh my gosh," you know, I tell her what's going on and then she gives me advice or what she thinks about the situation. So kinda like a little counselor." This staff member served as a resource and normalized asking for help. Nevaeh elaborated, "Because I talk to [my point of contact], like, maybe once a month, and when I do talk to her, what she says makes sense and does impact me … she does have a significant impact."

For Nevaeh, TLSC's ecology was valuable since "people who actually care about you." Her identity was represented and affirmed in the program, as were her perspectives, concerns, and struggles. Throughout her second year, Nevaeh succeeded academically and worked to become more engaged on campus. She continued to describe herself as shy, but she had the support she needed to make new friends and to get involved in campus activities rooted in her social identities and desire to be of service to others.

Third year of college. Nevaeh continued to thrive academically and deepened her engagement in campus activities related to her identities. She moved into a leadership role in a service organization. She was increasingly confident in her abilities to reach her academic and personal goals. She visited TSLC less frequently; however, Nevaeh was keenly aware of how TSLC helped with her transition to campus and served as a place of refuge as a Black woman. Nevaeh lamented being asked to serve as a spokesperson for her race in her non-TLSC courses: "Sometimes I feel like I have to speak for my race, and I don't feel like I should. I'll say something if – I don't know. It's weird. You have to speak for your race when you're just one person who is not the face of millions of other people."

Given this pressure, she felt relief having other Black women in TSLC: "I saw [a Black woman TSLC staff member], and it was refreshing. I didn't know I needed to see her." Reflecting on racial representation, Nevaeh said, "I think that makes a tremendous difference." The opportunity for sustained engagement with Black women throughout her time in the program and interactions with instructors who validated her identities was meaningful since it was in stark contrast with her experiences outside of the program.

Sadie's Story

Sadie, a White woman from Omaha, navigated health challenges in high school and provided support to a family member with a long-term disability. Given her prior experiences with physical and occupational therapy, she entered college as a pre-health student and planned on transferring to the University of Nebraska Medical Center to complete a nursing degree. Sadie's longtime boyfriend attended UNL, but did not receive a Buffett scholarship.

First year of college. Sadie was keenly aware of the differences between her TSLC and non-TSLC instructors:

> Well, the [TSLC] professors are a lot more genuine. They really care about – 'cause our [TSLC] professor, they're like … "If you need help, I will help you." They're like, "You just need to come to me about it." And they're just so much more personal, and they really care about you … They're just a lot more personable, 'cause I can sit down and have a conversation with them, no problem. I had a conversation with [a TSLC] professor about their granddaughter liking tree kangaroos … but my [non-TSLC] STEM professors are really cold, and they don't care about you, they're just there for the research.

Her TSLC instructors were interested in building genuine connections and talking about topics that did not relate to course content. In contrast, Sadie had the clear sense that some of her non-TSLC instructors did not care for her since their priority was research.

Throughout her first year, Sadie noted that she benefited from the diversity of identities and experiences among her peers in TSLC:

There's a lot of different people with very different ways of thinking and cultures and backgrounds, and I would say that we're pretty close-knit, because I went into my science class and I knew a lot of people because of TSLC and it made me feel more comfortable in that environment, because it's like 150 or 160 students and TSLC isn't like that with our classes, so it was nice to have them there sit together and study … I came from a very conservative family and being in TSLC has opened me up to so many different ways of thinking and I think that's – my parents have always warned me that college is going to change me and they always saw it, like, as a bad thing like going to college people get more like, like you're gaining more knowledge towards other people and their lifestyles and I don't know why they saw that as a bad thing cause I've learned a lot about different religions and, like, different ways of life and ways of living, and it's helped me grow as a person.

For Sadie, being in a "close-knit" community provided her opportunities for sustained engagement with people who were different from her. While she noted that it was nice to have people to sit next to in classes and to study with, the main benefit was being exposed to other perspectives which "opened [her] up." Sadie's identities and prior experiences were respected, as were her efforts to learn and grow. She explained how peers were "constantly making me think."

Sadie got involved in TSLC and served on a committee that planned social events. Her connection to TSLC deepened after she perceived one of her peers was engaged in self-harm:

Well, [my peer] came into my – well, first, they got up – they're in my [TSLC] class too and they're at my table 'cause we have group tables, and they just randomly just got up and left in the middle of class … so there's only maybe 20 kids in there, so our professor definitely knew something was up. And then, the next class, they came back and there was cuts on their arm, like self-harm, so I reported that to my mentor. And then I emailed the teacher 'cause the instructor was asking me what was wrong with them, and I was just like, "You might wanna reach out to the Buffett community and try and find them help."

Sadie became a part of the culture of ecological validation. She had concerns about a peer's behavior and reached out to her mentor, instructor, and the TSLC staff to ensure the student got the support needed. Given her proclivity to help other students and her desire to get more involved, Sadie applied to be a mentor and was selected for the role. Her hire validated her contributions to TSLC and signaled the staff's belief in her ability to succeed in the role.

Second year of college. Sadie had a challenging summer between her first and second years of college. Two of her grandparents fell ill. She spent extensive time with one who was receiving hospice care. The stress of caring for her terminally ill grandparent affected Sadie's health, and one of her strongest sources of support, her boyfriend, was away for the summer. Despite these challenges, Sadie completed Certified Nursing Assistant training and summer courses while maintaining her high GPA.

Given the stress of the summer, Sadie was tired coming into TSLC mentor training, but it provided her with the space she needed. Sadie recounted being told by a staff member that students would have the opportunity to share their stories and being overwhelmed by emotion when she had the chance to speak:

> I decided to get up there and … I was the first one to cry at this mentor retreat. I don't like crying, so that really made me upset that I was the first one to cry in front of everyone … So that really kind of hit my self-esteem a little bit, but I'm – I really didn't like talking about this, I didn't enjoy it, but I absolutely loved mentor training because I made a lot of good friends, a lot of dependable people. I got to really see that, although my summer was sucky and parts of my life were a little sucky growing up, there are other people in the same boat as me because they shared their stories and they were absolutely amazing.

Although it was difficult for Sadie to talk about herself, it ended up being an experience that she "loved." She was vulnerable and found that she was not alone. Her experiences and feelings were validated by her fellow mentors: "A lot of people came up to me and hugged me and thanked me for sharing my story, and they were really empathetic." Sadie's reflection within a supportive environment contributed to increased self-awareness.

Sadie's connections to TSLC continued to deepen during her second year:

> I have more friends now that I'm a mentor, because a lot of my friends are like mentors and they're nursing students too … But it's nice to have [staff point of contact] there and all of the other points of contact. Yeah, I feel like I'm more like rooted in Lincoln now than I was freshman year.

Sadie regularly met with her point of contact to "vent" about the stress of classes, relationships, and work and anticipated still being "really good friends" with her point of contact after she transitioned out of TSLC.

TSLC continued to be a space where Sadie enhanced her understanding of social issues and people who do not share her identities. Sadie became more conscious of how staff created a validating and inclusive environment:

> Probably that they're willing to talk about hard subjects and also because it is a diverse community so I'm around a lot of people that I normally never would've put myself around because I wouldn't have been comfortable but now I am. And plus, like, the – all the points of contact, they're not all White. They're from different backgrounds.

Sadie noted the value of compositional diversity and leveraging that diversity to talk about "hard topics." Her increased comfort and consciousness led her to think more about her role in supporting a validating environment for her mentees:

> It's making me realize that the social construction of our society with learning about my difference, like what my different mentees have gone through. It's making me realize that there is an imbalance in society with some social aspects with gender and racial differences … People don't eat for days on end because they don't make money because of where the system maybe put them in stuff. So that's something I'm learning from my mentees. It's affecting my mentoring because I have to be very cautious of what I say to them because I don't want to make it sound like I don't believe them. Like I don't want them to ever think I don't believe them, so I just kind of really had to pick my words wisely because I want them to be able to come to me and trust me with anything that they want or need.

Since Sadie did not share all her mentees' realities, she was conscious about her efforts to understand their experiences and to validate them. She tried as best she could to engage in identity-conscious mentoring to support the students in her mentor group.

Third year of college. Despite the many challenges Sadie negotiated, she continued to succeed academically and was admitted to UNMC to pursue nursing. Before formally beginning at UNMC in the fall of her third year, Sadie had the opportunity to complete a short-term study abroad over the summer. She also worked over the summer in a state-run healthcare facility that affirmed her career choice and gave her a firm sense of how she wanted to engage in care as a nurse. Once at UNMC, Sadie was closest with nursing peers that she knew from TSLC. Her TSLC peers engaged differently than other students she encountered at UNMC: "Nursing is kind of cutthroat … I also see that the TSLC students treat the patients with far more respect than people that haven't been in TSLC." Sadie and her TSLC peers demonstrated an ethic of care for patients that they saw modeled in TSLC.

The TSLC staff continued to demonstrate care for Sadie and her peers. A staff member reached out to students to invite them to celebrate the program's anniversary. Sadie reached out to her TSLC point of contact to talk; they occasionally had dinner. Although Sadie was a UNMC student, she was still a valued member of the TSLC community, and the staff worked to maintain those connections with her. Reflecting on her time in TSLC, Sadie summed up her experiences saying, "It really like affirmed – they made you feel valued that you were going to help other people and that they really cared that you were there to kind leave that legacy in TSLC."

University of Nebraska, Omaha

The University of Nebraska, Omaha is a four-year campus located in a metropolitan area of Nebraska. It was initially open-access and included a focus on serving students transferring from community colleges (or coming directly in) who would largely not be eligible for other selective institutions. The campus enrolls about 16,000 students, 34% are racially minoritized, 32% receive Pell grants, 30% are first-generation college, 90% are commuter students, and 5% were born outside the United States. The program ecology at UNO has several features that reflect the needs of students in TSLC. First, the program did not have a residential component given the large number of commuter students that attend UNO. Second, TSLC had a first-year and a second-year required seminar. The first-year seminar explored students' study skills, college knowledge, and their Gallup Strengths, while the second-year seminar focused on job and career exploration. TSLC students took their seminar with their mentor groups, and their peer mentors and TSLC advisors served as co-instructors. Third, one of the shared academic courses required of all TSLC students was an autobiographical reading and writing course known as Autobio (Perez et al., 2021). Finally, TSLC offered support for English language learners since the program served a number of students who were recent immigrants or refugees. To understand how students experienced the ecology, we explore Asher's and Mia's collegiate journeys.

Asher's Story

Asher was a White man from a small town in rural Nebraska. He considered attending UNK like his sibling, but was drawn to UNO after visiting campus and it "felt like home." Asher was the only person from his graduating high school class who decided to attend UNO, and he knew very few people at the institution when he began college.

First year of college. Since Asher's hometown was far from Omaha, he decided to live on campus and was placed in a building with other TSLC students. Living on campus helped Asher establish connections on campus:

Well, the first day we got here, I guess we had the breakfast. And that was the same day I moved in. And so that very first day at the TSLC breakfast, I had already made five friends at the table. And one of them actually lived in my building. So I had that person to share these new feelings with, so it wasn't as scary, I suppose, as doing it myself.

While Asher found his place socially at UNO rather quickly, it took him a bit longer to settle in academically. He was doing well in his classes, but he was uncertain about his major and career. As he considered changing his major, his peer mentor was a valuable resource:

When we have those [mentoring] meetings every month and we just talk about stuff, and [my mentor] was really helpful, because that's when I decided I didn't want to be a [social science] major anymore. [My mentor] gave me all these tips. And they said they'd changed their major a million times. So they gave me all of these tips about what to do. So I guess it's just nice to have somebody to ask.

Asher's mentor affirmed his decision to change his major and provided practical advice. His mentor normalized changing majors and supported his desire to find the right fit.

Throughout his first semester, Asher wondered about his place as a White man in a racially diverse community like TSLC. He appreciated the diversity and inclusiveness of TSLC:

Like if you just walk down this hallway and you walk by their offices, they just have all of these stickers of, like, different communities, and like how accepting they are … There's a bunch of different types of people on the staff, so I think that helps a lot too, just knowing that not only are us TSLC students different, but there's a lot of diversity in the staff, too.

Nonetheless, he had some discomfort discussing identity and politics in his TSLC autobiographical reading and writing class after the 2016 election; since "there's only two Caucasian people in class, I did feel a little bit out of place" when his instructor created space for students to share their feelings about the election. Although Asher did not share the same fears as some of his peers who are Latinx or undocumented, he "definitely empathize[d] with those people," and hearing his peers' perspectives was important to understanding their viewpoints. Asher's instructor validated his peers' identities and fears without targeting or denigrating him, which created an opportunity to cultivate empathy.

Asher was selected to read a narrative he had written about the loss of a family member at the public readings associated with Autobio:

> I was excited when I was chosen. I didn't think I was going to be chosen, because there were so many good writers in my class, so it was a little bit surprising. Because I don't consider myself to be a great writer, but I do enjoy it … I was a little bit nervous to read it, because it's – it's a big part of my life just to blurt out to people … I was glad that I did it, because I don't think – I've never shared anything that important before. I've done speech before so I wasn't afraid to speak in front of people, but I've never spoke about my life before. I was proud of myself for jumping that hurdle.

Being selected to read his narrative affirmed the value of Asher's story and validated his abilities. Being vulnerable in front of members of the TSLC community was challenging for Asher, but he had the support he needed to overcome his "fear of opening up."

The connections Asher built with his Autobio instructor were also present in his other TSLC courses. Comparing his course instructors, Asher said:

> I feel more connected to the TSLC [instructors] than I do my regular ones. My regular [classes] have a lot of people in them, so it's harder to get that one-on-one than it is in TSLC. It's just simple things like [TSLC instructors] know my name. They know a lot more about me than my other teachers would.

In addition to feeling connected to his TSLC instructors, Asher described his TSLC advisor as "more like emotional support, they're there to be your friend, to advise you in social situations. They're like your backbone almost." In effect, Asher had the academic and interpersonal support he needed to succeed during his first year, and he excelled academically and socially.

Asher applied to be a peer mentor. He described his selection to serve in the role as an act of validation: "I think that meant that I was ready to give back to what [TSLC] has given to me. I think that meant – for me it's a representation of giving back to what [TSLC] has given to me." He felt as though the TSLC staff believed in his potential, and he looked forward to giving back to the community that had supported him throughout his first year.

Second year of college. Asher sought to get more involved on campus and joined several organizations related to his academic interests. His affirming experiences in TSLC continued to help him as he developed confidence in his abilities. For example, he described how his TSLC co-instructor believed in his capacity to facilitate conversations in the first-year seminar they led:

> I taught the last class this Wednesday. He [Asher's TSLC staff co-instructor] said – I literally went to my meeting with them, our one-on-one for the class, and they're like, "I'm just gonna let you teach it. It's all you." … And I was so nervous. I was like, "Oh, my goodness. You can't make me do that." And then when I got into the classroom, they just made it a laid-back atmosphere. And then everything went well after that.

Although Asher was nervous to facilitate class, his co-instructor's complete confidence in his abilities eased his anxieties. Eventually, teaching seminars became one of Asher's favorite parts of being a mentor. The position also helped him develop increasingly close relationships with other mentors and TSLC staff members: "I feel way more connected to the advisors. I know the advisors so much better than I knew them anytime beforehand, which is really nice."

Given the structure of UNO's TSLC program, Asher also participated in the second-year seminar curriculum focused on career and major exploration. He was nervous about engaging in activities focused on professionalism, but came to see the value in cultivating these skills:

> I liked how they made us actually do these certain things, like résumé-build and go do interviews. The interview dinner was really cool. I actually really enjoyed that … I wouldn't say it was fun, but I think it was very necessary for us to do, to prepare all these things and get us ready for the future.

After taking the second-year seminar and participation in career preparation activities, Asher felt increasingly prepared to seek opportunities in the field of public health including the possibility of attending medical school or graduate school.

TSLC's professional preparation included further exploring social identity in the context of oppression. As in his first year, Asher wondered where he fit into conversations about diversity as a White man: "So that was hard to talk about, especially for me because I'm a White male. So I just felt like I didn't have a place." TSLC staff made efforts to create a safe space and cultivate respect during diversity conversations. The students and instructor co-created an environment that helped Asher feel comfortable sharing his learnings from an implicit bias test:

When I took the test, I had a slight bias towards White people. And what I said was, "Well, I'm from [Asher's hometown], Nebraska, which is predominantly White. There is no diversity. And any type of interaction I had with people who were different for me was through the media. And then I was like, "Well, we know that the media doesn't portray people as they are." So, then it was like I had these ideas of what people acted like who were different for me. But coming to UNO and having an open mind, the whole thing has changed, and I'm so grateful for that.

Asher's seminar became a brave space where he could be honest about his biases and his learning about his privileges. The TSLC staff constructed a seminar that was identity-conscious, and their efforts to validate students' experiences created space for their varied learnings about privilege. This approach cultivated Asher's openness rather than fostering resistance, and it affirmed that while difficult, he had a place in conversations about diversity as a White man.

As he finished his second year of college, Asher continued to succeed academically. His key insights from the year focused on being more self-assured in his abilities to succeed:

I think [TSLC] just further made me believe in myself and in everything I do. Because everyone is so encouraging and stuff. Because if you go to the TSLC office and you are like "Oh my gosh, I got an A on my test." Everyone is like, "Wow!" … . So, I just think that the support from them [TSLC staff] has really made me feel like I can do this.

He continued: "[TSLC] creates a path for you to be successful … [and] these resources that TSLC gives me is literally starting my path to my future."

Third year of college. Asher remained engaged in TSLC as a mentor and became increasingly involved in his major and field of interest. The TLSC staff was pivotal in shaping his experiences. For example, when he had doubts about seeking an internship at a nonprofit organization, a staff member encouraged him to explore the opportunity, saying, "That sounds like a great idea. I really think you'd be great at that." The staff member focused on his potential contributions to the organization and his learning from the experience.

After coming out as a member of the LGBTQ+ community, Asher was encouraged by different TSLC staff members to pursue an opportunity to engage in work that brought together his identity and professional interests. He had seen information about an opportunity to contribute to research in his field of interest with the LGBTQ+ community. The staff member was familiar with the community-based organization sponsoring the research and told him, "You should definitely go [to the informational meeting]." That was the nudge Asher needed, and over the year he became increasingly involved in the organization. Multiple TSLC staff members affirmed Asher's identities, assets, and potential to contribute to communities outside of TSLC.

Throughout his third year, Asher reiterated that TSLC had set him up to succeed in college and helped him move toward graduate school. Working as a mentor allowed him to develop relationships that set a foundation for validating interactions with TSLC staff members:

> As a mentor, "[I'm] almost more validated because they've gotten to know me a lot more. So, we've developed a lot more personal relationships. So, I think just feeling they care and that they remember conversations with me makes me feel validated, makes me feel they're invested in me and my success.

Although he was not planning to return as a mentor during his fourth year of college, Asher was confident that the TSLC staff would remain invested in him and his success going forward.

Mia's Story

Mia, an Asian American woman, was a transracial adoptee from the Omaha area. She had an older brother who attended UNO, but did not receive a Buffett scholarship. Mia worked as a healthcare assistant in high school and began college as a STEM neuroscience major with the goal of pursuing a career in medicine. She took several community college courses during high school and began college with credits toward her degree. Although she considered other colleges, she ultimately chose UNO since it was her best option financially.

First year of college. Mia lived with her family and commuted to campus. TSLC eased her transition to college and provided her with multiple ways to build connections with her peers:

> I was really nervous that it would be hard to make friends and everything but like, really through TSLC I've made two really good friends already and we're pretty close. And it's a lot easier than I thought it was going to be. I was nervous but it's been good. Like I've been hanging out with people and a lot of people are like, "Oh, if you don't live on campus it's impossible to have that college experience and stuff." So that was definitely my concern with coming to UNO because I knew I'd probably live at home because I'm so close, but it's turning out well.

Mia indicated that her TSLC courses and first-year seminar with her mentor group provided her with immediate opportunities to build connections. Her peer mentor was a valuable resource:

[My mentor] is really helpful. They're like, "Just text me or call me if you need anything or if you have any questions." And they've been good because they've been through the first year and being a TSLC student too, so they know what to expect and they know what to help us on and they can figure things out for us, so they've been a really good mentor.

Mia's mentor was open and accessible, and they were proactive in planning events to help members of their mentor group forge relationships.

Mia spoke highly of her experiences in TSLC courses during her first semester. She was nervous about taking communications, but her instructor created an affirming environment:

[The TSLC instructor] makes it known that they like care about, like, you and what your grade is and what's going on in your life and everything, and they just seem like very genuine in their teaching and they're really passionate about it and … they're, like, so good at communicating with you and making sure everything's going okay.

Her communications instructor's ethic of care helped Mia feel more comfortable giving speeches in front of others. Similarly, Mia's Autobio instructor created a classroom environment where she was challenged to develop her craft as a writer and affirmed in the process of doing so:

[My Autobio instructor] gives really good feedback, because we'll get into our groups and read what we wrote for our prompts and then we'll pick one to share to the class and after you read it [the instructor will] give you like advice to how, like further – dig deeper into it or expand on things. And they say a lot of positive things about everybody, and I think that's really good reassurance for people that, you know, they're good writers and all that kind of thing.

Mia's instructor provided feedback to students that was balanced and constructive. They affirmed students' stories and abilities as writers while also providing feedback on how to further develop the narrative. This instructor further validated Mia's abilities by selecting her to read a portion of her autobiography at the public readings for the course.

Mia's Autobio instructor continued to demonstrate confidence in her abilities as a writer and encouraged her to take a screenwriting class with them the next semester. In this course, she had the opportunity to pitch a story to a well-known director in Hollywood. She reflected:

I was freaking out. I was literally shaking. This is only my first semester of the class, so I still don't even know what I'm doing. And I was so scared, but it felt good to be outside my comfort zone … a couple days later, I met with my professor and I talked to them about the guest's feedback and stuff. And obviously, the director has his kinds of movies, I guess you'd say, that he likes to direct, and in a certain way. So obviously, his feedback is according to what he likes to direct, basically. So I don't know. I talked to my professor about what to take into account and what to work on and stuff. But it was a great opportunity.

Mia's instructor signaled confidence in her abilities as a writer and provided support after the experience to help her make sense of the feedback as she continued to develop her work.

As Mia more deeply immersed herself in writing, she struggled to some extent with her science courses and started to doubt her career path. She was unsure of how to proceed and turned to her mentor for support:

A lot of the help I get is from my mentor actually. When I meet with them for one-on-ones, they kind of just ask what I'm up to and what I'm thinking about classes and things like that. And so they definitely help out with just what I've been thinking about, what I'm working towards and things like that. And I've been thinking about going into pre-health actually and so having the mentor to talk about that topic is nice.

Her mentor created space for her to talk through her uncertainty and possible opportunities going forward. Rather than offering a solution, Mia's mentor helped her determine a path forward, and she eventually changed her major from a STEM field to an applied social science field.

After her first year, Mia described TSLC: "It's given me just a lot of confidence with my education and a lot of motivation, I guess, to do my best. And there's a lotta people that are supporting." She also benefited from the attention to diversity and inclusion in TSLC:

Part of the reason why I love TSLC is because it's so diverse on a lot of different levels. Just, you know that everyone in it has gone through something, and so they – I feel like everyone's more understanding of each other. The friends that I've made – it's just cool to learn other people's stories, and you – I don't know. I feel like there's just a mutual respect among everybody, and it's not "we're here to judge each other" or anything. It's just accepting the differences in us, and that's something that's really important to me, and I really enjoy it.

Mia decided to give back to the program by serving as a peer mentor during her second year.

Second year of college. Given Mia's increased engagement in TSLC, she decided to live in the residence halls during her second year to reduce her time commuting. Mentor training provided her with insight into TSLC's values and how they enact those values in practice:

> We just did a lot of things on inclusion and things with our strengths as well; TSLC focused a lot on strengths and using our strengths in the world. So, we just dug a bit deeper into that, and that was pretty cool to learn more about what they are focusing on for us as students and getting a third point of view of a first-year student because I think as a first-year student you don't do all the seminar stuff but then you actually get involved with being a teacher. It's pretty cool to see the mentee's reactions to it.

Mentor training highlighted the TSLC staff's proactive and intentional work to use strengths-oriented and identity-conscious approaches to creating curriculum. She leveraged her experiences to help her mentees: "It's nice to be able to share with them what I experienced my first year. That benefits them as they're going through their first year." She was nervous about her ability to "say the right thing" to support her mentees but found she could be a resource and friend for them.

Mia began to explore her career options more fully, which included questioning her interest in medicine since working as a healthcare assistant was physically and emotionally draining. Mia began to consider healthcare administration as a way to bring together her interest in helping professions and her communication skills. TSLC became a place where Mia started to cultivate her professional skills as she contemplated career options. In addition to being a peer mentor, she served as program assistant. She described her role, "I just thought it would be a really good experience, because you make the weekly and monthly newsletters ... And just like a lot of design things that I'm really interested in."

As Mia considered her career pathway, she found the TSLC second-year curriculum and programming helpful. She was nervous to participate in networking events and mock interviews but felt supported as she honed her interview skills:

> I felt really prepared, since in seminar we did a lot on just interviewing and what to wear and things like that. And we did actually, we have this

new program online, it's called Big Interview, and it's like a virtual interview. It's a person that's recording, they ask you questions and then you record yourself answering them, and then you send those videos in to a teacher and they critique you on that. So they give you this feedback before we have the actual interviews. So that was really helpful.

Receiving formative feedback from her advisor before participating in interviews helped her better understand her strengths and areas of development. This proactive and affirming approach contributed to Mia's skill development and eased her anxieties about interview processes.

The continued support from TSLC staff members was beneficial. She highlighted the benefit of mid-term meetings with her advisor:

It's really helpful to talk about just, like, what you're juggling. My teaching partner that is my advisor, too, I had my midterm meeting and we were talking about working in school. They related 'cause they were like, "I had to work three jobs when I was in college." It's nice to be able to, they've been through it, so it's like, they've been through it, it's going to be OK. But it's nice and they're really open with talking about stuff. They talk about their lives, too, which makes it more personal and comfortable … Second year, it's nice to be able to check in with your advisor and talk about how life is going.

In addition to using the mid-semester meeting to discuss her academic progress, this was a space where she could talk about her life. Her advisor affirmed her experiences working multiple jobs to pay for college, and Mia saw her advisor as a role model since they had a similar collegiate experience. Their presence signaled "it's going to be OK." Mia ended her second year with an increased sense of direction. She valued TSLC staff members' approach to supporting those who were exploring their options:

I think they're really supportive in helping you figure out what you want to do and they're not discouraging in that. It's okay if you don't know yet, you'll get there and just they provide a lot of information of places on campus where you can try and figure out more about the majors and what you want to do.

Although she was not certain of what career she wanted to pursue, Mia knew she had the support she needed to find her way. TSLC normalized exploration and uncertainty, which validated Mia's experiences and empowered her to create her path forward.

Third year of college. Mia continued to explore career options related to communications and began considering graduate school or law school. She had a summer internship running social media for an organization and used her work as a TSLC program assistant as an internship for credit within her major. Her work with TSLC was focused on developing the program's social media presence, which built upon her interests and skills. As a program assistant, Mia maintained relationships with TSLC staff members. She highlighted the benefits of these sustained relationships:

> Just knowing that you have a solid foundation of people supporting you and stuff and you always know that you can go to them about anything, I think just knowing that is kind of enough, especially when you get to your third year just knowing that you have people there for you. It's really helpful.

Although she did not need extensive support from the TSLC staff, knowing they were there as a safety net was comforting. She spoke to their efforts to provide holistic and tailored support:

> I think that the program does its very best to be there for students in every way that they can. I definitely think that there are certain things that are kind of outside of their reach, depending on – I just know some people have really hard home lives or how they were raised or the experiences they had kind of affects everything about their life. I think that [TSLC] does the very best that they can to be there for support, just be like a family to people who may struggle more than others, because everybody is different in the program.

She was aware that staff care and support did not end when students left the program or transferred institutions. Mia noted, "Just because they are not students here, they are still important." Students' presence and absence was noted, which led Mia to say, "You feel cared for and like people recognize you." Being cared for and acknowledged was vital to supporting Mia's experience as a commuter student who was engaged in ongoing career exploration.

Conclusions

In this chapter, we illustrate how students experienced ecological validation that is embedded within TSLC. Although Alberto, Lana, Nevaeh, Sadie, Asher, and Mia had different social identities and varied needs throughout college, they each highlighted similar benefits to participating in TSLC. Specifically, being in a program with sustained, validating, and holistic support across contexts was invaluable as students worked to build relationships, explored their beliefs, developed their academic and interpersonal skills, and determined their career pathways. Participants also reinforced the importance of identity-conscious practices and promoting inclusion. Advancing diversity and inclusion was central to supporting students' success, particularly for those who were racially minoritized. At UNL and UNO, the presence of a compositionally diverse staff was meaningful for students who did not see themselves represented elsewhere on campus like Nevaeh and Mia, and for those who were making new meanings of their identities like Asher.

Each of the students encountered a challenge or form of uncertainty during college. Their struggles were acknowledged by TSLC, and each student received the support they needed to move forward in a way that worked for them. Students needed TSLC in different ways over the course of time, and yet they trusted that TSLC would be there for them when they needed assistance. For example, Alberto and Lana noted how the UNK staff were proactive in reaching out to students who they knew were navigating familial challenges. These expressions of care were indicative of a holistic approach to practice that made these students feel supported.

While there were many similarities in the culture of ecological validation at the three campuses, there were also distinctions in how it operated based on the programmatic structure and the needs of the students within the respective programs. The programs at UNK and UNL had residential components for first-year students that Alberto, Lana, Nevaeh, and Sadie indicated were pivotal in helping them acclimate to campus, build peer relationships, and facilitate validating interactions with their peer mentors. In contrast, the autobiographical reading and writing course at UNO was a key site for relationship building and experiencing validation for Asher and Mia as first-year students. Furthermore, the focus on career and major exploration at UNK and UNO during the second year of TSLC was particularly valuable as Alberto, Lana, Asher, and Mia each considered their academic pathways and potential career opportunities.

Although we were only able to present six student narratives in this chapter, their stories are not an anomaly. Rather, they are representations of the diversity of student experiences in TSLC and the positive impact of the culture of ecological validation. We hope these students highlight the benefits of ecological validation and generate new possibilities for practice in other settings.

Reflection Questions

- To what extent do the students' narratives resonate with you? How might facets of their stories relate to your own? How did your collegiate experience differ from theirs?
- How do students experience engagement with your office or department over time? To what extent would they describe interactions as validating?
- How is your practice designed to validate students over the course of time?
- What barriers and opportunities exist to implementing ecological validation in your work?

SECTION 3

Expanding a Culture of Ecological Validation across the Campus

The final section focuses on how to leverage ideas presented in the first two sections to shift postsecondary institutions away from siloed approaches that undermine at-promise student success and toward a culture of ecological validation. Chapter 10 highlights how multiple stakeholders play important roles in creating an institutional culture of ecological validation. To meet the needs of students broadly, campuses need to rethink their institutional roles, structures, and culture so that they support ecological validation. One of the best ways to achieve this type of scale is to have all employees rethink their roles within this new framing of student success. There are different opportunities for various campus stakeholders to contribute to ecological validation, and this chapter helps articulate those specific opportunities. Chapter 11 focuses on the importance of shared leadership as an approach to scaling ecological validation in ways that shift the institutional culture. We also present professional learning communities as an important tool to orienting programs, departments, and faculty leaders across campus to a culture of ecological validation. We also share our experiences collaborating with three campuses to build professional learning communities focused on creating a culture of ecological validation. We include reflections from the educators who cofacilitated the professional learning communities.

DOI: 10.4324/9781003443711-12

10

STAKEHOLDER SUPPORT OF A CULTURE OF ECOLOGICAL VALIDATION

One of the challenges of Rendón's (1994) validation theory is that validation rests in the hands of individual educators – an instructor or a staff member. In practice, it relies on "kind" individuals who decide to commit to validating students. Rendón called for validation to be part of institutional structures; we suggest thinking about validation as a culture that can be scaled to reach all students and embedded into higher education processes, policies, structures, and practices, one that moves beyond the individual actions of educators or siloed campus support programs. All individuals who work at your campus – faculty, staff, paraprofessionals, faculty, administrators, peer leaders, and mentors – can serve as validating educators who work cross-functionally to enact the norms of ecological validation (i.e., proactive, identity-conscious, strengths-oriented, holistic, developmental, collaborative, and reflective practice.) Our study documented how validation can be embedded within campus cultures through ecological validation. In effect, we build upon Rendón's theory to make it scalable in a way that has not been documented or articulated before by demonstrating how it can become part of campus culture. Institutional culture operates at different levels – unit, department, college, and overall university. As a result, we discuss how stakeholders across the campus could play a role in creating a culture of ecological validation at your institution as well as within various subunits and colleges.

Revisiting Ecological Validation

In Chapter 6, we presented the concept of ecological validation and explored how the TSLC programs created a culture that included norms, structures,

DOI: 10.4324/9781003443711-13

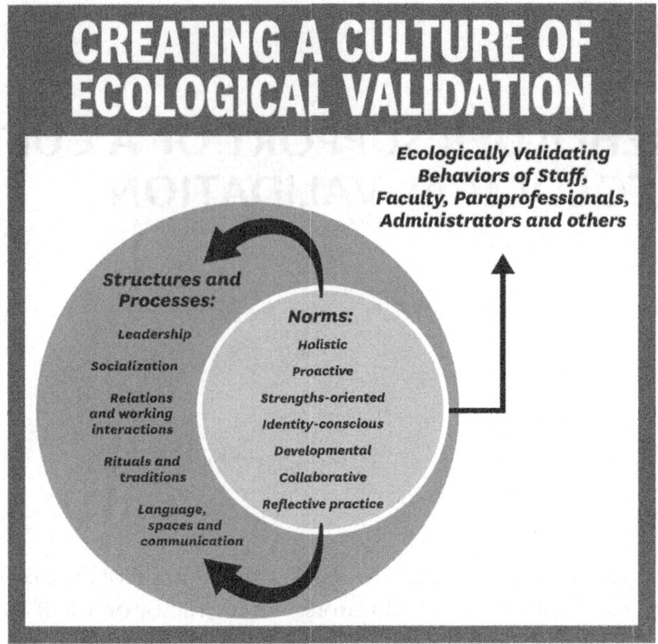

DIAGRAM 10.1   Revisiting a Culture of Ecological Validation.

and processes that resulted in ecologically validating behaviors of educators connected to the program (Diagram 10.1 summarizes the culture of ecological validation). While we documented the culture of ecological validation in three large comprehensive college transition programs, we believe the concept has applicability to postsecondary institutions more broadly. Similar to most postsecondary institutions, the TSLC programs supported a diverse group of students from different backgrounds (e.g., low-income, first-generation college status, immigration status), with different majors and aspirations, and different identities (e.g., gender, racially minoritized, sexuality). The programs navigated the complex silos of higher education to create a new culture that positively influenced students' experiences and outcomes. In addition, the postsecondary institutions used the TSLC programs as hubs of innovation and to identify promising practices and approaches that could be applied institution-wide (Kezar et al., 2021). We have also presented the culture of ecological validation to educators and leaders at multiple institutions, and they find the concept useful in thinking about how to create new approaches to at-promise student support.

As we previously explained, a culture of ecological validation involves seven norms that influence how educators engage in work practice to support at-promise students. Educators are *strengths-oriented* in believing in the potential of at-promise students and leveraging the students' experiences, assets, and strengths to help them achieve success. Educators *holistically* consider students as whole people with promising personal and academic assets, needs, and goals, which also means that the educator understands how the interpersonal and academic experiences influence each other. Educators *proactively* reach out early and consistently to understand student needs, goals, and assets and ensure challenges are addressed as well as connecting students to enriching opportunities. Educators are *identity-conscious* by being attentive to students' multiple identities, characteristics, needs, assets, and goals. Educators provide *developmental* support over the entire course of the students' academic career that is appropriate given their career, personal, and academic development. In addition to shaping how educators interact with students, ecological validation also frames the interactions between educators within a specific department or program as well as their interactions with staff, faculty, administrators, and other educators across campus. Educators individually and collectively *reflect* on what is working, what needs to change, and how to engage with other educators to improve student support. Educators engage in *cross-functional work* and *collaborate* with other educators, offices, and services to support student success and discuss strategies for supporting students in a systems-oriented way. In the remainder of this section, we provide a more detailed discussion and illustration of each practice.

Throughout the book, we have argued that *how* support is provided matters more than *what* support is provided. We leverage this key finding in thinking about how postsecondary institutions could create a culture of ecological validation at their campuses. Our findings suggest that it would not be as easy as a "five steps to success" approach that often gets utilized in education reform efforts. Rather, we believe that leaders in higher education would need to create space for a diverse group of educators (e.g., faculty, staff, administration, paraprofessionals) to engage with ecological validation and begin exploring how to apply those concepts across the institution. To assist in exploring how to work differently, the remaining sections provide guidance in starting to think about how educators could approach their work in ways that would create and sustain a culture of ecological validation.

Stakeholder Support of a Culture of Ecological Validation

Everyone at your institution plays a role in creating and sustaining a culture of ecological validation. Previous chapters discussed the role of faculty and staff members who work directly with students. In this chapter, we expand the focus to explore the role of other stakeholders on campus who can support a culture of ecological validation. Our discussion in this chapter is meant to build upon the important work already being done by educators on your campus.

In the sections that follow, we describe some of the ways that each group of stakeholders can engage in their work to create validating experiences for at-promise students. Specifically, we focus on the following campus stakeholders: executive leadership, faculty leadership, institutional research, peers, advancement, and alumni relations. The goal is not to create an exhaustive list of each stakeholder's role in creating ecological validation, but to explore some ways to move in that direction in order to start the conversation on your campus. We imagine that you will find additional strategies specific to your campus context.

Executive Leadership

The executive leadership – defined as senior-level administrators, often the cabinet – sets the tone and facilitates creating a mission that guides the entire campus. Campus administrators play important roles in setting campus priorities and goals. In particular, the president, chancellors, dean of students, college deans, and the provost create and oversee the policies and structures that could make ecological validation possible. Executive leadership also has the ability to bring people together from across campus to discuss the strengths and limitations of the current institutional culture in order to make decisions about how to shift in ways that benefit at-promise students. We provide a few examples of how executive leaders could support a culture of ecological validation.

Review Research and Data

Motivation to engage in a change often emerges from a combination of reviewing institutional data and engaging with current research. Postsecondary institutions generally have systems in place to facilitate continuous improvement, such as accreditation and program review, which involve critically examining institutional data to understand student outcomes, including investigating how subgroups of at-promise students are doing in terms of both academic and psychosocial outcomes. Executive leaders usually direct the priorities for institutional data collection, analysis, and review. They also signal how important the use of data is to decision-making. As discussed in Chapter 2, most postsecondary institutions have inequitable outcomes for some groups of students – often, those from low-income, racially minoritized, and/or first-generation college backgrounds. Having a clear understanding of the areas that warrant attention can be useful information needed to motivate institutional stakeholders. Furthermore, engaging in reflection about the institutional policies and practices that may contribute to potential inequities is necessary – as is being open to feedback about areas that can be improved to better serve at-promise students. Leadership can convene others on campus to review policies and practices in light of data they have collected and even have cross-unit comparisons that may motivate change.

Creating a Vision

The executive leadership can create a vision related to moving the campus toward a culture of ecological validation. Leadership can send a clear message that everyone on campus should be involved in creating validating experiences for at-promise students – all students get validated in all interactions with educators and staff. Leadership can set the expectation that interactions with students represent the norms of ecological validation: strengths-oriented, holistic, identity-conscious, proactive, developmental, collaborative, and reflective practice. A vision provides a sense of both direction and priority that can be aligned with campus plans. Working with the board of regents, leaders can also obtain broader support among alumni and key stakeholders for the new direction.

Strategic Planning

Executive leadership is responsible for developing planning initiatives on campus based on the review of data and vision. Such plans can then hold administrators, faculty and staff accountable for creating ecological validation. The plan helps members of campus on the journey to change their norms, which can take a long time to adjust. The plan provides goals, timelines, and action steps that help translate the idea into practice.

Budgeting and Resource Allocation

One of the most important ways to demonstrate support for ecological validation is to put resources toward its development. This means investing in people and professional development rather than programmatic efforts so that ecological validation is everyone's work rather than that of a few people. This is a major shift for campuses that have poured resources into programmatic and intervention efforts rather than into a major rethinking of investing in people's development and rewards in terms of evaluation and annual reviews. Senior leaders are also responsible for the priorities of development offices, and they can make resources to support ecological validation one of those priorities.

Communicating and Engaging Campus Stakeholders

Executive leaders have access to many communication vehicles – newsletters, campus email lists, publications, town hall meetings, speeches, and events – that can be used to engage administrators, faculty, staff, alumni, and student leaders in the ideas and norms of ecological validation. By repeatedly describing the importance and content of ecological validation, leaders can ensure that stakeholders understand the concept. They can also establish a professional learning community (see Chapter 11) as a way to have campus employees build their skills around ecological validation.

Create Professional Development

Professional development can be created at any level of the institution; however, professional development supported by executive leadership is much more likely to be engaged in by campus stakeholders. If leadership emphasizes the importance of professional development, it is likely to get the attention of employees. As noted under the budgeting section, leaders have not invested in professional development of employees as a strategy to better support at-promise students, and this is an important new area for their consideration and investment. We envision campuses creating an academy on campus that focuses on ways employees can support ecological validation. The academy can offer a certification that can also be used toward promotion or annual reviews.

Incentives and Rewards

Current reward systems are not aligned with faculty, administrators, or staff utilizing the norms of ecological validation. Changing reward structures signals what is valued on campus. For example, rewarding individuals and units that collaborate toward student success is a way that leaders can better align the incentive system with ecological validation. Providing merit based on involvement in professional development related to ecological validation is another strategy. Even if individual units create and conduct evaluations, leaders can review and provide guidance on overall merit and evaluation documents. One of the often-overlooked supports is rewards or incentives for collaboration. Current reward structures (annual review, promotion and tenure, and merit systems) support individual rather than group contributions. Faculty and staff are more likely to do the extra work of contributing to the overall organizational goals and objectives, such as implementing changes and supporting collective problem-solving, when they feel those efforts are rewarded by the organization. Leaders need to explore intrinsic and extrinsic motivators as different stakeholders in higher education are motivated by different types of rewards. Activities such as rethinking annual merit reviews to include ways members of the campus contribute to ecological validation, for example, can support collaborative work and implementation of a culture of ecology validation.

Revising Structures

The siloed, fragmented structures that employees work within have resulted in the approaches that faculty, staff, and administrators use in their work. Only executive leaders are able to dismantle or alter these structures in a comprehensive way. Reorienting campuses into more matrix organizations with more cross-functional teams is a task that only leaders can implement. Therefore, to make this work real and supported, leaders need to revise existing working relationships so there is more collaboration as well as examining structures for deficit approaches. Leaders are also responsible for facilities and physical plant. We have noted how spaces are generally not designed to support collaboration, which could change by engaging in new planning around physical spaces. The Learning Spaces Collaborative is one such initiative that helps campus leaders envision new spaces that support student success and new models of learning (https://www.pkallsc.org/about/about-learning-spaces-collaboratory/). For further reading on ways leaders can rethink campus structures to support at-promise student success, see: https://pullias.usc.edu/download/creating-a-diverse-student-success-infrastructure-the-key-to-catalyzing-cultural-change-for-todays-student/.

Environment of Organizational Learning, Risk-Taking, and Experimentation

Ecological validation is more complex to create than a single intervention or even a few aligned programs. It will take significant experimentation and failed efforts to identify ways to reach different groups, to make the complex culture change understandable, and to embed these ideas into the current siloed and White middle-class contexts. Collective action depends on an environment of risk-taking since the work breaks typical boundaries and working relationships and processes (Zhu et al., 2018). Leaders need to provide the support for risk-taking and experimentation. They can do this by modeling risk-taking and, more importantly, recognizing and rewarding this activity. As we noted earlier, adding learning and risk-taking toward a culture of ecological validation into merit reviews is a valuable step.

Faculty Leadership

Previous chapters illustrate the importance of faculty members in creating validating experiences for at-promise students. In Chapter 11, we discuss the role of shared leadership and governance, which play important roles in creating and sustaining a culture of ecological validation. Here, we focus on the role of faculty leaders in supporting individual faculty members. You may notice that we focus on support, not training. We appreciate why many research studies recommend one-time faculty training, but rarely is this practical or effective. As one of the faculty leaders in our study emphasized, "Faculty do not need another one-off training." Instructors and faculty leaders spoke about the benefit of information, guidance, and ongoing support. Our faculty participants discussed the importance of receiving support from people who understood the faculty role at their institution instead of mandated training that was disconnected from the realities of their work.

Department and Program Chairs

Faculty members often spend the majority of their time focusing on departmental tasks such as scheduling, hiring, or discipline-specific activities such as peer review. They may not be fully aware of the multiple resources across campus. Department and program chairs serve as gateways to information about institutional priorities, functioning, and information. As the executive leadership engages in a conversation at the institutional level about ecological validation, the department chair should localize the conversation. What does it mean for individual departments to support a culture of ecological validation? How can policies, practices, and rewards be adjusted at the departmental level? What resources, professional development, and support would faculty need to create validating experiences for at-promise students? How could the department move away from a siloed approach? Engaging in these conversations at departmental level can help move from an abstract idea to more practical and actionable areas for individual faculty members. The department chair can also help translate the concept of ecological validation within the specific discipline. While the general concepts may be the same across campus, the specific issues and actions may differ by discipline. For example, faculty in cultural studies may identify different challenges and opportunities for at-promise students than faculty in engineering. In addition, faculty in different departments may benefit from different resources and information. For example, the accounting department may have significant knowledge about how to connect students with professional experience and internships; they decide to focus on learning more about culturally appropriate and engaging pedagogy, so they connect with colleagues in education.

Faculty Governance Bodies and the Senate

Faculty leaders involved with shared governance make decisions about curriculum, pedagogy, professional development, faculty hiring, student support, and other key issues that can shape ecological validation. These leaders can support ecological validation by integrating ecological validation and the norms into their decision-making and policy development. When policies about student support are discussed by the faculty council or senate, faculty leaders can ask themselves whether the policy is identity-conscious, validating, and proactive, for example.

Identifying Lead Faculty Members as a Point of Contact for Instructors

Our research identified the importance of having a point of contact for faculty members who have questions about pedagogy, resources, student issues, and connecting students to opportunities. Faculty members at most universities receive a long list of email addresses and phone numbers at the beginning of each semester with information about the numerous student resources on campus. As our participants explained, navigating the list of resources when a student identifies an issue can seem overwhelming and discourage individual faculty members from engaging in conversations with at-promise students that could lead to identifying barriers to their success. Similarly, the "red flag" systems that many postsecondary institutions create were useful when the faculty member identified a significant issue, but were not as helpful in other contexts. For example, a faculty member may have a student who appears to have significant potential even though their grades are low, but the instructor does not know what strategies to use to engage the student. Or the instructor has a feeling that something is off with a student, but is not sure whether it rises to the level of a red flag. Or a faculty member may have a student who is excelling and is unsure of the opportunities on campus for that student to extend their learning.

Having a faculty leader to engage with can significantly shift how instructors think about their work and their willingness to engage in validating experiences with students. One approach that has promise is identifying faculty leads who serve as a point of contact for instructors (see faculty coordinator discussion in Chapter 8). We found that instructors are more comfortable and confident in engaging in holistic conversations with students when they know that any issues that emerge can be handed off to one person who will make sure the issue is addressed in an appropriate and validating way.

Institutional Data and Research Offices

Institutional data play an important role in being an organization that creates and sustains a culture of ecological validation. Most institutional research offices generate reports for administrative leaders that focus on student outcomes, including grades, course taking, retention, graduation, and other outcomes for both the overall student body and subgroups. These reports provide institutional-based information about where students may need support, which can be an important component of making decisions about how to adjust policies, structures, and interventions that support student outcomes. Intentional and critical analysis of data are important starting points for achieving equitable outcomes (Witham & Bensimon, 2012).

While institutional research offices have the potential to meaningfully contribute to a culture of ecological validation, barriers exist in many institutions. First, institutional research offices often focus on collecting and reporting data related to regulatory mandates instead of being oriented toward institutional improvement and learning (Kezar, 2018). As a result, the data rarely get shared with stakeholders across campus who make decisions about student supports and institutional structures. Scholars consistently call for institutional research offices to gather, analyze, and distribute data in ways that can inform decision-making and practice, such as through data dashboards at the department or unit level (Harris & Bensimon, 2007; Hrabowski, 2019; Kezar, 2018). Examples of such dashboards can be found at individual campuses as well as across systems such as the California State system. Second, the siloed nature of institutions means that data are gathered and analyzed in fragmented ways (Kezar, 2018). Individual departments and programs often gather data that are not shared with other stakeholders on campus. Scholars have called for taking a more holistic view of data in order to identify broad patterns and to explore the multiple factors that influence student success (Hrabowski, 2019). Finally, institutional research offices are not always trained or equipped to present data to stakeholders across campus in ways that could improve practice (Kezar, 2018).

New structures and cultural norms can be created that enable institutional research offices to contribute to developing and sustaining ecological validation. An important first step is providing training for institutional researchers concerning ecological validation in order to inform how they gather and analyze data. Connected with that, institutional researchers would benefit from training related to presenting data to the multiple different stakeholders on campus. Several examples of how to do such work have been offered by groups such as the Association for Institutional

Research, the National Survey for Student Engagement, and the National Institute for Learning Outcomes Assessment. The data need to be shared in ways that are easy to use and interpret by all stakeholders, including faculty in different disciplines, administrators, program directors, academic advisors, student leaders, and staff in all offices.

While institutional data tend to be provided to administrators, this information is not always easily accessible to all educators and staff on campus. The president or a dean may provide a broad overview of the data related to a specific area that will frame strategic planning. However, instructors rarely get more specific information that could inform their direct practice. Institutional research could generate reports at the program level that cover multiple years in order for instructors to explore patterns and opportunities to support students. In addition, the program leads and institutional research could engage in a discussion about the key areas where instructors want more information. Collaboration between instructors and institutional research has the potential to meaningfully inform practice in ways that general reports may not.

The research office can also explore ways to gather data and conduct analysis that are informed by ecological validation. The majority of current data gathered focuses on student outcomes. This information is essential. However, these data do not necessarily explore the structures, policies, and practices that frame these outcomes. Drawing from the discussions in Chapters 6 and 7, institutional research could gather data to explore how educators are working across disciplines to break down silos and build a culture of ecological validation. This may include surveys and focus groups of instructors and staff to understand the opportunities and challenges. In terms of student data, the current surveys could include questions related to if and how they experience holistic and validating support. When a sub-group of students is identified as having relatively low academic or psychosocial (e.g., belonging, mattering, self-efficacy) outcomes, focus groups could be created to understand the structures, policies, and experiences that frame these outcomes. These data could then be shared broadly to allow educators and administrators across campus to collectively engage in discussions about how to resolve these issues.

Students and Peers

Students and peers are often left out of discussions about creating validating experiences for at-promise students. However, we consistently heard from the students in our study that their peers were an important aspect of the culture of ecological validation. Before discussing the potential ways that students can support the culture, we want to acknowledge that at-promise students should not be expected to create their own validating experiences, and institutions should not create situations where at-promise students are asked to give free labor to compensate for things that institutional stakeholders should be doing. For example, creating "internship opportunities" with minimal or no financial compensation for students to be validating agents through opportunities to mentor each other, co-teach classes, provide tutoring services, or serve as a liaison for a department is problematic. While it may seem empowering to the student and a way for stakeholders to access valuable information that can support at-promise students, the result may be that students feel exploited and invalidated. Students providing a service to the institution should be compensated and appropriately supported through training and mentorship.

Solicit Student Perspectives on How They Want to Be Involved

Postsecondary institutions serve differing groups of students. The campuses we studied involved a traditional residential four-year campus as well as a metropolitan institution with a large number of commuter students and a rural campus whose students generally left campus each weekend to go home to assist with farming and other family needs. You may be at a community college with a large number of part-time students, a campus with primarily online classes, a small liberal arts college with a close-knit community, or a highly selective institution with a relatively small number of at-promise students. You will want to gather information from your students about gaps in support as well as how they would like to be connected to campus stakeholders. Gaining these insights will allow you to create opportunities that reflect the needs of your students.

Training for Student Leaders

Campuses generally have student leaders who take roles in student government, clubs, sports, Greek organizations, and other roles on campus. Many traditional four-year campuses have a robust assortment of student leaders across a multitude of different roles and groups. Other campuses serve commuter students who have less time available to participate in these sorts of organizations, so there are fewer leadership opportunities on campus. Student leaders play an important role in creating validating experiences for the students who participate in their groups; however, these leaders rarely understand how to create spaces where all students can fully engage and feel a sense of belonging. Campuses could create some basic training materials for new student leaders that provide an overview of the concepts of ecological validation and some strategies for working with a diverse group of students.

We would encourage campuses to also have training and/or support materials for campus stakeholders who oversee the student leaders.

Utilize Peer Mentoring and Support Programs

We consistently heard from our participants how much they valued the connections they built with peer mentors and tutors. In particular, our study focused on peer mentors and tutors who also identified as at-promise students. Seeing mentors – with whom they could identify – succeed and overcome challenges and pursue learning opportunities was validating for at-promise students. Moreover, the mentors received extensive training with information about research on at-promise student experiences, resources available on campus, and how to engage in culturally appropriate mentoring. While students at all campuses found peer mentoring important, this opportunity was particularly important for students who felt disconnected from the campus community (e.g., commuter students, first-generation college, parenting, and racially minoritized students). The students shared how the mentor did not need to have the same identities or backgrounds as long as they were trained to create validating experiences. With tutors, we also encourage training related to creating culturally appropriate and validating experiences. Tutors are often selected based on their content expertise, which is important. However, how they engage with at-promise students is equally important. Students generally solicit the support of tutors when they are struggling in class. A tutor can either affirm the student's potential and offer encouraging forms of support, or unintentionally send the message that the student may not be capable of succeeding.

Create Opportunities for Diverse Groups of Students to Build Community

The comprehensive programs we studied had a large group of students with diverse identities, backgrounds, majors, and career goals. The program created a shared vision and mission that all students agreed was important. The staff, instructors, and students were invested in creating a safe and supportive space where all students could thrive and succeed. The programs created shared experiences for all students that included clusters of students. For example, one campus created small groups of students who were assigned a mentor; these students sit together at the welcome event and community dinners as well as being in the same first-year seminar. The gathering of students together for shared experiences allowed students to see that they belonged on campus and enabled them to build connections with students from differing backgrounds.

Peer Validation in the Classroom

Foster opportunities in the classroom for students to learn about one another's backgrounds, share stories, and engage in validating peer feedback. Faculty must set the tone to ensure that students understand the classroom is an inclusive space where everyone's background, experiences, and assets have a place, and they must model validating feedback so that students can similarly engage in peer validation. For example, a faculty member might invite the class to share feedback and thoughts on an assignment a peer completed, prefacing the peer feedback opportunity with the question "what were some of the strengths of your peer's assignment?" to get students in the mindset of identifying those strengths, which would, in turn, be experienced as validating by the peer receiving that feedback.

Advancement Offices

Creating a culture of ecological validation begins with exploring how current resources can be used. However, advancement offices can play an important role in identifying additional funding sources that can expand current efforts or support new initiatives. Professionals working in advancement often have a broad view of the campus initiatives and try to align their fundraising with the needs, mission, and current resources of the institution. Advancement offices can use this knowledge to look for opportunities to create funding initiatives that encourage collaboration across units as well as provide resources for educators to support ecological validation. While some funders may be primarily interested in supporting narrow issues or specific programs, we encourage advancement officers to also look for funders who may be open to efforts that focus on broader issues.

Scholarships and Emergency Funding for At-promise Students

We recognize that advancement offices already focus on securing scholarship funds for underrepresented student groups, including low-income, racially minoritized, and first-generation college students. Our research affirms these efforts. Students consistently spoke about how scholarship funding influenced the decision to attend college, reduced their financial stress, and enabled them to remain enrolled. In addition, some postsecondary institutions have created emerging funding that can be made available for students who need a relatively small amount of money as a result of an unexpected financial issue (e.g., car repair) or expense (e.g., additional lab fees for class). For at-promise students whose families may have minimal expendable money, a small expense can create a financial crisis. Creating endowed funds that financial aid can access for small grants can make the difference in students remaining enrolled when an issue emerges.

Endowed Faculty Coordinator Positions

In the section on faculty leadership, we shared how creating a faculty coordinator role has the potential to support instructors in creating validating experiences for students. This also means that the faculty coordinators need a reduced course load in order to focus a portion of their time on supporting faculty. Securing funding to create an endowed faculty coordinator position reduces the impact on departments and colleges. The directed funding also allows for the faculty coordinator position to remain in place even during times when an institution experiences financial stress.

Adjusting Physical Spaces to Encourage Collaboration

Some colleges and universities have student services and resources spread across campus and/or have office spaces and buildings that inhibit collaboration. We previously spoke about one-stop student centers that bring all services and resources into one space, which can encourage collaboration and make it easier for at-promise students to access resources. The advancement office can play an important role in securing funding to renovate current structures or build new spaces that can help facilitate a culture of ecological validation.

Funding for Professional Learning Communities

In Chapter 11, we discuss building professional learning communities (PLCs) to allow administration, professional staff, and faculty leaders to explore how to break down silos and create ecological validation. PLCs require the educators to do considerable work, often for a few years. In addition, the group of educators may benefit from attending conferences together and visiting other institutions that are engaged in innovative strategies. A funding initiative could be created that included stipends, materials, course buyouts, and travel opportunities for the educators involved in the PLCs.

Alumni and Alumni Relations

Alumni relations professionals get the opportunity to connect with individuals who have successfully navigated their postsecondary institutions. Alumni possess knowledge and resources that can be leveraged by institutions as they create a culture of ecological validation.

Internships, Mentoring, Job Shadowing, and Employment Opportunities

At-promise students often have fewer individuals in their social and familial network who have completed college degrees and are working in careers in their professional field. Alumni relations can coordinate with career services and faculty members to help build bridges between current students and alumni. Alumni can be invited to speak in courses or at events about their professional experiences. Career services and academic departments can connect with alumni of their institution to get information about internships, job shadowing, and employment opportunities for their current students and recent graduates. Alumni are often willing to support their alma mater, but may not know how to do so beyond donating to fundraising campaigns. Faculty may be interested in connecting students with alums, but do not have the time, connections, or expertise concerning how to do so. The alumni relations office can serve as an important mediator and coordinator for these efforts.

The alumni relations office can also provide resources and training related to ecological validation. Depending upon the backgrounds and identities of individual alumni, they may or may not understand at-promise students' experiences, strengths, and challenges. Providing some general information can be important in helping alumni identify opportunities for students as well as how to provide validating support after students are selected for internships or jobs. Alumni will be best equipped to support the culture of ecological validation when they have a general understanding of why and how they play a role in the process.

Leveraging At-promise Alumni's Knowledge of the Institution

Alumni have experienced the process of navigating your institution. Gaining a deeper understanding of their challenges and successes can be useful information for faculty and administration. Alumni surveys can include questions about how they experienced the institution and solicit reflections about what may have been useful. These reflections from alumni can be particularly useful since they are considering their college experiences through the lens of their professional experiences. While this information can be useful in developing alumni engagement activities, it will also be valuable information to share with faculty who make the decisions about curriculum and pedagogy. Career services could use this information to prepare relevant support for students. Advancement and alumni relations could coordinate information sharing related to former students. At-promise alumni students can also be brought to campus to give talks about their lives and careers to serve as a source of inspiration to students. Students reported how impactful it was to hear from alumni who came from backgrounds like theirs and to see they succeeded.

Summary

Shifting to a culture of ecological validation provides all members of the institution an opportunity to collaboratively work toward at-promise student success. Each interaction with students gets viewed through the lens of creating a validating experience for students. While rules guiding a specific professional discipline remain important, the goal is to consider each student holistically. Instead of remaining in silos, each educator looks for opportunities to connect at-promise students with other services and programs on campus.

Guiding Questions

- Given your role on campus, how could you support building a culture of ecological validation at your institution?
- Given the office or unit where you work, in what ways could you imagine enacting a culture of ecological validation with your colleagues?
- What offices or individuals on campus might you collaborate with in support of student success?
- How could programs, departments, and offices across campus collaborate in ways that reflect a culture of ecological validation?

11
SHARED LEADERSHIP TO SUPPORT CREATING A CAMPUS-WIDE CULTURE OF ECOLOGICAL VALIDATION

This chapter highlights how campuses can scale ecological validation to create a campus-wide culture that supports at-promise student success. Now that you can envision ways you might support ecological validation in your role (see Chapter 10), it is important to consider how you could collaborate with others across campus to more broadly embrace these new ways of working. Shared leadership is essential for creating a culture that supports at-promise students through ecological validation. We highlight a set of approaches for engaging shared leadership in service of creating a culture of ecological validation. We begin with an overview of shared leadership, then articulate its importance to at-promise student success, and follow this with specific models of shared leadership. The final portions of this chapter provide an example and reflections for practitioners on how to implement a professional learning community focused on shared leadership and creating a culture of ecological validation.

Overview of Shared Leadership

Culture change is a complex activity that has eluded higher education institutions (Kezar, 2018). Studies of campuses engaged in culture change efforts face a series of barriers such as lack of buy-in among administrators, faculty, and staff; misunderstanding about the nature of the desired change among administrators, faculty, and staff; missing incentives or resources to support changes; political struggles that create conflict; leadership turnover; and external crisis that divert attention (Kezar, 2018). Researchers have offered detailed advice and approaches for leaders seeking to create culture

DOI: 10.4324/9781003443711-14

change (Kezar, 2018; Elrod & Kezar, 2016, 2017; Kegan & Lehay, 2009), which can be used in concert with the ideas presented in this chapter to improve the odds of being successful in institutional transformation efforts. One of the key findings from the research on culture change is the role of shared leadership. While many definitions of shared leadership exist, they share common characteristics:

1 A greater number of individuals in leadership than traditional models.
2 Leaders and followers are seen as interchangeable.
3 Leadership is not based on position or authority.
4 Multiple perspectives and expertise are capitalized on for problem-solving, innovation, and change.
5 Collaboration and interactions across the organization are typically emphasized.
6 Leadership is seen as a process that involves members throughout the organization.

Shared leadership is particularly suited as a strategy for advancing a culture of ecological validation since collaboration is a fundamental element of this approach. Pearce and Conger (2002) define shared leadership as "the dynamic, interactive influence process among individuals in groups for which the objective is to lead one another to the achievement of group or organizational goals or both" (p. 1). Shared leadership moves away from the leader-follower binary; capitalizes on the importance of leaders throughout the organization (which includes staff, faculty, and administrators across campus); and creates an infrastructure so that organizations can benefit from the leadership of multiple people. It involves more horizontal, lateral influence among colleagues or members of a team (Zhu et al., 2018). Further, shared leadership supports deeper changes by delegating authority to faculty and staff to make changes, creating a culture that supports risk-taking, and working in cross-functional arrangements to manage work processes in more holistic ways (Kezar, 2001; Wheatley, 1999). Shared leadership consistently emerges as a key factor for organizations that are better able to learn, innovate, and perform (Senge, 1990; Wheatley, 1999). It does so by building institutional creativity as well as enhancing memory and co-ownership over goals and strategies that could otherwise vanish when executive leadership turns over. Shared leadership does not mean the absence of executive leadership, but it changes the nature of executive leadership by working within a broad and distributed approach to leadership.

Generally, shared leadership draws upon a much broader range of people who work together across the traditional lines created by the structure of an institution, such as between academic and student affairs or across departments and colleges. Shared leadership is most effective when used for addressing complex problems or changes. Transformative change, like supporting at-promise college students, is ideal for using shared leadership as there are no clear answers, and an effective response will mean working together in new ways and learning as the challenge unfolds (Baer et al., 2008). These kinds of problems do not fit readily into a standard organization chart. Initiatives or efforts that require individuals to work interdependently to accomplish goals are good candidates for a shared leadership approach. Kezar and colleagues (2021) document how sharing equity leadership has been able to close equity gaps and support the success of racialized minority and low-income students.

Executive leaders, mid-level leaders, faculty, and staff play varying roles in advancing shared leadership (Kezar, 2018). Executive leaders in positions of authority have the ability to mandate changes, alter reward structures, create strategic plans, refine mission and vision statements, allocate resources, create support structures, and hire and train employees (Kezar, 2018). Leaders in the middle of the organization, such as department chairs, directors of a unit, or a dean of students, have access to some of the strategies and approaches of leaders in positions of authority such as hiring and planning, but often do not have access to altering reward structures or changing the mission. They are often ideally located within the organization to connect executive leaders and leaders on the ground, creating communication channels between the two. They also are uniquely positioned to connect work across units and help break down traditional boundaries. Faculty and staff can be local champions for a change by motivating and persuading colleagues as well as creating alliances with like-minded people. They can create networks and often utilize brown bag lunches and other informal learning opportunities to advocate for changes. Kezar and Lester (2011) identified how campuses that better support at-promise students and move toward culture change are able to maximize the leadership across executive, mid-level, and bottom-up leaders, which connects them into a shared leadership process that draws on everyone's expertise.

Shared Leadership and At-promise Students

There are three primary reasons that shared leadership is so critical to creating campus-wide ecological validation. First, shared leadership is a driver of culture change. Dozens of studies have validated its significance and importance to enacting transformational changes, which are the type needed to support at-promise students (Kezar, 2018). Second, cross-campus collaboration is fostered through shared leadership. As we have argued throughout the book, campuses struggle to break down silos, and shared leadership is one of the drivers to cross-campus collaboration that can create ecological validation. And lastly, top-down leadership has been unable to support at-promise students' needs. Those in leadership are largely removed from the experiences of at-promise students. Therefore, being able to tap the expertise and leadership of department chairs, assistant directors, faculty, and staff throughout campus ensures the right environment is created for at-promise students.

Studies of transformational change have consistently identified shared or team leadership – across administrators, faculty, staff, and students – as central to implementing changes (Eckel & Kezar, 2003). Top-down approaches to change rarely result in the type of buy-in or reach into the consciousness of faculty and staff needed for culture change. Creating a culture of ecological validation across a campus is a deep cultural change that requires the adoption of seven norms (holistic, strengths-oriented, proactive, identity-conscious, developmental, collaborative, and reflective practice). Shared forms of leadership engage stakeholders across the campus in sense-making processes (professional development, learning communities, campus dialogues, learning circles) that allow for pervasive change and belief systems necessary to scale transformation. Sensemaking involves helping groups that are tasked with changes to learn together. Additionally, if shared leadership focuses on at-promise student success, then an environment is created in which policies, practices, and processes are altered to support the new norms. Research consistently shows that norms and values shape institutional actions and establish direction and priorities (Morphew & Hartley, 2006). Shared leadership can also be paired with top-down forms of leadership that set direction and priorities through a strategic agenda focused on at-promise student success. Leaders can communicate, incentivize, align human and financial resources, and ultimately hold people accountable for progress, all documented to lead to culture change (Kezar, 2018).

Part of the challenge of breaking down siloed structures is that top-down leadership has not been able to alter the bureaucratic work of campuses because of turnover, inability to alter routines on the ground, and lack of ownership and buy-in by faculty and staff. In order to make this deeper cultural change, shared leadership across campus is needed to support cross-functional work and adjust typical working arrangements. Past efforts to break down hierarchical structures have failed due to a lack of support in terms of cross-functional structures and distributing work differently. Current structures and culture reinforce siloed work, and an enormous effort is needed to overcome these traditional structures – and shared leadership has been one of the only identified ways to achieve this type of change (Kezar & Holcombe, 2017).

Shared approaches to leadership that capitalize on the broader knowledge of institutional members and foster learning are needed for ecological validation. Kezar and colleagues' (2008) study of campuses that had made significant advances for racially minoritized students demonstrated that they used shared leadership. Interviewees spoke about a web of leadership that they created (or capitalized on, as it already existed on most campuses) across campus with change agents that developed coordinated support systems that would make racially minoritized students successful. Rather than look to the usual groups of people who might work on other leadership initiatives, campus leadership knew that they had to identify change agents on campus that were closely connected with racially minoritized students and understood the type of changes that were truly needed. Leaders stated that their colleagues that were less successful often depended on a small group of more formally appointed officers, such as a vice president for multicultural affairs or associate deans. While these individuals were important to include, they often lacked important information needed for success:

1 Close connection to the students and problems faced by racially minoritized students;
2 Information about possible on-the-ground solutions; and
3 Knowledge of the informal work going on to help racially minoritized students.

In order to create effective solutions for supporting at-promise student success, leadership needs to be aware of current issues and problems. Connecting to entry-level staff who work with student groups, for example, is important because they can talk about newer issues such as students exploring multiethnic identity or online racism. More recent studies also emphasize these findings (Kezar & Lester, 2011; Kezar et al., 2021). Shared leadership offers a wholly different approach, which can maximize expertise and knowledge that exist across campus, overcome siloed structures, and establish cross-functional knowledge needed to create sense-making necessary to develop new norms – all necessary for a culture of ecological validation.

Models of Shared Leadership

Several different models exist and can be used to foster shared leadership. Because shared leadership involves interactions that typically cross boundaries between units, roles, and responsibilities, it can be supported through new structures to support this type of work (Kezar & Lester, 2009).

We review three such structures in this section (cross-functional teams, steering committees, and professional learning communities), but other structures exist that could also be explored.

No matter what structure is used, the involvement of executive leadership, mid-level individuals, and those on the ground being connected through any of these models is ideal for establishing the type of shared leadership necessary to create a culture of ecological validation. Key administrators (e.g., chancellor, provost, vice presidents for student and academic affairs, and director of institutional research) can ensure support for priority setting, resources, incentives, and accountability to better support student success. For example, shared leadership groups benefit from access to student success data, knowledge of existing support systems, and information about systems that are accessible by upper-level administrators. Mid-level leaders (e.g., department chairs, deans, and directors of student support units) should be included in order to make sure that both academic and student support units are communicating and knowledgeable about the needs of students as well as connecting regularly about the ways their work can inform each other. These mid-level leaders are most integral to ensuring that collaboration happens between units, and often campuses do not have an ongoing mechanism for these groups to connect, work together, and plan. The distributed structure should also include faculty and staff that have direct contact with students on a day-to-day basis. Our study identified how faculty and staff received information on a regular basis that allowed for dynamic changes that responded to students' needs. (For additional information about building institutional capacity for shared leadership, see Kezar & Holcombe, 2017, or Pearce & Conger, 2002.)

Cross-functional Teams

Cross-functional teams are a model of shared leadership that involves bringing together individuals from different units/areas that typically do not work together (Yammarino et al., 2012). While not common in higher education, research related to siloed and bureaucratic programs hindering students have led to the creation of some cross-functional teams on campuses, particularly focused on retention. Interdisciplinary research groups, institutes, and centers have been formed to connect different departments and units to address complex problems like poverty and sustainability. Kezar and Lester (2009) found that the campuses with high levels of collaboration that support student success also have created cross-functional teams.

The Council for Advancement of Standards in Higher Education (2018) has recently released a framework for how campuses can implement cross-functional team structures in order to connect different offices, services, and programs within the first-year experience. The report was developed because of the continued problems with retaining first-year students and the lack of action to create cross-functional work that has been called for over the past two decades. The call for action is based on the mounting evidence for improved outcomes when students engage in thoughtfully combined and coordinated first-year success initiatives (Crissman, 2001; Hansen & Schmidt, 2017; Keup, 2005; Kezar & Holcombe, 2017). The guide outlines the establishment of a cross-functional team as well as suggests the individuals that should compose the team, mission statement for cross-functional teams, goals for teams, operating principles, recognition, accountability, authority, responsibilities, communication strategies, approaches to integrating the work of the first year, assessment, data collection, and interpretation. While this guide is focused on the creation of cross-functional teams for the first-year experience, the same principles could apply to teams for different purposes.

Steering Committee/Distributed Approach

A second model of shared leadership is distributed leadership. While this form of leadership is similar to cross-functional teams in that it also involves "flexible configurations that arise during particular projects or times of change," leadership is shared more broadly across multiple levels of an entire organization or even across organizational boundaries rather than just within a single team or group (Kezar & Holcombe, 2017). Research on distributed leadership tends to focus on demonstrating leadership as a process and activity that involves shared cognition and exchange of leadership roles within groups (Spillane & Diamond, 2008).

There has been less attention to specific models of distributed leadership. A few scholars have suggested that matrix organizations can be a model of distributed leadership. A matrix organization is defined as one in which there is dual or multiple managerial accountability and responsibility (Bolden, 2017). The matrix is a key structure in order to develop collaboration and work across boundaries. A matrix organizational structure is a workplace in which employees report to two or more managers rather than one manager overseeing every aspect of a project. For example, an employee may have a primary manager they report to as well as one or more project managers they work under. This leads to greater innovation, flexibility, and enhanced service or products (Kezar & Holcombe, 2017). Other studies have identified steering committees as entities that can help to distribute leadership (Clark, 1998). But much of the research on distributed leadership is focused on altering existing bureaucratic structures to be flexible and emergent to share leadership. Thus, the emphasis on specific structures is downplayed in comparison to rethinking existing roles within current organizations. Rather than new structures for leadership, it is about rethinking individual roles throughout the organization.

One of the campuses in our study created a steering group that brought together administrators, staff, and faculty to help improve the TSLC program. The space was also an avenue to learn about best practices within the program and distribute them across the campus. The steering committee connected to several other campus committees/groups, which helped create a culture of ecological validation. This sort of group fits more with a distributed leadership approach in that it did not have a formal set of goals, but a loose set of guidelines around learning from and informing each other as well as connecting work groups from across campus.

Another example of a distributed approach to leadership in higher education that involves a whole institution moving toward a campus-wide model similar to ecological validation is described in a recent book by Freeman Hrabowski and his colleagues (2019). Their book provides essentially an extended case study of the development and practice of a distributed approach to shared leadership at University of Maryland Baltimore County in support of at-promise students. They provide examples of people leading from various positions and roles within the institution: students advocating for changes to the campus racial climate and response to sexual assault, faculty leading course redesign or faculty diversification efforts, staff "infusing entrepreneurship into the academic core and the student experience" and innovating within the spaces of information technology and data analytics (Hrabowski et al., 2019, p. 52).

Professional Learning Communities

A third model of shared leadership – professional learning communities (PLCs) – includes many of the aspects of distributed leadership and cross-functional teams while also adding a shared learning component. PLCs are common in K-12 education, and they bring together teachers in groups to improve their practice or administrators, staff, and teachers to improve overall school function. A PLC generally involves the collaborators learning together and working toward achieving a shared vision (DuFour & Eaker, 2009; Kezar et al., 2022c; Reichstetter, 2006). While there are two different types of PLCs (a group where all members have a similar professional role or a group where members have different professional roles from across campus), they tend to have similar processes of bringing together groups to ask questions, examine or look at data, and conduct action-oriented research that aims at learning that can improve practice.

PLCs have been less common in higher education, although faculty learning communities have gained in prominence over the last decade (Kezar, 2018). Faculty learning communities involve bringing together 10 to 12 faculty members to meet monthly over the course of a year, read texts in common, engage in changes in pedagogy, and end in the culmination of a final project – often a new syllabus or curricular element (Kezar, 2018). We argue for PLCs that bring administrators, faculty, and staff together explore how to create a campus-wide culture of ecological validation.

PLCs have at least one facilitator who is typically trained to lead discussions and help encourage risk-taking and innovation, particularly across stakeholder groups. Groups are structured for ongoing interaction and reflective dialogue. They start by setting goals and structures to ensure progress on learning and shared values, as well as norms to guide the group's work. Educators building a PLC recognize that they must work together to achieve their collective vision. Therefore, they create structures to promote a collaborative culture within the group and emphasize interdependence. And as we have stressed throughout this book, a collaborative culture is essential for ecological validation, and this makes PLCs particularly attractive for promoting shared leadership.

PLCs can enhance teaching practice, address complex problems, improve working relationships, and help individuals and groups to stay more engaged with ongoing research and data related to their practice (Reichstetter, 2006). These benefits are accrued when PLCs are well structured, have a skilled facilitator, establish clear goals, achieve a shared set of values for working together, involve the right individuals, are connected to institutional resources to implement their changes, and utilize assessment to obtain feedback (Stoll & Louis, 2007). A PLC would be ideal for creating campus-wide ecological validation, which requires working across various campus stakeholders, learning about at-promise students at their particular campus, and exploring new norms of institutional practices (Kezar et al., 2022c).

We are currently leveraging PLCs in our work with the three campuses featured in this book. In collaboration with our campus partners, we created a PLC on each campus that would engage with the concept of ecological validation as well as other research and case studies in order to make decisions about how to shift campus culture. We encouraged the campuses to invite a compositionally diverse group, which included personal identities, professional roles, level of leadership, length of time at the institution, and direct or indirect student support. The members committed to a year of learning together and then two years engaged in rethinking the work within their individual units as well as reimagining the policies, practices, and structures across campus in order to move toward a culture of ecological validation. While these PLCs committed to three years together, another campus may navigate the learning and action processes within a shorter or longer timeframe. The final section of this book includes reflections from the educators who cofacilitated the PLCs.

We have identified a few insights related to how the educators learned together within the PLC (Kezar et al., 2022c). The groups:

- Learned more about the different roles on campus and discussing the realities of the work being done;
- Had permission to learn together, build trust, and imagine new ways to support at-promise students before moving to action;
- Empowered everyone in the group to share their perspectives and concerns without consequences given the political dynamics of having staff, faculty, and administrators in one space;
- Encouraged educators to move beyond focusing on their particular units in order to consider how to shift campus systems;
- Leveraged the culture of ecological validation to create a shared language related to problems, challenges, and solutions; and
- Learned how to access and interpret campus data.

As the PLCs moved toward exploring ways to support the campus cultures, they used several strategies (Kezar et al., 2022c), including:

- Examining how to map the existing student advising and support resources to identify where the gaps in support exist;
- Identifying pockets of success on campus, and discussing if/how those might be scaled across campus;
- Exploring how to leverage the cross-functional nature of the group to create more collaborative approaches to at-promise student support;
- Rethinking the hiring and onboarding processes for new educators through the lens of ecological validation;
- Reviewing messages students receive from educators across campus to look for opportunities to be more identity-conscious, strengths-oriented, proactive, holistic, and developmental as well as looking for ways to be more collaborative in order to reduce redundant or conflicting messages from different offices;
- Developing new assessment tools to evaluate if and how the campus is leveraging ecological validation; and
- Creating professional development opportunities to enable faculty, staff, and leadership across campus to learn about ecological validation.

So, what does this all look like together? In the next section, we provide an illustration of a PLC that could be created to develop campus-wide ecological validation on a campus. We constructed this hypothetical example based upon our research with campuses. Following this example, we share reflections from educators who are currently facilitating PLCs focused on creating a culture of ecological validation.

An Example of Shared Leadership

After years of incremental success in supporting at-promise students, Antelope College decided they need a new approach. Things have been improving, but students are disappointed with the progress and pushing the campus to do more. The president and his cabinet meet with students. After hearing their wide-ranging concerns, the executive leadership decides that the campus community broadly needs to learn how to better serve their students. The president establishes a PLC and appoints key members of his administration (chief diversity officer, vice president for student affairs, director of institutional research, vice president for community engagement, chief financial officer, director of alumni affairs); several staff members including the directors of the multicultural center, TRIO program, student support services, and advising; and individuals from academic affairs including the dean of arts and humanities, six department chairs, and five faculty members.

The president identifies a faculty member – Juan – who has experience with PLCs to lead the group. The president lets Juan know that he has access to the resources he may need to support the PLC. Juan asks for a stipend for the staff and faculty members who he knows serve on several different groups and are overburdened. The president agrees to the stipend. Juan also asks about how the PLCs work will be used to inform campus decision-making, priority setting, and policies. If the group is not empowered, they will not fully engage. The president explains that he plans to review and implement the group's recommendations and agrees to come to the initial meeting as well as to come periodically to hear the group's discussion. After reviewing the list of participants, Juan appreciates the group's diversity in terms of race, gender, sexual orientation, and role. However, Juan notices there are no Native Americans, which is a subgroup the campus wants to serve better; so they identify another member of the team. He also suggests adding a representative from the nontenure-track faculty members who teach most introductory courses on campus.

At the meeting with the president, Juan obtains all the information that has been received from the students recently as well as data about historical issues related to at-promise student success. Juan uses the data to develop a set of discussion questions for the PLC as well a set of activities to engage in over the next term. The first meeting is set. The president welcomes everyone and invites them to make deep and comprehensive changes. Juan helps the group to understand their charge – to better support at-promise students and to look for broad institutional-level changes that can have a more scaled impact than previous initiatives that have come out of committees such as the retention committee. Juan explains that this group represents a much greater cross section of the campus and can/should think about overall institutional changes. The group engages in an activity to ensure that each of them has a clear understanding of their charge and goals. They work together to map out a set of activities for the next year.

At the second meeting, they work on ground rules for working together and some shared values including respect, pushing each other to see beyond their normal perspective or unit, everyone's voice is valuable, and people have had different experiences that should be acknowledged. They recognize that having some individuals in positions of authority with others that have much less power in the organization will be a challenge. Juan will meet with everyone after the third meeting to see how things are going and if everyone is feeling the power to speak. Juan will also be observing the meetings for these kinds of dynamics and may pull people aside to ask them to speak less or be conscious of how much space they are taking. As an experienced facilitator, Juan notes he will use techniques to draw out different people in the group (e.g., round robin discussions). After the third meeting, Juan reaches out to individuals to see how they are doing and finds out that two of the faculty members, the chief financial officer, and one of the directors are not clear about their roles within the PLC. The director also feels her comments are dismissed by the group. As Juan reflects on the meetings, he can appreciate her comments. At the next meeting, he specifically calls on her and validates her perspective in front of the group.

For the first few months, they reviewed data gathered by the president and office of institutional research. They also read two research-based books about at-promise students' experiences in college. After the fourth meeting, themes emerge from the data: students have multiple and different needs, making simple solutions difficult; students do not think that the overall community cares about them, and they feel like a number; when students hit an inevitable challenge, there are not enough safety nets like a food pantry, study support, or emergency finances; often their family members are not able to support them in their studies; they are having trouble juggling multiple responsibilities; and they do not understand why they are taking many of their classes. Juan sees the connection between the issues identified and readings related to ecological validation. Juan brings this framework for the group to consider. He also asks the president to attend this meeting to hear about a possible direction forward. After some discussion, the group decides it will spend the next semester learning about ecological validation and developing a plan for creating it, including a gap analysis for understanding what resources (human, financial, and otherwise) might be needed to move forward on the plan.

The president is excited about the direction. He asks the group to consider incentives to do the work and to set up an assessment plan to go along with their emerging strategic plan. He also empowers them and underscores that he wants them to take risks; if they do not meet some of their items in their assessment, this will not jeopardize the to move forward. The group meets for another semester, becoming familiar with key concepts of validation, sense of belonging, being proactive, identity-conscious, holistic, and related ideas, as well as developing the plan. Juan asks each member to take a turn at a meeting to describe how ecological validation would fundamentally change their work and role. Each member gets feedback on the reconceptualization and has an individual meeting with Juan to go over their new role and unit description. The plan is for each of them to present again and reconsider their practice.

During this time period, one of the faculty members who felt his role was unclear and did not feel he had much to contribute to the group becomes disengaged. He starts to have side conversations and distracts some of the others. Juan meets with the faculty member to try to encourage him to contribute his expertise to the discussions around ways that faculty members can be validating, proactive, and collaborate to support students. Also, Juan points out concerns about making courses relevant for students and better connecting them to majors. Yet at the following two meetings, things do not improve. Juan privately asks the faculty member if he would prefer to leave the group, which he chooses to do.

After ten meetings, the group members have become experts on ecological validation and developed a plan. They ask the president to attend their next meeting. They recommend a cross-campus convening to share ecological validation as the vision for the campus and get feedback on their plan. The president agrees to fund the convening and allocate some of his staff to do the planning work. He applauds their bold thinking, including the development of five cross-functional working groups, required training on validation, adding support for a culture of ecological validation to annual merit reviews, consolidation of several units and divisions, a new approach to hiring, orientation that includes information about at-promise students, designation of career planning as part of most units' work, and many other bold steps. The convening is a success. Because the planning group was so broad and their learning so deep, they can describe the new culture in detail to their colleagues. They organize retreats within their respective divisions.

Reflections on Leading a Professional Learning Community

By Sarah Edwards, Aaron Estes, Amy Goodburn, Toni Hill, Sammi Kaiser, and Kelli King

We collaborated with the PASS research team to develop PLCs at each of our campuses. While our general approach was similar, we also considered our campus contexts as we facilitated the development and implementation of the PLCs, including our campus mission, student body, structure, and needs. While still engaged in this work, we share some reflections on our experiences.

Each campus PLC was cofacilitated by a leader from student affairs and academic affairs. The Kearney campus was led by Aaron Estes (Director of the Academic Success Offices) and Toni Hill (Professor and Assistant Department Chair of Family Sciences). The Lincoln campus was led by Amy Goodburn (Senior Associate Vice Chancellor and Dean of Undergraduate Education) and Kelli King (Assistant Vice Chancellor for Student Affairs). And the Omaha campus was led by Sarah Edwards (Assistant Vice Chancellor for Curriculum and Programs) and Sammi Kaiser (Assistant Vice Chancellor for Student Success). The cofacilitators recruited PLC members (approximately 10–20 members) that included senior leaders, mid-level faculty and staff, and front-line professionals to create the stage for rich, data-informed, and practical conversations.

Initially, PLC meetings focused on creating norms, trust, and a shared vision and purpose. Monthly topics focused on the ecological validation norms. Group members committed to reading materials prior to the meetings. We discussed what was working on our campuses as well as considering how to draw from the readings to build upon our current successes. The cross-unit relationship building enabled the PLC members to collaborate with one another to identify and address challenges that at-promise students were facing on our campuses. As one fellow noted, these relationships "have impacted the lives of many students and their ability to be successful here simply because a handful of campus adminis-trators happen to know one another better and can pick up the phone and problem-solve together." The members began actively looking for oppor-tunities to implement the norms within their professional spaces on campus in order to move toward a culture of ecological validation on our campuses.

Each of our campuses developed a strategy to inform the campus's senior leadership about ecological validation and the work of the PLC. We recognized the importance of having support from senior leadership who would be able to help us elevate the ideas that emerged from the group. We looked for opportunities to connect our work with the campus mission and leadership initiatives. Two of the campuses also invited members of senior leadership to serve as ex officio members to ensure a stronger connection to current and future goals, initiatives, and challenges.

PLC members recognized the need to develop avenues to share ecological validation with other faculty, staff, and campus leaders across campus. One of our campuses used a system of cascading presentations about ecological validation and the work of the PLC by starting with senior leadership and then working across the organization chart. Another campus decided to use the PLC work as part of its university's quality initiative proposal for its ten-year accreditation review, including milestones to identify campus units for dissemination of PASS findings and designing tools to evaluate institutional campus change.

Each campus hosted a forum and intentionally invited educators from across campus to engage in and experience the power of ecological validation. One campus organized a symposium to create a "mini learning community" experience for attendees by utilizing shared pre-readings about ecological validation and vignettes we created based on common issues that students on our campus face across academics, career development, co-curricular experiences, and campus support units. Rather than inviting only the people who always show up for events related to at-promise student support, this campus included individuals who are not typically considered "student facing." For instance, individuals who process transfer credit, military benefits, and classroom scheduling were intentionally invited. Attendees were placed in small groups to discuss the student vignettes, attending to elements of ecological validation and considering how they might collectively understand the vignettes from the various perspectives and expertise across the units they represented. This forum was designed to build relationships through the mini PLCs that could support the integrated and collaborative elements of ecological validation in the future. One attendee noted: "I want to talk to the rest of my staff about the ecological validation norms we discussed at the forum. I learned so much from my small group discussion, that I would like to share that feedback with the rest of my team."

Based upon our experience leading the PLCs, we provide the following insights:

- While our primary focus was conceptualizing a validating ecology for at-promise students, we began to apply the ecological validation framework to our faculty and staff ecology as well, understanding that we could not create such a campus for students if we, ourselves, did not feel validated in our work. Acknowledging and validating the strengths and identities of our PLC members as well as the importance of the work

that they do to support students was critical in building community and providing continued motivation for the PLC's efforts.
- We needed to conceptualize our PLCs in relation to existing campus networks, councils, and working groups that might already be engaged in identifying institutional barriers that affect at-promise students.
- We have found ourselves balancing PLC members' aspirational goals for systemic change with realistic understandings and expectations of constraints and limits – we encourage our members to celebrate victories of all size that result from our work.
- We are developing ways to assess the impact of our PLCs in terms of process (building relationships across units, developing shared expertise) and product (are the ideas that they raise/sponsor making a difference for at-promise students?).
- We are considering how to maintain momentum for implementing change once the PLC officially ends, including evolving into a co-ordinating committee that continues to engage in cross-functional conversations about creating and sustaining a culture of ecological validation.

The work and learning that our PLCs have done collectively has certainly influenced the ways members approach their work outside of the PLC. Ecological validation has been spreading across our campuses through each member's sphere of influence. PLC members infuse ecological validation norms into department processes, discuss them at staff meetings, and use them to influence the work of other camus-wide committees on which they serve. This allows the cause to be advanced in real, tangible ways, even as the broader aspirational goals are being developed.

Resources to Support Your PLC

We have publicly available resources on our website (https://pass.pullias.usc. edu). We created a syllabus to guide the learning year that complements the information shared in this book. We also have several practitioner briefs and videos that explain ecological validation, the norms, and other ideas emerging from our research. We plan to continue adding more resources as the PASS Project continues.

Reflection Questions:

- Which shared leadership model might work best at your campus to implement ecological validation at scale?

- Have you utilized the group and organizational capacity building levers to ensure the success of the shared leadership approach?
- What relationships or opportunities might you need to cultivate to better leverage shared leadership on your campus?
- Given the nature of your work and aims, how do you think implementing ecological validation would affect the students you serve?
- What might your next action steps be, based on your learning and the areas you have identified as potential areas for future growth?

Concluding Thoughts

Throughout this book, we argue that supporting at-promise student success requires providing these students with educational environments that are ecologically validating. We recommend moving from siloed programs or individual interactions toward coordinated and collaborative approaches. Based upon our analysis of research and theory, we encourage institutions to consider implementing ecological validation.

Students' experiences with ecological validation were transformative. Not only did students persist and graduate, but their experience in college was a positive one that helped them flourish or thrive. Ecological validation provided them enriched experiences by the strengths-oriented, identity-conscious, holistic, proactive, and developmental support from staff, faculty, and other educators. Throughout this book, we explored how a comprehensive college transition program (CCTP) supported at-promise student success. For readers who are considering developing a CCTP at their institution, we hope the TSLC model provides guidance in how to create a program grounded in ecological validation that will positively influence at-promise student experiences. In addition, institutions can leverage a CCTP as a hub of innovation by piloting interventions and identifying successful practices that can be brought to scale at the campus level (Kezar et al., 2021). For institutions that are ready to create institutional systems that reflect ecological validation, we provided guidance about how to move toward a culture of ecological validation. We argue that all at-promise students should have validating experiences when engaging with all educators, which requires a shift in norms that become embedded in institutional structures and processes.

REFERENCES

Abelman, R., & Molina, A. (2002). Style over substance reconsidered: Intrusive intervention and at-risk students with learning disabilities. *Nacada Journal, 22*(2), 66–77.

Altieri, F. M. (2019). The next generation of one-stop student service centers, Part II. *College and University, 94*(3), 53–56.

Angrist, J., Autor, D., Hudson, S., & Pallais, A. (2015). *Leveling up: Early results from a randomized evaluation of post-secondary aid* (No. w20800). National Bureau of Economic Research.

Arbona, C., & Jimenez, C. (2014). Minority stress, ethnic identity, and depression among Latino/a college students. *Journal of Counseling Psychology, 61*(1), 162–168.

Ardoin, S., & Martinez, b. (2019). *Straddling class in the academy: 26 stories of students, administrators, and faculty from poor and working-class backgrounds and their compelling lessons for higher education policy and practice.* Stylus.

Aspen Institute. (2019). *From a nation at risk to a nation at hope.*

Astin, A. W. (1984). Student involvement: A developmental theory for higher education. *Journal of College Student Personnel, 25*(4), 297–308.

Bailey, T. R., Jaggars, S. S., & Jenkins, D. (2015). *Redesigning America's community colleges: A clearer path to student success.* Harvard University Press.

Baer, L. L., Duin, A. H., & Ramaley, J. A. (2008). Smart change. *Planning for Higher Education, 36*(2), 5.

Becker, M. A. S., Schelbe, L., Romano, K., & Spinelli, C. (2017). Promoting first-generation college students' mental well-being: Student perceptions of an academic enrichment program. *Journal of College Student Development, 58*(8), 1166–1183.

Bettencourt, G. (2020). "When I think about working class, I think about people that work for what they have": How working class students engage in meaning making about their social class identity. *Journal of College Student Development, 61*(2), 154–170.

Berg, G. (2010). *Low-income students and the perpetuation of inequality: Higher education in America*. Routledge.

Bettencourt, G. M., Irwin, L. N., Todorova, R., Hallett, R. E., & Corwin, Z. B. (2023). The possibilities and precautions of using the designation "at-promise" in higher education research. *Journal of Postsecondary Student Success, 2*(2), 16–29.

Betz, N. E., & Luzzo, D. A. (1996). Career assessment and the career decision-making self-efficacy scale. *Journal of Career Assessment, 4*(4), 413–428.

Bronfenbrenner, U. (1994). Ecological models of human development. *Readings on the Development of Children, 2*(1), 37–43.

Bronfenbrenner, U., & Morris, P. A. (2006). The bioecological model of human development. In R. M. Lerner & W. Damon (Eds.), *Handbook of child psychology: Theoretical models of human development* (pp. 793–828). Wiley & Sons Inc.

Bullock-Yowell, E., McConnell, A. E., & Schedin, E. A. (2014). Decided and undecided students: Career self-efficacy, negative thinking, and decision-making difficulties. *NACADA Journal, 34*(1), 22–34.

Buultjens, M., & Robinson, P. (2011). Enhancing aspects of the higher education student experience. *Journal of Higher Education Policy and Management, 33*(4), 337–346.

Cabrera, N. L., Watson, J. S., & Franklin, J. D. (2016). Racial arrested development: A critical whiteness analysis of the campus ecology. *Journal of College Student Development, 57*(2), 119–134.

Carnevale, A., & Smith, N. (2018). *Balancing work and learning: Implications for low-income students*. Center on Education and the Workforce, Georgetown University.

Chambliss, D. F., & Takacs, C. G. (2014). *How college works*. Harvard University Press.

Cheese, M., & Vines, J. (2017). The importance of support networks for at-promise students. *Journal of Research Initiatives, 3*(1), 14.

Chickering, A. (1969). *Education and identity*. Jossey-Bass.

Chickering, A., & Reisser, L. (1993). *Education and identity* (2nd ed.). Jossey-Bass.

Clotfelter, C. T., Hemelt, S. W., & Ladd, H. F. (2018). Multifaceted aid for low-income students and college outcomes: Evidence from North Carolina. *Economic Inquiry, 56*(1), 278–303.

Clotfelter, C., Hemelt S., & Ladd H. (2017 June). *Multi-faceted aid for low-income students and college outcomes: Evidence from North Carolina (Working Paper No. 2217)*. National Bureau of Economic Research.

Cole, D., Culver, K., Kitchen J., Rivera, G., & Swanson, E. (2020). *How and why a comprehensive college transition program works. Promoting at-promise student success policy brief.* Retrieved from https://pullias.usc.edu/wp-content/uploads/2020/10/Formative-TSLC-policy-brief-PUBLIC-FINAL.pdf

Cole, D., Culver, K., Rivera, G., & Swanson, E. (2020). *How and why a comprehensive college transition program works: Promoting at-promise students' success in the Thompson scholars learning communities*. Pullias Center for Higher Education, University of Southern Californa.

Cole, D., Kitchen, J. A., & Kezar, A. (2019). Examining a comprehensive college transition program: An account of iterative mixed methods longitudinal survey design. *Research in Higher Education, 60*, 392–413.

Colyer, J. (2011). Strangers to a strange land: Low-income students and the transition to college. In A. Kezar (Ed.), *Recognizing and serving low-income students in higher education: An examination of institutional policies, practices, and culture* (pp. 121–138). New York, NY: Routledge.

Conrad, C., & Lundberg, T. (2022). *Learning with others: Collaboration as a pathway to college success.* Johns Hopkins University Press.

Culver, K. C., Perez, R. J., Kitchen, J. A., & Cole, D. G. (2021, April 12). *Promoting equitable engagement for Students of Color: Mixed-methods exploration of a comprehensive college transition program.* Paper presented at the American Educational Research Association Conference.

Culver, K. C., Swanson, E., Hallett, R. E., & Kezar, A. (2021). Identity-conscious strategies to engage at-promise students in a learning community: Shared courses in a comprehensive college transition program. *Teachers College Record, 123*(8), 146–175.

Cushman, K. (2007). Facing the culture shock of college. *Educational Leadership, 64*(7), 44.

Dawson, R. F., Kearney, M. S., & Sullivan, J. X. (2020). *Comprehensive approaches to increasing student completion in higher education: A survey of the landscape* (No. w28046). National Bureau of Economic Research.

DuFour, R., & Eaker, R. (Eds.). (2009). *On common ground: The power of professional learning communities.* Solution Tree Press.

Eckel, P. D., & Kezar, A. J. (2003). *Taking the reins: Institutional transformation in higher education.* Greenwood Publishing Group.

Elrod, S., & Kezar, A. (2016). *Increasing student success in STEM: A guide to systemic institutional change.* Association of American Colleges and Universities: Washington, DC.

Elrod, S., & Kezar, A. (2017). Increasing student success in STEM: Summary of a guide to systemic institutional change. *Change: The Magazine of Higher Learning, 49*(4), 26–34.

Engle, J., & Tinto, V. (2008). *Moving beyond access: College success for low-income, first-generation students* (pp. 1–38). The Pell Institute for the Study of Opportunity in Higher Education.

Espiritu, D., Rawls, K., & Wimer, T. (2019). The undergraduate student perspective. In S. Ardoin & b. Martinez (Eds.), *Straddling class in the academy.* Stylus.

Ehrmann, S. C. (2021). *Pursuing quality, access and affordability: A field guide to improving higher education.* Sylus.

Felton, P., Gardner, J., Schroeder, C., Lambert, L., & Barefoot, B. (2016). *The undergraduate experience: Focusing institutions on what matters most.* Jossey-Bass.

Flores, L. Y., & Heppner, M. J. (2002). Multicultural career counseling: Ten essentials for training. *Journal of Career Development, 28*(3), 181–202.

Gloria, A., & Hird, J. (1999). Influences of ethnic and nonethnic variables on the career decision-making self-efficacy of college students. *Career Development Quarterly, 48*, 157–173.

Gopalan, M., & Brady, S. (2020). College students' sense of belonging: A national perspective. *Educational Researcher, 49*(2), 134–137.

Gupton, J., Castelo-Rodriguez, C., Martinez, D., & Quintar, I. (2008). Creating a pipeline to engage low income, first generation college students. In S. Harper & S. Quaye (Eds.), *Student engagement in higher education*. Routledge.

Guiffrida, D. (2005). Othermothering as a framework for understanding African American students' definitions of student-centered faculty. *Journal of Higher Education, 76*(6), 701–723.

Guiffrida, D. A., Kiyama, J. M., Waterman, S. J., & Museus, S. D. (2012). Moving from cultures of individualism to collectivism in support of students of color. In S. D. Museus & U. M. Jayakumar (Eds.), *Creating campus cultures: Fostering success among racially diverse student populations* (pp. 68–87). Routledge.

Hackett, G., Betz, N. E., Casas, J. M., & Rocha-Singh, I. A. (1992). Gender, ethnicity, and social cognitive factors predicting the academic achievement of students in engineering. *Journal of Counseling Psychology, 39*(4), 527–538.

Hallett, R. E., Crutchfield, R., & Maguire, J. J. (2019a). *Addressing homelessness and housing insecurity in higher education: Strategies for educational leaders.* Teachers College Press.

Hallett, R., Kitchen, J. A., Perez, R., & Reason, R. (2019b). *College transition and success model: Integrating validation, belonging, and mattering.* Paper presented at the annual conference of the Association for the Study of Higher Education Portland, OR

Hallett, R.E., Kexar, A., Kitchen, J.A., Perez, R.K., & Reason, R. (2020). *Qualitative narrative of methods: Promoting At-promise Student Success (PASS) project.* USC Pullias Center for Higher Education.

Hallett, R. E., Kezar, A., Kitchen, J., & Perez, R. J. (2020a). A typology of college transition and support programs: Situating a two year comprehensive college transition program within college access. *American Behavioral Scientist, 64*(3), 230–252.

Hallett, R. E., Reason, R., Toccoli, J., Kitchen, J., & Perez, R. J. (2020b). The process of academic validation within a comprehensive college transition program. *American Behavioral Scientist, 64*(3), 253–275.

Hallett, R. E., & Venegas, K. M. (2011). Is increased access enough? Advanced placement courses, quality, and success in low-income urban schools. *Journal for the Education of the Gifted, 34*(3), 468–487.

Harper, S. R. (2009). Race-conscious student engagement practices and the equitable distribution of enriching educational experiences. *Liberal Education, 95*(4), 38–45.

Harper, S. R. (2010). An anti-deficit achievement framework for research on students of color in STEM. *New Directions for Institutional Research, 2010*(148), 63–74.

Harper, S. R., & Quaye, S. J. (2009). Beyond sameness, with engagement and outcomes for all. *Student Engagement in Higher Education*, 1–15.

Harper, S. R., Wardell, C. C., & McGuire, K. M. (2011). Man of multiple identities: Complex individuality and identity intersectionality among college men. In *Masculinities in higher education* (pp. 81–96). Routledge.

Harris III, F., & Bensimon, E. M. (2007). The equity scorecard: A collaborative approach to assess and respond to racial/ethnic disparities in student outcomes. *New Directions for Student Services, 2007*(120), 77–84.

Hart Research Associates. (2013). *It takes more than a major: Employer priorities for college learning and student success.* Hart Research.

Hrabowski III, F.A. (2019). *The empowered university: Shared leadership, culture change, and academic success.* JHU Press.

Hurst, A. (2012). *College and the working class: What it takes to make it.* Sense Publishing.

Hurtado, S., & Carter, D. F. (1997). Effects of college transition and perceptions of the campus racial climate on Latino college students' sense of belonging. *Sociology of Education,* 324–345.

Hurtado, S., Milem, J., Clayton-Perderson, A., & Allen, W. (1999). *Enacting diverse learning environments: Improving the climate for racial/ethnic diversity in higher education* (ED430514). ERIC. https://files.eric.ed.gov/fulltext/ED430514.pdf

Hypolite, L., Kitchen, J. A., & Kezar, A. (2020, April). *Developing major and career self-efficacy among marginalized students: Impacts of a comprehensive college transition program.* Paper for the annual meeting of the American Educational Research Association, San Francisco, CA.

Jayakumar, U., & Museus, S. (2012). Mapping the intersection of campus cultures and equitable outcomes among racially diverse student populations. In S. Museus & U. Jayakumar (Eds.), *Creating campus cultures: Fostering success among racially diverse student populations.* Routledge.

Jenkins, S. R., Belanger, A., Connally, M. L., Boals, A., & Durón, K. M. (2013). First-generation undergraduate students' social support, depression, and life satisfaction. *Journal of College Counseling, 16*(2), 129–142.

Jochman, J., Cheadle, J., Goosby, B., Tomaso, C., Kozikowski, C., & Nelson, T. (2019). Mental health outcomes of discrimination among college students on a predominately white campus: A prospective study. *Socius, 5,* 1–16.

Jury, M., Smeding, A., Stephens, N. M., Nelson, J. E., Aelenei, C., & Darnon, C. (2017). The experience of low-SES students in higher education: Psychological barriers to success and interventions to reduce social-class inequality. *Journal of Social Issues, 73*(1), 23–41.

Keeling, R. P., Underhile, R., & Wall, A. F. (2007). Horizontal and vertical structures: The dynamics of organization in higher education. *Liberal Education, 93*(4), 22–31.

Kegan, R., & Lahey, L. L. (2009). *Immunity to change: How to overcome it and unlock potential in yourself and your organization.* Harvard Business Press.

Kezar, A. (2001). Investigating organizational fit in a participatory leadership environment. *Journal of Higher Education Policy and Management, 23*(1), 85–101.

Kezar, A. (2011). *Recognizing and serving low income students in higher education: An examination of institutional policies, practices, and culture.* Routledge.

Kezar, A. (2018). *How colleges change: Understanding, learning, and enacting change* (2nd ed.). Routledge.

Kezar, A. (2019). *Creating a diverse student success infrastructure: The key to catalyzing cultural change for today's student.* Pullias Center for Higher Education.

Kezar, A., Eckel, P., Contreras-McGavin, M., & Quaye, S. J. (2008). Creating a web of support: An important leadership strategy for advancing campus diversity. *Higher Education, 55*(1), 69–92.

Kezar, A., Hallett, R. E., Kitchen, J. A., & Perez, R. (2022a). Mapping the connections of validation and high-impact practices. In J. Zilvinskis, J. Kinzie, J. Daday, K. O'Donnell, & C. Vande Zande (Eds.), *Delivering on the promise of high-impact practices: Research and models for achieving equity, fidelity, impact, and scale* (pp. 30–39). Stylus Press.

Kezar, A., Hallett, R. E., Perez, R. J., & Kitchen, J. A. (2022b). Scaling success for low-income, first-generation, and racially minoritized students through a culture of ecological validation. *Journal of Diversity in Higher Education*. 10.1037/dhe0000401

Kezar, A., Corwin, Z. B., Hallett, R. E., Hypolite, L. I., & Nagbe, M. (2022c). Creating systemic culture change and solving vexing problems on campus: The promise of professional learning communities in higher education. *Academic Leader*. https://www.academic-leader.com/topics/institutional-culture/creating-systemic-culture-change-and-solving-vexing-problems-on-campus-the-promise-of-professional-learning-communities-in-higher-education/

Kezar, A. J., & Holcombe, E. M. (2017). *Shared leadership in higher education*. Washington, DC: American Council on Education, 1–36.

Kezar, A., Holcombe, E., Vigil, D., & Dizon, J. P. M. (2021). *Shared equity leadership: Making equity everyone's work*. American Council on Education; University of Southern California, Pullias Center for Higher Education.

Kezar, A., Hypolite, L., & Kitchen, J. A. (2020). Career self-efficacy: A mixed-methods study of an underexplored research area for first-generation, low-income, and underrepresented college students in a comprehensive college transition program. *American Behavioral Scientist*, 64(3), 298–324.

Kezar, A., Kitchen, J., Estes, H., Hallett, R. E., & Perez, R. J. (2023). Tailoring programs to best support low-income, first-generation, and racially minoritized college student success. *Journal of College Student Retention*, 25(1), 126–152.

Kezar, A., Kitchen, Joseph A., Estes, H., Hallett, R., & Perez, R. (2020). Tailoring programs to best support low-income, first-generation, and racially minoritized college student success. *Journal of College Student Retention: Research, Theory & Practice*, 25(1), 126–152. 10.1177/1521025120971580.

Kezar, A., & Lester, J. (2011). *Enhancing campus capacity for leadership: An examination of grassroots leaders in higher education*. Stanford University Press.

Kezar, A., & Lester, J. (2009). Supporting faculty grassroots leadership. *Research in Higher Education*, 50(7), 715–740.

Kezar, A., Perez, R. J., Kitchen, J., & Hallett, R. E. (2021). Learning how to tailor a program to support low-income, first-generation, and racially minoritized student success. *Journal of Postsecondary Student Success, 1*(1), 25–57.

Kezar, A., Perez, R., & Swanson, E. (2021b). *Hubs of Innovation to scale changes needed to support at-promise students* [Brief]. USC Pullias Center for Higher Education.

Kezar A., Perez, R. J., & Swanson, E. (2022). The potential of and mechanisms for a hub of innovation on campus to support changes for low-income, first generation, and racially minoritized college students. *Research in Higher Education*, 63, 1237–1260.

Kiang, P. (2009). A thematic analysis of persistence and long-term educational engagement with Southeast Asian American college students. In L. Zhan (Ed.), *Asian American voices: Engaging, empowering, enabling* (pp. 21–58). NLN Press.

Kitchen, J. A. (2023). Developing low-income college students' sense of belonging: The role of validation. *Journal of College Student Development, 64*(2), 231–238.

Kitchen, J. A., Cole, D., Rivera, G., & Hallett. R. (2021a). The impact of a college transition program proactive advising intervention on self-efficacy. *Journal of Student Affairs Research and Practice, 58*(1), 29–43.

Kitchen, J. A., Kezar, A., & Hypolite, L. (2021b). More than a pathway: Creating a major and career ecology that promotes the success of low-income, first-generation, and racially minoritized students. *About Campus, 25*(6), 4–12.

Kitchen, J. A., Kezar, A., & Hypolite, L. (2021c). At-promise college student major and career self- efficacy (MCSE) ecology model. *Journal of Diversity in Higher Education*. Online First.

Kitchen, J. A., Perez, R., & Hallett, R. (2021d). Validating approaches to proactive advising: A promising practice to promote college success among low-Income, first-generation, and racially minoritized students in a comprehensive college transition program. In G. Martin & S. Ardoin (Eds.), *Social class supports: Programs and practices to serve and sustain poor and working-class students through higher education* (pp. 209–222). Stylus.

Kitchen, J. A., Perez, R. J., Hallett, R. E., Kezar, A., & Reason, R. (2021e). Ecological validation model of student success: A new student support model for low-income, first-generation, and racially minoritized students. *Journal of College Student Development, 62*(6), 627–642.

Kitchen, J. A., Cole, D., Rivera, G., & Hallett, R. E. (2021f). The impact of a college transition program proactive advising intervention on self-efficacy. *Journal of Student Affairs Research and Practice, 58*(1), 29–43.

Kitchen, J.A., Sonnert, G., & Sadler, P. (2018). The impact of college- and university-run high school summer programs on students' end of high school STEM career aspirations. *Science Education, 102*(3), 529–547.

Kitchen, J. A., & Williams, M. S. (2019). Thwarting the temptation to leave college: An examination of engagement's impact on college sense of belonging among students of color. *Journal for the Study of Postsecondary and Tertiary Education, 4*, 67–84.

Kiyama, J. M., & Rios-Aguilar, C. (Eds.). (2017). *Funds of knowledge in higher education: Honoring students' cultural experiences and resources as strengths.* Routledge.

Komarraju, M., Swanson, J., & Nadler, D. (2014). Increased career self-efficacy predicts college students' motivation, and course and major satisfaction. *Journal of Career Assessment, 22*(3), 420–432.

Kuh, G. D. (1991). *Involving colleges: Successful approaches to fostering student learning and development outside the classroom.* Jossey-Bass.

Kuh, G. (2002). Organizational culture and student persistence: Prospects and puzzles. *Journal of College Student Retention, 3*(1), 23–39.

Kuh, G., Kinzie, J., Buckley, J., Bridges, B., & Hayek, J. (2006). *What matters to student success: A review of the literature.* National Postsecondary Education Cooperative.

Kuh, G., Kinzie, J., Buckley, J., Bridges, B., & Hayek, J. (2007). *Piecing together the student success puzzle: Research, propositions, and recommendations.* ASHE higher Education Report, 32(5). Jossey-Bass.

Kuh, G. D., & Hall, J. E. (1993). Using cultural perspectives in student affairs. In G. D. Kuh & M. D. Lanham (Ed.), *Cultural perspectives in student affairs work* (pp. 1–20). American College Personnel Association.

Kuh, G. D., Kinzie, J., Schuh, J. H., & Whitt, E. J. (2005). Never let it rest lessons about student success from high-performing colleges and universities. *Change: The Magazine of Higher Learning, 37*(4), 44–51.

Kuh, G., & Love, P. (2000). A cultural perspective on student departure. In J. M. Braxton (Ed.), *Reworking the student departure puzzle* (pp. 196–212). Vanderbilt University Press.

Kuh, G., & Whitt, E. (1988). *The invisible tapestry: Culture in American colleges and universities.* ASHE-Eric Higher Education Report.

Lent, R. W., Lopez, A. M., Jr., Lopez, F. G., & Sheu, H. B. (2008). Social cognitive career theory and the prediction of interests and choice goals in the computing disciplines. *Journal of Vocational Behavior, 73*(1), 52–62.

Locke, L. A., & Trolian, T. L. (2018). Microaggressions and social class identity in higher education and student affairs. *New Directions for Student Services, 2018*(162), 63–74.

Lopez, S., & Louis, M. (2009). The principles of strengths-based education. *Journal of College & Character, 10*(4).

Lumina Foundation. (2015). *Beyond financial aid how colleges can strengthen the financial stability of low-income students and improve student outcomes.* Retrieved from https://www.luminafoundation.org/files/resources/beyond-financial-aid.pdf

Manning, K., Kinzie, J., & Schuh, J.H. (2013). *One size does not fit all: Traditional and innovative models of student affairs practice.* Routledge.

Mayhew, M. J., Rockenbach, A. N., Bowman, N. A., Seifert, T. A. D., Wolniak, G. C., Pascarella, E. T., & Terenzini, P. T. (2016). *How college affects students: 21st century evidence that higher education works* (pp. 523–574). Jossey-Bass.

Mayhew, M., Rockenbach, A., Bowman, N., Seifert, T., & Wolniak, G. (2016). *How college affects students.* Jossey-Bass.

McNair, T. B., Bensimon, E., Cooper, M. A., McDonald, N., & Major Jr, T. (2016). *Becoming a student-ready college: A new culture of leadership for student success.* John Wiley & Sons.

Miller, C. Headlam, C., Manno, M. S., & Cullinan, D. (2020). *Increasing community college graduation rates with a proven model: Three-year results from the Accelerated Study in Associate Programs (ASAP) Ohio Demonstration.* Retrieved from https://www.mdrc.org/publication/increasing-community-college-graduation-rates-proven-model

Mireles-Rios, R., Rios, V., Auldridge-Reveles, T., Monroy, M., & Castro, I. (2020). I was pushed out of school: Social and emotional approaches to a youth promotion program. *Journal of Leadership, Equity, and Research, 6*(1), 2–21.

Mitchell, M., Leachman, M., Masterson, K., & Waxman, S. (2018). *Unkept promises: State cuts to higher education threaten access and equity.* Report from the Center on Budget and Policy Priorities. Retrieved from https://www.cbpp.org/sites/default/files/atoms/files/10-4-18sfp.pdf

Melguizo, T., Martorell, F., Swanson, E., Chi, W. E., Park, E., & Kezar, A. (2021). Expanding student success: An experimental evaluation of a comprehensive college transition program. *Journal of Research on Educational Effectiveness*, *14*(4), 835–860.

Morphew, C. C., & Hartley, M. (2006). Mission statements: A thematic analysis of rhetoric across institutional type. *The Journal of Higher Education*, *77*(3), 456–471.

Museus, S. D. (2011). Generating ethnic minority student success: A qualitative analysis of high-performing institutions. *Journal of Diversity in Higher Education*, *4*(3), 147–162.

Museus, S. D. (2014). The culturally engaging campus environments (CECE) model: A new theory of success among racially diverse college student populations. In M. Paulsen (Eds.), *Higher education: Handbook of theory and research* (vol 29, pp. 189–227). Springer.

Museus, S. D., & Jayakumar, U. M. (Eds.). (2012). *Creating campus cultures: Fostering success among racially diverse student populations*. Routledge.

Museus, S. D., & Maramba, D. C. (2011). The impact of culture on Filipino American students' sense of belonging. *Review of Higher Education*, *34*, 231–258.

Museus, S. D., Lâm, S. C., Huang, C., Kem, P., & Tan, K. (2012). Cultural integration in campus subcultures: Where the cultural, academic, and social spheres of college life collide. In *Creating campus cultures* (pp. 116–139). Routledge.

Museus, S. D., Griffin, K., & Quaye, S. (2020). Engaging students of color. In S. J. Quaye, S. R. Harper, & S. L. Pendakur (Eds.), *Student engagement in higher education*. Routledge.

Museus, S. D., & Quaye, S. J. (2009). Toward an intercultural perspective of racial and ethnic minority college student persistence. *The Review of Higher Education*, *33*(1), 67–94.

Museus, S. D., Zhang, D., & Kim, M. J. (2016). Developing and evaluating the culturally engaging campus environments (CECE) scale: An examination of content and construct validity. *Research in Higher Education*, *57*, 768–793.

National Center for Education Statistics (NCES). (2021). *Digest of Education Statistics, 2019* (NCES 2021-009), Chapter 3.

Nunn, L. M. (2021). *College belonging: How first-year and first-generation students navigate campus life*. Rutgers University Press.

Page, L., Kehoe, S., Castleman, B., & Sahadewo, G. (2019). More than dollars for scholars: The impact of the Dell Scholars Program on college access, persistence, and degree attainment. *Journal of Human Resources*, *54*(3), 683–725.

Pajares, F. (1996). Self-efficacy beliefs in academic settings. *Review of Educational Research*, *66*(4), 543–578.

Patton, L. D., Renn, K. A., Guido, F. M., & Quaye, S. J. (2016). *Student development in college: Theory, research, and practice*. John Wiley & Sons.

Pearce, C. L., & Conger, J. A. (2002). *Shared leadership: Reframing the hows and whys of leadership*. Sage Publications.

Peet, M. R., Reynolds-Keefer, L., Gurin, P., & Lonn, S. (2011). Fostering integrative knowledge and lifelong learning. *Peer Review*, *13*(4/1), 15.

Pendakur, S. L. (2016). Empowerment agents: Developing staff and faculty to support students at the margins. In Pendakur V. (Ed.), *Closing the opportunity gap: Identity-conscious strategies for retention and student success*. Stylus Publishing, LLC.

Perez, R.J., Acuña, A., & Reason, R.D. (2021). Pedagogy of validation: Autobiographical reading and writing courses for first-year, low-income students. *Innovative Higher Education*, 46(6), 623–641.

Peterson, S., & DelMas, R. (2001). Effects of career decision-making self-efficacy and degree utility on student persistence: A path analytic study. *Journal of College Student Retention*, 3(3), 285–299.

Purnell, R., & Blank, S. (2004). *Support success: Services that may help low-income students succeed in community college.* MDRC. https://files.eric.ed.gov/fulltext/ ED484621.pdf

Quaye, S., & Harper, S. (2007). Faculty accountability for culturally inclusive pedagogy and curricula. *Liberal Education*, 93(3), 32–39.

Quaye, S., Harper, S., & Pendakur, S. (2020). *Student engagement in higher education* (3rd ed). Routledge.

Quaye, S., Poon, T., & Talesh, R. (2009). Engaging racial/ethnic minority students in predominantly white classroom environments. In S. Harper & S. Quaye (Eds.), *Student engagement in higher education.* Routledge.

Rayle, A. D., & Chung, K.-Y. (2007). Revisiting first-year college students' mattering: Social support, academic stress, and the mattering experience. *Journal of College Student Retention: Research, Theory and Practice*, 9(1), 21–37.

Reeves, R., & Halikias, D. (2017). *Race gaps in SAT scores highlight inequality and hinder upward mobility.* Brookings Institution. Retrieved from https://www.brookings.edu/research/race-gaps-in-sat-scores-highlight-inequality-and-hinder-upward-mobility/

Reichstetter, R. (2006). Defining a professional learning community. *E&R Research Alert*, 6, 1–4.

Rendón, L. I. (1994). Validating culturally diverse students: Toward a new model of learning and student development. *Innovative Higher Education*, 19(1), 33–51.

Rendón, L. I. (2002). Community college Puente: A validating model of education. *Educational Policy*, 16, 642–667.

Rendón, L.,I. (2006). *Reconceptualizing success for underserved students in higher education.* Retrieved from https://nces.ed.gov/npec/pdf/resp_Rendon.pdf

Rendón, L. I., Jalomo, R. E., & Nora, A. (2000). Theoretical considerations in the study of minority student retention. In J. Braxton (Ed.), *Rethinking the departure puzzle: New theory and research on college student retention* (pp. 127–156). Vanderbilt University Press.

Rendón, L. I., & Muñoz, S. M. (2011). Revisiting validation theory: Theoretical foundations, applications, and extensions. *Enrollment Management Journal*, 2(1), 12–33.

Renn, K. A. (2003). Understanding the identities of mixed-race college students through a developmental ecology lens. *Journal of College Student Development*, 44(3), 383–403.

Renn, K. A., & Arnold, K. D. (2003). Reconceptualizing research on college student peer culture. *Journal of Higher Education*, 74(3), 261–291.

Renn, K. A., & Reason, R. D. (2021). *College students in the United States: Characteristics, experiences and outcomes* (2nd ed.). Stylus.

Rios, V., Mireles-Rios, R. (2019). *My teacher believes in me! The educator's guide to at-promise students.* Five Rivers Press.

Rivera, G., Kitchen, J., & Cole, D. (2022). Program staff as facilitators of academic self–efficacy, academic behavioral change, and achievement among low–income, first–generation, and minoritized students. *Journal of Student Affairs Research and Practice*, Online First.

Robb, C. (2017). College student financial stress: Are the kids alright? *Journal of Family and Economic Issues, 38*, 514–527.

Rodgers, K., Blunt, S., & Trible, L. (2014). A real PLUSS: An proactive advising program for underprepared STEM students. *NACADA Journal, 34*(1), 35–42.

Schee, B. (2007). Adding insight to proactive advising and its effectiveness with students on probation. *NACADA Journal, 27*(2), 50–52.

Schiele, J. (1994). Afrocentricity: Implications for higher education. *Journal of Black Studies, 25*(2), 150–169.

Schlossberg, N. K. (1989). Marginality and mattering: Key issues in building community. *New Directions for Student Services, 48*, 5–15.

Schreiner, L. (2010). The "thriving quotient": A new vision for student success. *About Campus, 15*(2), 2–10.

Scrivener, S., & Weiss, M. J. (2013). *More graduates: Two-year results from an evaluation of Accelerated Study in Associate Programs (ASAP) for developmental education students.* Available at SSRN 2393088.

Seidman, A. (2005). Minority student retention: Resources for practitioners. *New Directions for Institutional Research, 125*, 7–24.

Senge, P. M. (1990). *The art and practice of the learning organization.*

Shapiro, D., Dundar, A., Huie, F., Wakhungu, P., Bhimdiwali, A., & Wilson, S. (2018). *Completing college: A national view of student completion rates (Signature Report No. 16).* National Student Clearinghouse Research Center.

Shapiro, D., Dundar, A., Huie, F., Wakhungu, P. Bhimdiwala, A., & Wilson, S. (2019 February). *Completing college: A state-level view of student completion rates (Signature Report No. 16a).* Herndon, VA: National Student Clearinghouse Research Center.

Soria, K. M., & Stebleton, M. J. (2012). First-generation students' academic engagement and retention. *Teaching in Higher Education, 17*(6), 673–685.

Soria, K. M., & Stubblefield, R. (2015). Building a strengths-based campus to support student retention. *Journal of College Student Development, 56*(6), 626–631.

Stevens, C., Liu, C., & Chen, J. (2018). Racial/ethnic disparities in US college students' experience: Discrimination as an impediment to academic performance. *Journal of American College Health, 66*(7), 665–673.

Stewart, S., Lim, D., & Kim, J. (2015). Factors influencing college persistence for first-time students. *Journal of Developmental Education, 38*(3), 15–20.

Stoll, L., & Louis, K. S. (2007). *Professional learning communities: Divergence, depth and dilemmas.* McGraw-Hill Education (UK).

Strayhorn, T. L. (2012). Satisfaction and retention among African American men at two-year community colleges. *Community College Journal of Research and Practice, 36*(5), 358–375.

Strayhorn, T. L. (2018). *College students' sense of belonging: A key to educational success for all students.* Routledge.

Strayhorn, T. L., Long, L. L., III, Kitchen, J. A., Williams, M. S., & Stentz, M. (2013). *Academic and social barriers to Black and Latino male collegians' success in engineering and related STEM fields.* Proceedings from 2013 ASEE Annual Conference and Exposition, Atlanta, GA.

Swanson, E., Chi, E., Martorell, F., Melguizo, T., Park, E., & Kezar, A. (2021). *Creating a context for at-promise students to thrive: Relating psychosocial and academic outcomes* [Brief]. USC Pullias Center for Higher Education.

Swanson, E., & Cole, D. (2022). The role of academic validation in developing mattering and academic success. *Research in Higher Education*, Online First.

Swanson, E., Culver, K., Cole, D., & Rivera, G. (2021). Promoting at-promise students' success in 4-year universities: Recommendations from the Thompson Scholars Learning Communities. *Journal of Diversity in Higher Education, 14*(4), 457–462.

Swanson, E., Kitchen, J., Melguizo, T., & Martorell, F. (2020). *Examining STEM performance within a comprehensive college transition program.* (EdWorkingPaper: 20-287). Retrieved from Annenberg Institute at Brown University: 10.26300/t0d9-mr28

Swanson, E., Melguizo, T., & Martorell, P. (2021). Examining the relationship between psychosocial and academic outcomes in higher education: A descriptive analysis. *AERA Open, 7*(1). 10.1177/23328584211026967

Tate, K., Caperton, W., Kaiser, D., Pruitt, N., White, H., & Hall, E. (2015). An exploration of first-generation college students' career development beliefs and experiences. *Journal of Career Development, 42*(4), 294–310.

Taylor, M., Turk, J., Chessman, H., & Espinosa, L. (2020). *Race and ethnicity in higher education: 2020 supplement.* American Council on Education.

Ting, S. M. R., Grant, S., & Plenert, S. L. (2000). The Excellence-Commitment-and-Effective- Learning (EXCEL) group: An integrated approach for first-year college students' success. *Journal of College Student Development, 41*, 353–360.

Tinto, V. (1988). Stages of student departure: Reflections on the longitudinal character of student leaving. *Journal of Higher Education, 59*(4), 438–455.

Tinto, V. (2012). *Completing college: Rethinking institutional action.* University of Chicago Press.

Toccoli, J. S. (2021). *Supporting instructors to promote at-promise students' success: How faculty coordinators facilitate TSLC's ecological validation* (Doctoral dissertation, University of the Pacific).

Toccoli, J., & Hallett, R. E. (2022). *Supporting validating teaching practices for instructors who work with at-promise students.* Presented at the Annual Conference of the American Educational Research Association, San Diego, CA.

Torres, V. (1999). Validation of a bicultural orientation model for Hispanic college students. *Journal of College Student Development, 40*, 285–298.

Tovar, E., Simon, M. A., & Lee, H. B. (2009). Development and validation of the college mattering inventory with diverse urban college students. *Measurement and Evaluation in Counseling and Development, 42*, 154–178.

Toven-Lindsey, B., Levis-Fitzgerald, M., Barber, P. H., & Hasson, T. (2015). Increasing persistence in undergraduate science majors: A model for institutional support of underrepresented students. *CBE—Life Sciences Education, 14*(2), 1–12.

Tudge, J. R., Mokrova, I., Hatfield, B. E., & Karnik, R. B. (2009). Uses and misuses of Bronfenbrenner's bioecological theory of human development. *Journal of Family Theory & Review, 1*(4), 198–210.

U.S. Commission on Civil Rights. (2018). *Public education funding inequity: In an era of increasing concentration of poverty and re-segregation.* https://www.usccr.gov/pubs/2018/2018-01-10-Education-Inequity.pdf

U.S. Department of Education. (2018). https://nces.ed.gov/pubs2018/2018421.pdf

Witham, K. A., & Bensimon, E. M. (2012). Creating a culture of inquiry around equity and student success. In S. D. Museus & U. M. Jayakumar (Eds.), *Creating campus cultures: Fostering success among racially diverse student populations.* Routledge.

Weissman, E., Cerna, O., Geckeler, C., Schneider, E., Price, D. V., & Smith, T. J. (2009). *Promoting partnerships for student success.* https://mdrc.org/sites/default/files/full_482.pdf

Weiss, M. J., Ratledge, A., Sommo, C., & Gupta, H. (2019). Supporting community college students from start to degree completion: Long-term evidence from a randomized trial of CUNY's ASAP. *American Economic Journal: Applied Economics, 11*(3), 253–297.

Wheatley, M. J. (1999). *Leadership and the new science (2nd ed.).* San Francisco: BerrettKoehler.

Yammarino, F. J., Salas, E., Serban, A., Shirreffs, K., & Shuffler, M. L. (2012). Collectivistic leadership approaches: Putting the "we" in leadership science and practice. *Industrial and Organizational Psychology, 5*(4), 382–402.

Yosso, T. J. (2005). Whose culture has capital? A critical race theory discussion of community cultural wealth. *Race, Ethnicity and Education, 8*(1), 69–91.

Young, D., Schreiner, L., & McIntosh, E. (2015). Investigating sophomore student success: The national survey of sophomore year initiatives and the sophomore experiences survey. *Research reports on college transitions No. 6.*

Zhu, J., Liao, Z., Yam, K. C., & Johnson, R. E. (2018). Shared leadership: A state-of-the-art review and future research agenda. *Journal of Organizational Behavior, 39*(7), 834–852.

INDEX

Made in the USA
Las Vegas, NV
12 November 2023